AF556220

UNDERSTANDING TAXONOMY

UNDERSTANDING TAXONOMY

By

Dr. P.R. Yadav

Lecturer

Dept. of Zoology

D.A.V. College

Muzaffarnagar (U.P.)

(India)

DISCOVERY PUBLISHING HOUSE PVT. LTD.

NEW DELHI-110 002

Reprinted - 2019

First Published - 2010

ISBN: 978-81-8356-521-9

Understanding Taxonomy

Published by:

DISCOVERY PUBLISHING HOUSE PVT. LTD.
4383/4B, Ansari Road, Darya Ganj
New Delhi-110 002 (India)
Phone: +91-11-23279245, 23253475; 43596065
E-mail: discoverybooksindia@gmail.com
discoverypublishinghouse@gmail.com
web: www.discoverypublishinggroup.com

Printed at:
Infinity Imaging Systems
Delhi

Preface

The present title "Understanding Taxonomy" has been written for those students interested in careers in diverse fields of biological sciences. It provides a structured approach to learning by covering all the important topics in a uniform, systematic format. The book has been comprehensively designed incorporating recent advances in this fast moving field. It also provides accessible information on taxonomy in compact form for undergraduate students in biology and related life sciences. It is intelligible to the educated layman, though it deals with some complex ideas. It is an adequate text for all the requirements of students in this area. In addition, busy lecturers who require a quick reference compendium will find it useful, particularly for tutional planning. Simple, yet hopefully clear figures and tables are provided throughout the book.

The over-riding goal of this book, and indeed of the whole *Understanding series*, is to present the essential information concering taxonomy in a compact, readily accessible form which leads itself to student learning and revision. The convergence of various approaches has generated a rich panorama of detail, the significance of which we are still attempting to unraval. The present text has been written as an introduction to this rapidly growing field.

To make the work more comprehensive and informative, the author has consulted many authoritative books, research journals, abstracts, monographs etc., so there can be no claim to originality except in the manner of treatment.

The author expresses his thanks to his friends and colleagues whose continue inspirations have initiated him to bring out this book.

The author expresses his gratitude to Mr. Wasan and staff of M/s Discovery Publishing House Pvt. Ltd. for their whole hearted co-operation in the publication of this book.

In the mean time, the author will remain sincerely responsible for any shortcomings of the book and be grateful to the readers for their suggestions and constructive criticism for the continuous betterment of the book. He takes this opportunity to appeal to the readers to send their suggestions straightaway to his Publisher.

Author

Preface

Contents

1

INTRODUCTION

By the time a person is old enough to take a course in taxonomy, he will already have been involved in a good deal of such taxonomy. He will know how to tell apart some kinds of animals, even if they are only man and various kinds of domestic animals. He will know that not all members of one kind are alike-that some young animals are noticeably different at first from their parents, that male and female may be clearly different, and that some horses are bay, some chestnut, some white, etc.

He will, unconsciously at least, have compared different kinds with each other, distinguishing the features in which they differ from the features in which the members of each kind differ. He will have classified many things. When he says, "Rover is a dog," he is using dog in a group sense and Rover as one of the included individuals.

He will doubtless know that dogs are part of the larger group called mammals. He will very likely have applied a new name to some pet. Although taxonomy doesn't usually give names to individuals, there is no difference between the naming of individual groups and the naming of individual animals.

He may have made a collection, if not of animals, then perhaps of minerals, fossils, plants, postage stamps, or postcards. Some of the features of collecting, and some of the possibilities for studying the collection, will have been illustrated. He may have identified an unknown bird or other animal by looking it up in a book. Whether this involved use of a key or merely a search through pictures, it was identification.

These and other aspects of elementary taxonomy are part of his everyday life. He cannot exist as a thinking being without using some of the ideas and devices of taxonomy. All zoology students must learn a classification of animals, even if it is only two subkingdoms and ten phyla. This classification is one of the principal products of taxonomists, who have been kept busy erecting it for two centuries.

Of course, the ten-phylum scheme is much simplified. The student then studies comparative anatomya study of how certain representatives of major groups differ in their major anatomical features. He studies embryology, in which the development of certain customary species, for example "the pig," "the chick," shows him a little of how species (representing entire groups) differ in the anatomy of early stages and in the details of developmental processes.

He studies genetics, in which he learns some of the factors that make the members of each kind alike from generation to generation, and also some of the factors that make individuals within the kind different from their fellows in color, size, ability, sex, etc. He soon comes to know that species receive a dual name and that all groups of species receive a single name, such as the names he learned for the subkingdoms and phyla.

He soon finds out that some groups have received more than one name, so that he must choose between Mastigophora and Flagellata, for instance.

What Taxonomists Do

Inasmuch as taxonomy is defined as the work done by taxonomists, it would seem to be a simple thing to show what that includes. But unfortunately one can only list several major aspects of their work and indicate some of the things involved in each.

Obtain Specimens

This may be by collecting in the field, exchanging, purchasing, going to a museum, or all of these.

Obtain Literature

All the literature back to the first description of a species in the group is required in most real taxonomic studies and is usually best obtained in a library, preferably the one attached to the museum containing the specimens. Further, some papers are obtainable upon request, or exchange, from the authors, and some books are obtainable by purchase from book stores or used-book dealers.

Study Specimens

Under this heading must be included not only the taxonomic study of the particular specimens but also the pertinent background knowledge, listed in other chapter of this book, such as comparative anatomy, life history, development, and natural history. The taxonomic study *must* employ all appropriate and necessary methods, which will vary greatly from group to group.

Study Literature

This goes on simultaneously with the study of the specimens, but there must also be a considerable knowledge of previous work before study of the specimens can usefully proceed. Unless the literature is quite restricted in volume, it will be necessary to organize it in some way, usually by some sort of cataloging; however, if catalogs and bibliographies have already been published, this will help.

Identify Specimens

After the specimens and the literature have been sufficiently studied, the taxonomist will be able to identify some of the specimens. He will presumably know whether some of his specimens do not correspond to any of the species in the group and therefore represent new species.

Publish Conclusions

Having worked out the species and groups, he may prepare descriptions, keys, new descriptions, or monographs for publication. These embody his taxonomic conclusions, whether they are about the newness of a species or group, its position in the classification, or an easier way to distinguish it from other species or groups.

Propose New Names

If any of the species or groups are new, the taxonomist must propose names for them. To do this he must be thoroughly familiar with the procedures and rules of nomenclature accepted by taxonomists. He must also have a working knowledge of the Latin and Greek employed in scientific names.

Classify Species

He must classify the new species, at least to the extent of assigning them to genera. Eventually he must go much further and classify the genera into groups and these groups into more inclusive groups-prepare a classification, which is a sort of synthesis of all he knows about the species and the groups.

Although these are the principal scientific tasks of the taxonomist, he must usually perform some other tasks that make the taxonomic work possible. Delegation of these more routine tasks to a non-taxonomist is usually not a satisfactory arrangement.

Maintain Collections

As most of the work of the taxonomist is based on specimens of the animal species and the data recorded about them, it is necessary to maintain permanent collections so that specimens will be available when needed. Moreover, future taxonomists will use these collections to recheck the work and for later studies. Maintenance of the libraries is equally important.

Study New Methods

Although conventional methods are usually the basis for any taxonomic study, many cases require development or adoption of new methods before a successful solution can be achieved. It is always desirable to be on the lookout for new techniques that offer better results, and the taxonomist should try to adapt these to his work whenever the advance of the science requires it.

Study Nomenclature

The highly technical nature of the rules under which zoological names are formed and used makes necessary not only an understanding of their provisions by all taxonomists but also the study of the rules themselves by certain taxonomists, who become in effect nomenclature specialists. These nomenclaturists attempt to make the rules more effective in making names serve the needs of all zoologists. They also serve as consultants to other taxonomists on questions of the use of names.

THE EMPLOYMENT OF TAXONOMY

Historically, the fields of zoology appeared in about this order: taxonomy (the recognition of kinds), natural history (the life history in general), comparative anatomy, classification, cytology, evolution, embryology, genetics, ecology, speciation, and biochemistry. The first five of these were comparative. They sought out and recorded the pertinent facts for different kinds of animals.

If there had been no ability to recognize and refer to the kinds (species), it would have been impossible to build up any comparative field, so that when a dissection was made, or a life history worked out, there would have been no way to record to which animal it applied. Embryology, genetics, ecology, and biochemistry, for example, are also partly comparative in nature.

Embryologists work out the normal development of each species. Gene maps are comparative, and one of the results of genetic work shows the pattern of characters and determinants of the various species. Part of ecology studies the reactions of individuals to various factors, but another, part studies the environmental preferences, ranges, and so on of each species. Biochemistry is taking a great interest these days in how kinds differ in their biochemical components.

It is possible to view most of biochemistry as a prelude to comparison of the species in respect to their components and chemical reaction systems. Taxonomy not only produces knowledge but organizes it from all fields, thus providing the essential framework needed to make the data widely usable. This framework is the classification of organisms, and the keys to the data in the classifications are the names of the species and groups.

All other zoological specialties use this framework and the key names. It is impossible to go very far in the study of organisms, whether one is studying ecological, anatomical, distributional, physiological, biochemical, or genetic factors, without a means of referring to the different kinds and a means of relating the data discovered to previous data. Taxonomy is the means of doing both. The abilities to recognize kinds, to associate them with names that are distinctive, and to recognize the groups into which they fit with similar species are used constantly by all zoologists.

Without these abilities there could be no biological science. It is entirely the result of taxonomic work that these essential tools are available, and it is due primarily to continuing taxonomic work that they are constantly revised and corrected. Two aspects of taxonomy are constantly depended upon by zoologists or biologists, and most other scientists dealing with animals.

The first of these is the ability to recover information from the system by use of the name of the species or group. For example, a person encountering the name *Taenia pisi formis* in a textbook or medical literature or veterinary practice, can without difficulty extract from indexes and publications all that is known about this tapeworm species, including hundreds of reports on its occurrence, development, vectors, and hosts, together with the aetiology of disease it produces.

Again, a person studying a little fruit fly would not get very far in genetics unless he found out which species of *Drosophila* he was using. After identification, the name would lead him to all the genetic and other work done on that species. A study made of just "a fruit fly" would be useful only as a training exercise. It could produce useful data only if the identity of the fly were definitely established.

The second aspect used by all zoologists is the association of the species at hand with other species in some taxon of the classification. For example, mention of any species of *Drosophila* immediately associates this species not only with the other species in this genus but also with the order Diptera, the class Insecta, and the phylum Arthropoda, so that it will display the features distinctive to each of these groups.

It is not necessary to ask if it has four wings or two, because it is assumed that all normal adult Diptera have only two; nor to inquire if it breathes by means of tracheal tubes, because it is assumed that all active adult insects do; nor to wonder if it has a chitinous exoskeleton and a body divided into regions, because these are characteristics of all adult Arthropoda. Underlying virtually all important biological work, although sometimes unrecognized, is the knowledge of not only what the species is, but also where the organism fits into the system.

Without this, it is doubtful if any of the major advances in biology could have been made. Both evolution and genetics were made possible by the ability of taxonomists to identify species and relate them to a classification. It is difficult to imagine a part of zoology which is not sooner or later dependent upon this taxonomic capability built up over two centuries by generations of taxonomists. It is *not necessary* to conclude from this that taxonomy is more important than any other subject.

It is *appropriate* to recognize that the more "modern" and "glamorous" fields of zoology are possible today because taxonomy did not fail in its task of identifying and classifying animals. It is to be hoped that taxonomy can keep its system adequate to the future needs of all zoology. It may be thought that this is a personal exaggeration of the importance of one field of specialization, but the importance of taxonomy has been recognized by a variety of modern writers.

In *The New Systematics* at least two writers commented on the dependence of biology on taxonomy: "Systematics, in our understanding, is the basis of knowledge of the plant and animal kingdoms. It was not by mere chance that the greatest evolutionist, Charles Darwin, started his work from systematics" (N. I. Vavilov). Again, ". .. as if biology as a whole could possibly advance when the essential work of systematics is allowed to lag behind" (W. H. Thorpe).

An entomologist primarily concerned with non-taxonomic aspects has written: "Taxonomy is the focal point and basis for all the biological sciences," and "Taxonomy must precede all other forms of biological investigation and furnishes the foundation and frame upon which may be built the results of the researches of all the natural sciences". Another non-taxonomist, forty years ago, saw this relationship and expressed it in direct terms: "It is the systematist who has furnished the bricks with which the whole structure of biological knowledge has been reared.

Without his labors the fact of organic evolution could scarcely have been perceived, and it is he who to-day really sets the basic problems for the geneticist and the student of experimental evolution" (Raymond Pearl). A paleontologist and evolutionist who is also a systematist of note has described the place of taxonomy in these terms: "It is impossible to speak of the objects of any study, or to think lucidly about them; unless they are named.

It is impossible to examine their relationships to each other and their places among the vast, incredibly complex phenomena of the universe, in short to treat them scientifically, without putting them into some sort of formal arrangement. . . . Taxonomy is at the same time the most elementary and the most inclusive part of zoology, most elementary because animals cannot be discussed or treated in a scientific way until some taxonomy has been achieved, and most inclusive because taxonomy in its various guises and branches eventually gathers together, utilizes, summarizes, and implements everything that is known about animals . . ." (G. G. Simpson).

A conference on systematics was held in 1953 under the aegis of the National Research Council in Washington, D.C. It was organized by the Society of Systematic Zoology for the purpose of acquainting government agencies with the importance of systematics in biological research.

The organizer was Dr. Waldo L. Schmitt, whose principal remarks are quoted in full in a later paragraph. Various other speakers discussed aspects of biology that are substantially dependent upon prior or concurrent systematic work. It was there pointed out by a parasitologist that one who knows the systematics can predict life cycles, vectors, and avenues of infection, and in consequence the necessary preventive measures or treatment.

The identification of organisms and the resulting correlation with known data are the keys to the study and control of many diseases. As to paleontological taxonomy, much emphasis was placed on its dependence upon the systematics of living organisms. Paleontology is largely a science of inference from the known to the unknown. Most of the "facts" about fossils, other than the structure of hard parts, are inferences from their nearest relatives among living organisms.

This dependence is so great that some paleontological agencies have had to hire and train taxonomists for work on Recent species, because paleontological investigations could not wait for biologists to study these groups. In September 1962, a conference' was held at Lawrence, Kansas, on Taxonomic Biochemistry, Physiology, and Serology. The necessity was clearly shown, in these experimental fields, for a real understanding of the nature of classification and taxonomic procedures. A large number of the biologists in specialized fields discussed their experimental results on particular animals.

They all attempted to show how their discoveries agreed or disagreed with the "accepted" classifications, and it appeared they all wished to show that their data and methods could be of value in taxonomy. Unfortunately, it became obvious that few of these scientists understood the nature of classification and taxonomic procedures sufficiently to show the effect of their own data or judge whether it really was of value.

Many speakers refused to accept their own results if they failed to agree with whatever classification they thought was the one accepted in taxonomy. Some highly interesting conclusions were brushed aside because of the lack of this agreement. A taxonomically trained person would have seen the implications and known how to study them further. Taxonomy has not only been important in biological science but has contributed substantially to the biological arts, which are the fields known as the applied sciences, including economic entomology, parasitology, biological control, conservation, veterinary medicine, and public health.

To indicate the scope of the use of taxonomy in applied fields, one can do no better than quote in full the paper read by Dr. Schmitt at the 1953 conference on systematics.

APPLIED SYSTEMATICS: THE USEFULESS OF SCIENTIFIC NAMES OF ANIMALS AND PLANTS

"It is an error to suppose as many do that classification is an outmoded phase of natural history. It affords a continuing test of evolutionary doctrine. The increasing refinement of biological study requires greater certainty than ever before of the identity of animals and plants used in experimental work. The fact that all organisms are now considered to be part of one great family tree is a challenge to the intelligence and skill of the classifier who must reconstruct that tree. Actually the business of classification has today greater vitality and significance than ever before . . ."

—Paul B. Sears

The field of biological systematics is a broad one, and within it are brought together at least a part of all natural-science disciplines. It represents the orderly understanding and the sum total of our knowledge of the animal and plant kingdoms. However, to name animals and plants intelligently you need to know a great deal about them, their makeup, lives, growth, behavior, and geographic distribution; in short, their biology in the broadest sense of the word.

SYSTEMATICS IN EVERYDAY LIFE

Everyone at heart is a taxonomist, either by virtue of necessity or because of mere curiosity. From childhood up we want to know the names of things. What is this, that, or the other object-how, where, why, and what? Children at an early age readily learn to distinguish a number of common things-birds, the various wild-flowers, poison-ivy, bees, wasps, yellow jackets-according to their experience.

Every good housewife can identify the tiny moth flitting through the bedroom or the parlor if it be a clothes moth. This knowledge has a dollarsand-cents value, for the name of a beast or a pest indicates the method of control to be applied.

With further experience she can distinguish this kind or species from one that may more rarely flutter through the house but in more disturbing numbers-the moth that sometimes appears in your packaged grain or cereals. Or perhaps it is the winged ant coming out from under the house that catches her attention.

In mere self-interest she will want to know if it is an ant or a termite, which, by the way, is not an ant but an insect of quite another order and family. There are also wooddestroying ants, the carpenter ants, infesting houses, yet these rarely if ever become serious pests.

With the identification comes the scientific name, which is the key, the index entry, indeed the only device which will open up for one the world's literature containing the extant information regarding any object, animal, mineral, or plant. If a name cannot be found for it, the object is probably new and undescribed, in which case the information regarding it is yet to be developed.

Indeed, wherever man comes to grips with the problems of life and living, the importance of the names of things is most vital, whether he be concerned with disease, the production of food, or merely safe drinking water. The physical fitness of drinking water can readily be determined by chemical analysis, but only by identifying the organisms existing in it, or rather determining the absence of certain of them, can its safety be assured.

Among the biological contaminants that need to be distinguished are to be numbered first of all the enteric bacilli and amoebae, the "germs" of typhoid and cholera; copepods, which are the intermediate hosts of the broad tapeworm of Europe now established in parts of this country; and a host of other organisms that vary as to locality.

Unknown waters are not safe to drink even in the high Arctic with its extremely low, often killing temperatures, for there the melting ice and snow in the spring expose and redistribute the well-preserved refuse of the long winter months from human habitations.

But please do not look askance at the glass of drinking water before you. Our modern municipal waterworks take pains to treat and filter it carefully. Yet accidents happen and plumbing installations have been found faulty, as in Chicago, where carelessness in this respect resulted in 70 deaths from amoebic dysentery a few years ago.

Whether the water be fresh or salt, pollution not only renders it unfit for use, but, if in sufficient degree, will also destroy the inhabitants useful and economically important to man. Dr. Ruth Patrick, curator of limnology, specializing in diatoms at the Academy of Natural Sciences of Philadelphia, as the result of her investigations in certain Pennsylvania streams, was perhaps the first to stress the importance of the specific naming of the organisms present in the evaluation of stream pollution, its kind or type, and duration.

She found that the heretofore frequently tried method of using indicator organisms simply did not supply the data needed to make such evaluations. All groups of plants and animals living in a stream, particularly the sessile or attached forms, or those which moved about in only a small area, merited serious consideration definitely at the species level.

This entailed extensive collecting in relatively shallow water, the area in which the majority of such forms live, and required the cooperation of a number of experienced taxonomists to identify specifically the material collected, especially the algae, rotifers, worms, mollusks, Crustacea, insects, and fishes.

Sooner or later we all discover, as did Dr. Patrick, that there is no satisfactory shortcut to the solution of a biologic problem, ecologic, medical, agricultural, or otherwise, that ignores names of the species involved.

Engineering

Ordinarily you would not expect an electric light company to have a biological problem, let alone one in which mollusks were involved. Six or seven years ago a heavily armored power cable lying on the bottom of the bay between Palm Beach and West Palm Beach suffered one of a series of blowouts as the result of the penetration of the outer insulation and the heavy-load casing by marine mollusks.

The company's officials naturally wanted to know what manner of shell-fish this was and what could be done to prevent further damage. Though the animal was found to be a new species, which was subsequently described, it was at once recognized by the expert to whom it was submitted as belonging to a genus of boring mollusks which would quickly be suffocated if the cable were buried several inches below the bottom of the bay.

This would also prevent further damage of the same sort. In the 8 years preceding, the cable had suffered 15 failures, entailing repairs costing upwards of $12,000. Here an identification solved a costly engineering problem.

The Field of Ecology

Engineering problems accompanied by specimens are easier to solve than ecological ones unsupported by specimens. Recently an ecologist was discussing the behavior of a green parrotfish in the waters about a tropical island. You can imagine his consternation when he was asked to which of 10 possible species he was referring!

The importance of specific names to ecologists may be illustrated by this excerpt from a letter received by one of our Museum curators from a well-known student of jungle life: "I have all of my voluminous field notes ready and only await the names of the [specimens] which I sent you a long time ago. Have you had a chance to go over them? I have the names of most, but there are still many left and I can publish nothing until I get them."

And Charles Elton, in his book "Animal Ecology," writes: "One of the biggest tasks confronting anyone engaged upon ecological survey work is that of getting all the animals identified. Indeed, it is usually impossible to get all groups identified down to species, owing to lag in the systematic study of some of them.

The material collected may either be worked out by the ecologist himself or he may get the specimens identified by experts. The latter plan is the better of the two, since it is much more sensible to get animals identified properly by a man who knows them well, than to attain a fallacious sense of independence by working them out oneselfwrong."

Evolution and Genetics Studies

The abundance of the pasturage in what are known as "the meadows of the sea" is being evaluated these days by the oceanographers in terms of the chlorophyll collected by their continuous plankton recorders without having to take the pains of identifying the many species of which the plankton mass is composed.

At least samplings of the organisms involved should be specifically determined, for there are bad as well as good planktoners in the sea, just as there are good and bad plants on some of our western ranges. Pasturage in meadows on land, by certain tests, may yield a very high chlorophyll rating, but a lot of it could be locoweed.

If the marine chlorophyll ratings are to have real significance, the species on which they are based need to be known. In evolutionary and genetic studies, it is especially important to know well the species dealt with and the literature about them. Years of effort can go for naught if pertinent taxonomic finds, procedures and discoveries are disregarded.

An unfortunate instance of this sort was a rather impressive report on "An Investigation of Evolution in Chrysomelid Beetles of the Genus *Leptinotarsa,*" published some years ago, a 320-page volume illustrated with 31 text figures and 30 plates, some in color.

Aside from a number of unnecessary nomenclatorial mistakes, records of distribution and occurrence were far out of line with published work on these beetles. Although the author stated that three species were found in the United States, and that life histories were almost entirely undescribed, actually eight species were known from the States at the time, and seven life histories had been published previously.

Several forms which he enumerated as species were invalidated by evidence given in his own work, and to have given it standing he should have supplied or published elsewhere satisfactory descriptions of the new forms he mentioned but concerning which his text was insufficient and unclear. As the informed entomologist who reviewed this work remarked, "Even a slight acquaintance with the literature of the subject would have saved [the author] from errors which are surprising in a man who claims to have devoted eleven years to his subject."

Is it not to be regretted that so much time and money were expended on work so deficient for want of adequate taxonomic background? For "it is the systematist," said Raymond Pearl, "who has furnished the bricks with which the whole structure of biological knowledge has been reared. Without his labors the fact of organic evolution could scarcely have been perceived and it is he who today really sets the basic problem for the geneticist and the student of experimental evolution."

The National Museum's Contribution to Systematic Studies

The U.S. National Museum is one of the world's great centers for systematic research. The studies that the Museum is unable to accomplish with its own staff it tries to encourage others to undertake. That is how it happened that the late Dr. J. A. Cushman became interested in working up the Museum's collections of Foraminifera.

In his day he knew more about the classification and distribution in time and space of Foraminifera than perhaps any other man. His great knowledge of these shelled protozoans was derived in great measure from the vast collections that had been dredged up from the seven seas and stored in the National Museum, largely unstudied, before his time.

When these microscopic organisms came into prominence as primary indicators of oil-bearing strata, particularly in the Gulf of Mexico region, Dr. Cushman was the authority to whom the oil companies turned for help in applying this information.

His special taxonomic knowledge of the group enabled him to predict from the species brought up in drillings the proximity of a given sample to oil-bearing strata within several hundred feet. His determinations were worth millions of dollars in revenue to the oil companies and in taxes to the United States Government.

Though other techniques, electronic and geophysical, are now frequently employed in prospecting for oil, the Foraminifera are still important in identifying and correlating strata and in subsurface mapping in oil-producing areas.

The foregoing is perhaps the most outstanding example of the eventual successful application of purely systematic studies and the naming of species to economic ends. It can safely be said that most, if not all, systematic work has a dollar-and-cents value, perhaps not today or tomorrow, but certainly in time.

Biological Controls

In looking over some recent literature dealing with biological controls, I saw reference to the classical example with which I became acquainted in my earlier days in the Government service some 40 years ago. It was the story of the identification of an insect that played the role of a villain threatening the destruction of the sugar industry of

Mauritius back in 1910, and how it was circumvented in the best tradition of the popular "whodone-its" by a systematic entomologist. The villain was a destructive white grub that bored in the roots of the sugarcane, killing the plant.

It appeared very suddenly in such alarming numbers and spread so rapidly that the threat of the ruination of the plantations of sugarcane, the big money crop of the island, could not be ignored. With such information as was at hand, the best guess was that the borer was the larva of an African genus of beetle represented on the island by two species and the only remedies that suggested themselves were to dig up the root stumps to destroy the larvae or to catch the beetles as they flew about at night in search of food.

The invader, lurking unknown in introduced cane cuttings, and finding itself a favorable environment without enemies, in reproductive capacity far outstripped all human efforts to control it despite the fact that in less than 6 months more than 27 million insects were accounted for.

Meanwhile, the aid of the specialists in the British Museum was sought. With the extensive reference collections and library there available, it was soon determined that the beetle was not an African one, but a New World form, of which, however, no record or specific description could be found.

In an ensuing search through the large collections of that Museum three specimens of this selfsame beetle, labeled "Trinidad," turned up. The fact that this native of the West Indies had never been mentioned in literature implied that it was of so little economic importance that it had failed to attract the attention of any entomologists stationed in the islands. What kept its numbers down at home?

With specimens for comparison, a trained entomologist soon located both the beetle and its larval stages in cane roots on Barbados. It further developed that there it had two natural enemies. The only one in evidence at the time was a so-called blackbird which eagerly followed field hands rooting up cane stumps, to eat the grubs turned up, but unable to reach those beneath the ground.

The other natural enemy, a tiny, inconspicuous wasp, was discovered by a neat bit of detective work on the part of the entomologists. Attached to one of several Barbados root borers transmitted to the British Museum was observed a tiny white grub. In the manner of its attachment it suggested the larval stage of a small wasp common in Barbados, one of the family of solitary wasps known to parasitize beetle larvae but not heretofore the cane borer. The wasp lays her eggs upon the borers after paralyzing them with her sting so that they will serve as food for her own young on hatching.

Introduced into Mauritius, this little wasp soon turned the tables on the cane borer. One cannot leave the subject of biological controls in the field of agriculture without touching upon one of the most remarkable successes of all time. This particular one was made possible by the taxonomic studies that preceded and were undertaken in connection with it.

It was the conquest of the prickly pear in Australia by the cactus moth borer, *Cactoblastis*. Cactuses are peculiar to the New World. As horticultural curiosities, and also as hosts of the cochineal insect, they were introduced shortly after their discovery into many other lands. The dates of the early introductions of the prickly pears, or Opuntias, into Australia are not known.

Some planted as hedges and in gardens escaped to run wild in the surrounding country. As with the cane borer in Mauritius, in a favorable environment and without natural enemies to keep them in check, they spread at a tremendous rate. The rapidity of their increase has been called one of the botanical wonders of the world.

In a period of 20 years the land area preempted by these prickly pears increased from 10 million to 50 million acres. It was imperative that something drastic be done if the Opuntias were not to take over the land. Millions of acres had become veritable wildernesses of prickly pears. The Australians soon discovered that the cost of eradicating cacti by hand, poison, or mechanical means so greatly exceeded the value of the land that it was prohibitive.

Some less costly method would have to be employed if the land was to be reclaimed. Biological control seemed to offer the greatest hope. Forthwith, the systematic literature of the world was searched for all pertinent information-the kinds, distribution, and habits of the prickly pears, and especially the literature relating to the animals and plants that have been reported to live in or upon them.

Australian entomologists searched the world, so to speak, for the known and yet unknown enemies of prickly pears, studying those preserved in museum collections, as well as the living ones in the field. The most favorable places for these investigations were Argentina and the United States, where the great natural stands of "pears" existed. Some 150 to 160 different kinds of insects injurious to the cacti were found, of which 50 proved to be new to science.

Twelve of the most promising ones were introduced, and of these one, *Cactoblastis cactorum,* described in 1885 from South America, proved so successful that further introductions were unnecessary. From an original shipment of about 2,800 *Cactoblastis* eggs in 1927, 10 million were reared in the next 2 years. In the course of 6 years 3 billion eggs were released. The cactuses literally disintegrated before the onslaughts of the *Cactoblastis* grubs feeding within their tissues.

Within 15 months after the first trial liberation, huge stands of cactus lay rotting on the ground and in the next 7 years the last large area occupied by the pears collapsed. By 1940 less than 100,000 acres were believed to be infested with patches of dense or moderately heavy cactus growth, whether of regrowth or seeding origin, as compared with the hundreds of square miles of a few years before.

In Queensland, the worst-affected state, it would have cost from four to five hundred million dollars to have cleared the infested areas of prickly pears by poison and mechanical means. Following a careful study of the problem, and, I would emphasize again, especially the taxonomic literature bearing on it, by introducing and distributing eggs of *Cactoblastis,* the Commonwealth Prickly Pear Board accomplished the task at a cost of less than a million dollars.

Thus, the formerly useless acreage regained for settlement because of its suitability for grazing, dairying, and agricultural purposes became an asset valued at 40 to 50 million dollars, to say nothing of the worth of new improvements and the future yield of the land, which, in time, will amount to many times its present value. Moreover, the benefits of the Australian experiences extended to South Africa and India, where prickly pears had also been giving considerable trouble.

The Australian entomologists give due credit to the work of the taxonomists who preceded them in the study of cactuses and cactus insects for their share in the accomplishment of this latter-day miracle, but who could have foreseen 65 years ago that the then published description of an insect found to be new by an Argentine zoologist making known to science the animal life of his part of the world would, half a century later, be instrumental in saving a continent from a pest run wild?

Insect Quarantine

To prevent such unwitting introductions as this cane borer, the prickly pear, and other pests, our Department of Agriculture has a farflung inspection service at all ports of entry and at border stations. Indicative of the importance that the Department attaches to the necessity of having all "immigrants" of agricultural import promptly identified is the fact that it maintains insect, plant, and phytopathological identification services.

The division of insect identification, located in part in the National Museum in Washington, comprises a staff of about 40 entomologists and technical assistants, and elsewhere in the Department an equally alert staff of taxonomic botanists and plant pathologists. They handle many thousands of identifications each year and in the course of making them have detected many harmful insects and other forms of life which might otherwise have become serious agricultural pests.

Epidemiological Applications

Malaria ranks as one of the great scourges of mankind. We hear a great deal of the wonder drugs developed to overcome it, but very little of the role that taxonomy played in furthering its control.

From the time that Ross first discovered that the causative parasites were transmitted by anopheline mosquitoes, it was thought that the problem could be solved quite simply by a reduction of the mosquito population-by treating their breeding places with larvacides, by introducing the little mosquito-eating fish *Gambusia,* by clearing out aquatic vegetation, and by drainage.

The results in the States, and in Panama in the course of the construction of the Canal where expense was no object, were most gratifying, but when the Rockefeller Foundation tried to apply these methods in southern Europe, the same successes were not achieved.

The carrier abroad was a different species, to be sure, with different habits and capable of breeding at the edges of running water, where its North American congener was a pool breeder. Nevertheless, it was impossible to establish any correlation between the incidence of intense malaria and the relatively few anophelines found in houses. On the other hand, there were localities with incredible numbers of the anophelines, tens of thousands in a single stable, and no malaria whatever; there were swamps without malaria, and a great deal of malaria without swamps.

It was not until two important and, at the time, unrelated discoveries were brought to bear on the problem that the apparent anomalous behavior of the common malaria mosquito abroad was cleared up. The first was the precipitin test, permitting the exact identification of blood, both human and animal, a serological and purely taxonomic procedure by means of which, no matter where a mosquito was lurking at the time of its capture, its host or hosts could be determined.

The other discovery, which to my mind is one of the most important discoveries in the history of malariology, and certainly in its European aspects, was the discovery by Falleroni that females of the apparent European carrier, which he carefully raised, deposited five different types of beautifully ornamented but consistently different eggs, and that a given female always laid the same type of egg.

Today it seems incredible that 7 long years elapsed before this significant discovery was properly appraised and applied to the taxonomy of mosquitoes. By means of these discoveries, what had been formerly considered a single but unpredictable and widely distributed form, was found to be in reality several distinct species and distinguishable races. Thus, the hitherto inexplicable behavior of the European malaria mosquitoes was resolved with the aid of taxonomy, and the way cleared for effective control.

Species Sanitation

The exact knowledge of the species of mosquitoes found in any given area is of greatest importance in preventing the waste of effort and funds on unnecessary control measures and permitting full attention to be paid to the dangerous species. Species identification insures a maximum of effective control at minimum cost; we have, therefore, today "species sanitation," as it is called, as the accepted practice in mosquito control.

A notable instance where species sanitation was most successfully carried out was in the Natal, Brazil, area from 1938 to 1940. It was here that the late Raymond Shannon, formerly with the U.S. Department of Agriculture, and, at the time, with the Rockefeller Foundation, made the startling discovery in 1930 that the dread African carrier of malaria, *Anopheles gambiae,* was on the loose in the New World.

Probably shipborne, it brought about, in all, what is said to have been the worst malaria epidemic in historysome 300,000 cases, with enormous mortality, in a comparatively limited area. At once steps were taken to eliminate this exceedingly efficient carrier from the immediate vicinity of Natal. This was accomplished in the next 12 months, but, rather strange to say, no efforts were made to look farther afield for this highly dangerous insect.

It apparently made the most of the opportunity so afforded. Nothing is known of its ravages in the interim. In 1938, however, it caused a serious epidemic of malaria some hundreds of miles inland. This time there was no hesitation. All possible means of control were directed against this much to be feared species.

Nothing was left undone to completely eradicate it. In 2 years of intensive effort complete success was apparently achieved. No trace of *Anopheles gambiae* seems since to have been found in Brazil. A few airborne individuals, however, have been detected in planes from Africa and promptly destroyed.

Here again, species identification proved to be the important thing. It made species sanitation possible, and definitely effective, in a comparatively short space of time, and today enables the Brazilian Government to keep this dangerous enemy out of the country.

THE BLACK DEATH

The story of the plague-bubonic plague, the highly fatal Black Death of the Middle Ages-and of its spread and control in India, Ceylon, and elsewhere parallels that of malaria, and, like it, turns upon the critical recognition of species of insects-in this case, fleas.

Much of our knowledge of the dissemination of plague by fleas we owe to two men, L. Fabian Hirst, health officer at Colombo, Ceylon, and Nathan Charles Rothschild, an authority on the kinds of fleas, who discovered that the prevalent rat fleas of India and the Orient did not constitute a single species.

It was Hirst who first suggested and then demonstrated that these fleas had quite different biting habits and different appetites for human blood, and thus varied in their effectiveness in transmitting plague from rat to rat, and rat to man. Their discoveries established the geographic distribution of the different species of rat fleas as one of the most important factors governing the spread of plague, and for the first time furnished a logical explanation for the relative immunity of certain parts of India and Ceylon to both epidemic and epizootic bubonic plague.

This discovery was the natural outcome of the purely zoological researches of Rothschild and others on the systematics of fleas.

In Time of War and in National Defense

Though not accorded recognition in the headlines of the daily press or rewarded with oak-leaf clusters, the taxonomists made many noteworthy but unheralded contributions to the waging and winning of the late great war with their prompt identification of the many things about which vitally important information was urgently needed.

In war we have much the same problems in medicine, epidemics, disease, and health as in times of peace, only more intensified and more urgently calling for solution or alleviation. The immobilization of armies by attacks of malaria in the European theater and the casualties, if we may call them that, from the same cause and insect-borne diseases in the Pacific became so serious that it was of utmost importance that the mosquitoes, fleas, ticks, and other pests or vermin be identified without delay.

Those that could not be named by the sanitary and medical units in the field were given the very highest priority to Washington for immediate determination. During World War II a well-known news commentator, for want of a more timely subject perhaps, took it upon himself to ridicule a systematic treatise of the fleas of North America. It is the type of technical work that is of utmost value to the specialist desiring to make prompt and accurate determinations.

He described this Government publication as a waste of paper, containing no useful information because it did not tell how to free your dog of fleas. But it was just the sort of book that would have enabled Rothschild to distinguish the species of flea that was the chief carrier of bubonic plague in India from the less harmful kinds.

Moreover, this publication has in it the very information which enables one to identify this particular oriental plague carrier, which, by the way, has become established in this country, but happily, so far as we know, is not here infected with that most serious of diseases. A museum friend of mine, though not a scientist, was utterly shocked by the low regard that the commentator had for work so important. He wrote the commentator a letter which I believe is still pertinent, and I quote part of it:

"Having for many years been connected with a scientific establishment, and not being a scientist myself, I have come to realize the real value of such scientific works as you disparaged, and for the first time in my life I am moved `to write to the editor."

"This impulse was perhaps strengthened by the fact that the very next morning [after your broadcast] I was pointedly reminded of it by the receipt from the medical officer at one of our outlying bases of *a single* specimen of flea which he particularly desired to have identified with reference to its function as a possible carrier of disease.

Only by knowing the exact identity of an insect can information of this character be given promptly, and the scientific entomologist turns instantly to such works as you ridiculed just as you would seize 'Who's Who' or the Encyclopedia Britannica, or some report of the Department of Commerce for data you might need.

"A steady stream of mosquitoes, ticks, and the like is pouring into Washington each day by airplane under highest priorities from our farflung battle fronts, in order that the local specialists may make prompt identifications, thereby furnishing the medical officers in the field the guidance necessary for applying the most effective control measures.

"The mere knowledge of the precise name of `resident' fleas and other insects will enable the medical and sanitary services of our Armed Forces to quickly ascertain which of several towns in plagueinfested areas are the safest for quartering men.

"Such works as the one under discussion are a distinct contribution by the home front to our forces on the battle front. In this connection I am moved to quote a line from one of Kipling's `Barrack Room Ballads':

'Making fun of uniforms
    That guard you while you sleep
Is cheaper than them uniforms
    And they're starvation cheap.'"

Men, expendable I assume, were landed from submarines on more than one occasion to reconnoiter the places and the islands to be attacked. They were also instructed to bring back what they could of the animal life encountered.

As important as was the knowledge of the numbers and disposal of the enemy was the identity of the insect vectors in calculating the risks of attack and casualties from disease, which, more times than we care to admit, laid out more men than the enemy. The identification of dangerous insects in the war areas can be speedily accomplished only because of the stores of knowledge that the taxonomists have accumulated over the years.

They supplied much exceedingly valuable information in other directions also. Something had to be done about floating mines drifting into our coastal waters to menace shipping. Our patrol fleet needed to know the paths they traversed through the sea, so that they might be intercepted before their hostile mission could be accomplished.

It was also imperative to determine where the far more dangerous German submarines sinking tons of shipping in the western Atlantic and Caribbcan areas had their bases for overhaul, refueling, and the replenishment of stores.

From the surfaces of the mines and submarines were scraped marine growths and from the ballast and trimming tanks of the few submarines that were captured intact were recovered traces of bottom mud and sediments pumped into the tanks as the submarines were anchored near, or rested on, the bottom of the shoal bays of their rendezvous. These growths and the sediments, their mineral constituents and contained organisms, were carefully examined and named by appropriate specialists.

When the identifications were checked against the known distribution of the various materials it became possible to plot the probable paths of the mines and also to trace the submarines to their bases where they could be destroyed. You may well remember the paper balloons with which the Japanese so ingeniously took advantage of the currents of the upper atmosphere for dropping bombs on the States during the war with a minimum of effort and cost to themselves.

Until recently it was not known that during the 6 months that the Japanese continued this unique barrage over 9,000 such balloons had been launched and evidence had been found that 300, perhaps many more, had reached this country, some traveling as far east as Michigan. These balloons and the bombs they carried might have been frightfully dangerous.

They could kill and maim, start devastating forest fires, and, had they been so employed, would have been capable of spreading disease and noxious insect pests. How were we to stop them? The balloons were so constructed that after the last of their bomb load was dropped an explosive charge destroyed the balloon. To keep the Japanese from learning of the success of their efforts, the strictest censorship was imposed, but word was also quietly sent out to appropriate State officials that an intact balloon must be recovered at all costs, so that it could be carefully examined.

One was fortunately secured by an Oregon sheriff. The resulting identification of the sand ballast that the balloon carried, along with some of the remains of microscopic plants that were found in the sand, pointed to five possible launching sites. Armed with this information, our Air Force promptly bombed all five sites and, in so doing, must have hit the right one or ones, for soon thereafter this menacing offensive ceased.

Fisheries Biology and Conservation

I do not have space to tell of many examples in other fields of study in which the name of a species or organism solved a biologic problem. But because of their special pertinence I should like to cite three little instances that bear on the economics of fisheries.

Some months ago an American specialist on sipunculid worms was asked for copies of his technical publications by an Alaskan cod fisherman who had found that where these worms occurred he always made good hauls of fish. He wanted to plot the distribution of the worms in order to do better and to extend his operations.

A matter of weeks ago an ardent sport fisherman brought in a mantis shrimp about which he wanted to know its mode of life, its distribution, and where it could be obtained in quantity. Of course, to make a search for information, the species had to be identified. In turn, we learned something also-that this stomatopod was the favorite food of certain desirable panfish much sought after by fishermen in the Chesapeake Bay area.

In the Carolinas, where shad enjoy a certain amount of legal protection, the State conservation agent must be able to distinguish between four or five species of fish, all superficially more or less alike, if he is to catch violators of the law and avoid congesting the courts with the innocent. So, even in the enforcement of conservation laws, a knowledge of the species involved must be had.

Some Botanical Applications

Recently I was discussing some of these things with a friend of mine who is a systematic botanist. He spoke of cortisone and yams, and mentioned how much and how often the plant taxonomists are being called upon these days for information regarding not only the names of plants, but also their phylogeny and systematic relationships.

If a plant contains a rare alkaloid or drug, what about its relatives? Knowledge of kinship has facilitated many such investigations. The lore of ancient, primitive, and often unlettered peoples contains much of interest and value to us if only we can find the scientific names for the animals and plants of which they had learned the properties, good or bad, useful or harmful, by long and often sad experience.

Curare is one of these. Botanists these days work with maintenance crews in keeping clear fire lanes and electric-power and telegraph rights-of-way for the purpose of identifying the plants, so that the appropriate herbicides may be used to kill off unwanted vegetation. The result desired and achieved is a dense growth of low shrubbery that will so occupy and shade the ground that all other growth will be inhibited, yet itself will not hinder or impede the passage of inspection, maintenance, and repair crews.

Manual as well as mechanical clearing of ways, uphill and downdale, in these days of high labor and operating costs, is an expensive proposition, which, at best, only temporarily controls the situation. Spraying, too, can be a costly affair, as well as ineffective, if indiscriminate, without regard to the kinds of plants involved. Again we are moved to remark that wherever one turns, a thorough knowledge of the kinds of organisms, whether of plant or animal origin, sooner or later proves of real value and often of considerable economic importance in the most unexpected ways and places.

And finally, may we repeat what George Gaylord Simpson once so well stated:

"It is impossible to speak of the objects of any study, or to think lucidly about them, unless they are named. It is impossible to examine their relationships to each other and their places among the vast, incredibly complex phenomena of the universe, in short to treat them scientifically, without putting them into some sort of formal arrangement. . . . Taxonomy is at the same time the most elementary and the most inclusive part of zoology, most elementary because animals cannot be discussed or treated in a scientific way until some taxonomy has been achieved, and most inclusive because taxonomy in its various guises and branches eventually gathers together, utilizes, summarizes, and implements everything that is known about animals. . . ."

2

THE DIVERSITY

It is an evident truism, scarcely ever put into words, that animals are not all alike; they exist in a variety of forms, sizes, and colors and perform a variety of activities. It is also evident that individual animals do not occur with random combinations of features, but that there are large groups of individuals with substantially the same features, clearly set off from other groups of individuals possessing different sets of features.

These facts have long been tacitly assumed in the recognition that there are different *kinds* of animals. The word kind sometimes signifies groups of considerable size, as birds are recognized as being different *in kind* from fishes, but it is more often applied to the narrowest or most restricted concept; for example, a cottontail is not the same *kind* as a jack rabbit.

These kinds are in general what the scientist calls species. The members of each kind are recognized because they share certain features. This does not mean that they are exactly alike, however-one recognizes different house cats by minor features in which they differ from each other, just as one recognizes different human individuals. It is common knowledge, too, that within a given species there may be a difference in appearance between the young and the adult individuals, and between male and female.

There may also be differences due to the season of the year, the amount of food consumed, or the activities of the individual. The preceding remarks have suggested several of the ways in which animals are diverse-different kinds, developmental forms, seasonal forms, growth differences, functional forms, and all the differences between individuals and between parts of individuals. These cover a tremendous range of variety, at many levels.

This variety is oftentimes forgotten in the current tendency to enlarge upon the unity of all living things. There is basic similarity, but the similarities do not extend as far up the scale of organization as is sometimes implied, and the dissimilarity is frequently substantial at several levels. All animals and plants consist of protoplasm and its products, and .this protoplasm consists basically of immensely complex molecules of a few types.

These molecules are principally chains of carbon atoms with side chains and a variety of prosthetic groups. But different organisms possess many complex molecules that differ from those of other organisms, and they combine to form cells, structures, and organ systems of an almost endless variety. Unity or similarity is interwoven with multiplicity and diversity.

Taxonomy is based on the fact of diversity, and it records both similarities and diversities. Up to this point the term diversity has been used in a broad sense to cover all of the ways in which two individual animals may be different, whether they belong to the same species or not, or even the same group. It is useful to make a distinction between the diversity shown by the million kinds and the variability shown within one kind.

The word diversity implies both of these, so it is appropriate to refer to the first as *diversity of groups* (or group diversity). The word variation does not generally cover features of group diversity, so it can be restricted to the variability within the species.

However, variation will not readily include the gross forms in which animals appear (here called polymorphs), so the general term for all the diversity within the species must remain the *diversity of individuals* (or individual diversity). Although many of the same features are involved in these two levels of diversity, there is generally a marked difference in the expression at the two levels. They can thus be discussed separately in large part.

THE VARIETY IN THE DIVERSITY

The following list shows some of the ways in which the diversity appears. The numbered forms of diversity are stated in general terms, some more technical conditions are cited, and sometimes examples for clarification. The items are not mutually exclusive but are intended to suggest different aspects of diversity.

A. Two individual animals (specimens) may be different although belonging to the same species:

1. Different *age* (even among adults, age alone may produce differences).
2. Different *sex* (male or female; see also item 16 below).
3. Different physical *castes* (queen, drone, worker, soldier, replete, etc.).
4. Different phases of a *life cycle* (developmental stages; e.g., egg, larva, cyst, embryo, juvenile, nymph, pupa, adult).
5. Differing *body forms (polyp,* medusa, medusoid, dactylozooid, gonangium).
6. Were in differing positions in a *colony* (terminal individuals or basal ones, performing different functions, differing in structure).
7. Were living at different *seasons* or in different climatic cycles (spring and summer forms, and cyclomorphosis).
8. Were living in different physical *habitats* (ecophenotypes; arctic and temperate individuals).
9. Had responded in color to differing *backgrounds* (color changes produced by integumentary chromatophores in response to environment).
10. Were living in different *hosts* (in absence of complete host specificity, or in presence of host variability, a parasite may differ in or on different hosts).
11. Were feeding on different prey or plants *(food)* (difference similar to that in item 10 above).
12. Were living under different *crowding* conditions (density-dependent variation, sometimes related to availability of food).
13. Were differently *parasitized* (mechanical distortion response to presence of a parasite, as in stylopization).
14. Differ in *karyotype* principally (diploidy and haploidy, homozygosity and heterozygosity with dominance; sex chromosome differences would normally also result in sex differences as in item 2 above).
15. Had developed disproportionately in *size* (size alone would be a difference; sometimes large size is correlated with

excessive growth of one part; size may be due to differences in food supply, age, etc.).

16. Differing in *sex combination* (gynandromorph, intersex; in some species there may be male, female, hermaphroditic, and sexless individuals).
17. From different extremes of continuous *character expression.*
18. From differing sectors of *a discontinuous character expression.*
19. Were *deformed* at birth or any time during development (normal vs. teratological; at least sometimes due to factors in item 20 below).
20. Had suffered an *accident* (leaving permanent physical damage).
21. Was *diseased,* in the sense of infection by germs or poisons (normal vs. pathological but usually temporary).
22. Underwent *post-mortem changes* (due to preservation of specimens or lack of it-color, size, oiliness, etc.).

C. Two individuals, while belonging to different species, may differ in any of the ways 1-22 (specimens of different species may differ in any of these ways but real differences between species may be found in the ability to differ in these ways, and in the limits or frequency of these differences) and the following:

23. Differing in one or more relatively *minor feature,* structural, physiological, behavioral, or other (these are the customary specific characters).

D. Two individuals, while belonging to the same group but not the same species, may differ in any of the ways 1-23 (specimens of different groups may differ in any of these ways but real differences between groups may be found in the ability to differ in these ways, and in the limits or frequency of these differences) and the following:

24. In *most gross features* (as any two phyla differ).
25. In *some gross features* but not most (as any two classes in a phylum, or orders in a class).
26. In *a major structural feature* or combination (as any two families or genera).
27. In a basic *body arrangement* (symmetry, segmentation,

strobilation, cephalization).

28. In *a primary ecological adaptation* (fins for swimming, wings for flying; air-breathing vs. aquatic).
29. In an important *metabolic process* (use of different hydrogen acceptors in muscle metabolism).
30. In a major *activity capability* (winged, sessile, sense organs).
31. In being *solitary or colonial* (earthworms and bryozoans, jellyfish and corals).
32. In having a drastically different *life history (such* as juvenile-toadult in Nematoda, or miracidium-to-sporocyst-to-redia-to-cercariato-metacercaria-to-adult in Trematoda, or larva-to-pupa-to-adult in Insecta).
33. In basic *cleavage pattern* (the direction of the first planes of cleavage and distribution of egg contents thereby).
34. In any of the multitudinous body systems, functions, activities, distributions, etc., not cited above.

This list is by no means exhaustive, especially B and C. There are innumerable variations of these diversities, intermediates between them, and combinations of them. (Items 1-22 include polymorphism and individual variation (within the species). Item 23 consists of the usual features distinguishing species.

The Diversity within a Species

Before a taxonomist can classify species, he must know these species. Whether he believes that he can classify individual specimens into species or that he must infer the species from the sample (specimens) before him, there are many differences between individuals which will not be used to distinguish the kinds. These are the differences found between individuals of the same species.

If these characteristics are not to be used in classification, they must be recognized and consciously rejected. Man happens to be a species that occurs in relatively few forms. Thus, there are no normal physical coloniality, no functional hermaphroditism, no distinct seasonal forms, no parthenogenesis, no asexual generations, and no physical castes.

Nevertheless, the variation from individual to individual seems to us to be great, involving male and female, babies, youths, and adults, tall and short, hirsute and bald. We tend to forget the more extreme examples such as *dwarfs*, *megalocephalics*, and *Siamese twins*. That these all belong to one species might not be obvious if it happened not to be the one most familiar to us. Although such differences between individuals will not be useful in classification, they must be recognized and understood, else all the males will be classified together and all the females.

Many errors in classification have been made because of failure to recognize the variation within the species. The diversity within a species, often called variation or individual variation, can be in the form of continuous change, such as growth, or of discrete types, such as sexes or castes. Either of these may be part of a sequence of forms (growth or alternating generations) or not sequential (climatically induced or castes existing together).

The word variation has been used in various ways. It is restricted here to the difference (whether structural, functional, behavioral, chemical, or other) that exists between the offspring of the same parents or between individuals of the same species.

These are the differences that might appear among the progeny of one asexual parent, or one parthenogenetic parent, or two parents that could themselves have been offspring of another such pair. The amount of variation within different species is extremely diverse, but no species are known in which there is no detectable variation (except where there are too few specimens for comparison).

Theoretically, the nearest approach to this is found among the asexually produced populations (clones), in which the basic gene complements may at first be identical and environmental pressures relatively uniform.

The Causes of Diversity

There are many brief statements of the causes or sources of variation. None of these seems entirely adequate to explain all of items 1-21 in the previous tabulation. These causes or sources have been classified as intrinsic or extrinsic, inherited or non-inherited, continuous or discontinuous, and constant or sporadic.

However, the two most useful ways of distinguishing causes or sources of variation seem to be the following: *First,* the distinction between those that occur normally in the life cycle and those that occur only sporadically or accidentally; *second,* the distinction between those that are produced by genetic factors and those that are determined by the environment (within limits set by the genes).

There are five main subdivisions of variation: polymorphism, other normal cyclic changes, mutations, normal genetic differences, and externally induced differences. Examples or a brief discussion of each of the causes of variation are given here:

(1) ***Normal developmental processes*** produce the stages in the life cycle (developmental polymorphism), growth and aging, alternating generations, and obligate seasonal forms (including cyclomorphosis).

(2) ***Sexuality*** refers to sexual polymorphism (male, female, hermaphrodite, neuter), sequence of sexes (protandry and protogyny), sex-linked characters (those of one sex only, such as male plumage and ovipositors of females), and some castes.

(3) ***Colonial division of labor*** refers to the polyp and medusa, and the polymorphic colonies (such as *Obelia, Physalia,* and the Bryozoa).

(4) ***Genetic recombination*** accounts for a large part of general variation but can seldom be recognized except by genetic analysis. *Ploidy* involves the haploid and diploid conditions as well as the rarer polyploids. Gynandromorphs and intersexes are also due to genetic aberrations.

(5) ***Mutations*** may produce either apparently continuous variation or discontinuous variation. The number of mutations normally present in populations of most species is unknown, but they are doubtless a real part of the individual variation.

(6) ***Response to environment*** results in a variety of sorts of variation:

(a) habitat-induced;
(b) host-determined;
(c) density-dependent (crowding);
(d) climatically controlled (e.g., arctic forms);
(e) food (prey or plant food, some castes);
(f) disease (response to pathogenic organisms);
(g) parasite-induced;
(h) color changes;
(i) seasonal forms (if not obligate); and
(j) terata and accidental mutilations.

There are also some that can scarcely be classified. One of these is autotomy, self-mutilation, in response to accident but determined by intrinsic decision. Another case is the effect of domestication. Still another is the effect of fossilization and preservation in sediments and rocks.

The word variation is most likely to bring to mind the small differences, particularly those that are continuous or not obviously discontinuous. This variation is accounted for in large part by the following items: growth and aging, sex-linked characters, recombination, mutations, habitat and food effects, color changes, and very diverse mixtures of these, affecting diverse features of the animals.

The forms of diversity. Some of the kinds of diversity may be tabulated thus:

A. Inherent diversity
   1. Part of the life cycle
      Age variation and change
      Growth (normal stages or heterogonic growth)
      Seasonal (including cyclomorphosis)
      Alternating generations
      Sex arrangement (protandry, protogyny, extra form of neuter or hermaphrodite)
      Developmental stages
      Body forms (polyp and medusa, functional forms)
   2. Genetically produced (but not in usual life cycle)
      Castes
      Sexes
      Gynandromorphs
      Intersexes
      Genetic polymorphism (recombination)
      Ploidy
      Mutations (discontinuous)
      Variation of any feature
B. Externally induced
   3. Environmentally induced
      Ecological
         Habitat
         Host-determined
         Density-dependent
         Climatic (arctic forms)
         Food (prey or plant food)
         Disease
      Parasite-induced
      Neurogenic or neurohumeral color changes
C. Occasional and abnormal
   4. Autotomy

5. Teratological changes
6. Accidents
7. Post-mortem changes
8. Fossilization
9. Artifacts

D. Indistinguishable combinations of these

10. Continuous variation of any features or of the combination of many features

In discussing below some aspects of this variation, it will be helpful to use still another arrangement of the factors. Among the causes listed above are several which produce strikingly different body forms (correctly called polymorphism in the classical sense). There are others which produce continuous change during the life of the individual *(development)*. There are some that involve *sexuality* and the distribution of the sex organs.

There are some that are clearly an aspect of the normal *environment*. And there are some that consist of *willful or accidental* events. These are not clearly distinct, and this overlap is one of the factors that makes this variation hard to recognize and make allowance for.

POLYMORPHISM

Five forms of diversity produce sharply different forms within some species: developmental stages, alternating generations, body forms, castes, and sexes. These occur regularly in the normal life of the species, which is to say in the lives of the individuals which make up the species. Polymorphism is defined here as the existence of individuals of more than one form within a species.

This situation is very nearly universal among animals, for different forms may be assumed by males and females, by young and adults, by successive "generations," by individuals receiving different food, and by others. In the zoological books which refer to polymorphism in detail, sexual and developmental forms are often omitted, but if we exclude them by definition we would have to set up a new term to include all the regular *intraspecific* but discontinuous diversity.

All polymorphism is genetically controlled in the sense that nothing can take place which is not provided for in the genetic constitution. Most polymorphism is directly produced by genetic means, such as sexual, developmental, alternating, and allometric. Some is produced or controlled by the environment, such as nutritional, seasonal, and occasionally sexual.

It has not been found useful to classify the various types of polymorphism. There is too much overlap in causes, too little known about how the various types arise, and little real difference in the manner of expression. It is possible to group some types as involving two or more forms simultaneously as against those appearing successively. Cr those that perform different functions as against those that do not.

Or those that exist in a united colony as against those that are completely separate individuals. But no useful classification results, so the different types will here be discussed separately under the most appropriate headings, beginning with those that occur simultaneously.

Functional Polymorphism

In several groups of animals there is a real division of labor between individuals. This is seen among bees, ants, and termites, where individuals may be specialized for breeding, tending the young, protecting the colony, gathering food, storing food, and so on.

These forms are called *castes,* and the individuals are, of course, completely separate. In the colonies of connected individuals, such as occur in Coelenterata, Bryozoa, and Tunicata, the individuals may be very highly specialized, with as many as six different kinds of individuals in one colony.

Again these specialized individuals may each perform one function, such as grasping food, reproduction, anchoring or floating the colony, nursing other individuals, feeding, swimming, or protection. In each of these types of colonies its very existence depends upon the presence of these specialized individuals.

We can thus look upon this as obligatory polymorphism. Sexual dimorphism, which is of course also functional, is sometimes obligatory, and 'it is sometimes partly facultative in the sense that it is not essential to species continuance, although the individuals do not have any choice in the matter.

Sexual dimorphism. Substantial difference in appearance between the two sexes in any species is a form of polymorphism. It is almost universal among sexual animals. In a few cases, there are more than two sexual forms, described below, and some forms of general structural polymorphism are correlated with the sex of the individuals.

The simplest animals to show clear dimorphism of the sexes are Acanthocephala, Neinatoda, and Rotifera. In some of the echiuroid worms, the difference between male and female reaches such an extreme that the male becomes an internal parasite in the body of the female, bearing almost no resemblance to her in form, size, or activity. In many groups of Arthropoda there is a marked size difference between the sexes, or evident modification of some external feature in one sex. In some insects the ovipositor of the female is very distinct.

In some the antennae or mouthparts may be very different in male and female. Sometimes color pattern is strikingly different. There are all degrees of difference, ranging from sexes which differ only in the cryptic fact that the gonad produces sperm in one and ova in the other to the almost complete dissimilarity between the sexes in scale insects and Strepsiptera (with parasitic females).

Perhaps mainly because of greater size, the differences between the sexes in many vertebrates are well known. Probably none are so extreme as *Bonellia* or *Lecanium,* but they are none-the-less obvious. In many birds the dimorphism is striking. Sexual polymorphism, in the sense of more than two sexual forms, occurs in Protozoa, Coelenterata, Gastrotricha, Calyssozoa (Endoprocta), and such colonial forms as may possess neuter individuals (Coelenterata, Bryozoa, Pterobranchia, and Tunicata).

It is easy to let sexuality get beyond the proper range of polymorphism, as defined above. Mere separation of sexes does not produce polymorphs, unless the individuals are noticeably different. In the Gastrotricha at least one species can have males, females, or hermaphrodites, but striking differences in appearance seem to be lacking. In the Calyssozoa at least one species occurs as male, female, or hermaphrodite, but again no great differences are found in appearance. None of these, therefore, is truly polymorphic.

In social insects there may be males, females, and neuters of several sorts. These may be clearly distinguishable and may be considered polymorphic. (They are also properly treated as castes.) In ciliate Protozoa, the mating types described by Sonneborn seem to be very similar in nature to sexes. There may be as many as six mating types in one species.

However, the absence of differences in external appearance would make it inappropriate to call this polymorphism. Developmental polymorphism. Most familiar animals originate from zygotes or fertilized eggs formed in each case by the union of sperm and ovum from its parents. We cannot say all, because there are two classes of exceptions.

In a wide variety of groups, some individuals originate by asexual means, and in other groups unfertilized ova may develop into new individuals. (There are even groups in which males are not known to exist at all.) In animals that originate from ova, either fertilized or parthenogenetic, there is always a considerable change of form during development. Even if the egg gives forth a miniature of the adult, which simply grows larger to become mature, there are two forms of the individual-the egg and the adult.

In most such animals, the individual which hatches from the egg is somewhat different, perhaps almost entirely different, in appearance from the adult (as well as from the egg). In these animals the newly hatched individual is called a larva. The change from the larva to the adult is sometimes called metamorphosis.

It is part of development. The occurrence of these structurally, and sometimes functionally, different stages in the development of an individual is polymorphism in a successional sense. It is obligate in the sense that the stages cannot be avoided by the individual, which must pass through the sequence to attain adulthood (usually sexual maturity).

If the animal is viviparous, that is if it retains the egg within its body until after the egg hatches, or if there is no egg covering after cleavage begins, the form is judged upon birth. There appears to be no difference between this and oviparity so far as developmental polymorphism is concerned. There are three principal types of developmental polymorphism, arising from the general habits of the animals.

Marine organisms frequently hatch from the egg as a motile larva different in appearance from the adult, which may change into another larval form or directly into the adult. Internal parasites frequently produce eggs which develop through a succession of larval forms, often with asexual multiplication at one or more points, and with the final larval form developing into the adult.

Terrestrial Arthropoda usually lay eggs from each of which hatches a grub-like larva, which may later enter a different resting or pupal stage before metamorphosing into the adult form. In all of these, the egg, larva, and adult are distinct in form, and additional larval forms or a pupal form may be interpolated.

Polymorphism in development thus can involve either sexual or asexual processes. In some animals it may involve both in turn, in an alternation of generations. (Some of the ways in which these alternations can occur are diagrammed in the next chapter.)

VARIATION

Variation in development. In addition to the polymorphic forms cited above in the life cycle of many animals, other kinds develop with little or no evidence of such forms. In Nematoda a juvenile hatches from the egg and grows into an adult with no stages or quick changes in form.

The only distinct stages left are egg and adult. In asexually reproducing forms, such as *Hydra,* by the time the new individual is separated from the old it is already an adult. It never passes through any larval or egg stage. In these, there is gradual change-in size, proportions, external features, internal organs, and so on. This is developmental variation. It occurs in all forms even when there are polymorphic stages.

Other difficulties appear to perplex the zoologist: when adults of some species are larviform, when larvae become sexually mature before assuming the adult form, when regeneration produces structures different from those lost by mutilation (heteromorphosis), and when there are alternations of asexual and sexual forms.

Sexual Variation

As indicated above, sexuality does not always result in dimorphism. The sexes may look alike; hermaphrodites may look like unisexual individuals; and even neuters may be indistinguishable. On the other hand, there may be numerous sex-linked features which show any amount of variation due to genes or environment.

This is a major source of the continuous variation. Genetic variation. Although all variation, like all diversity, is either controlled directly by the genes or limited by them, much small variation is the sole result of various genetic processes.

Although this can be confidently stated to apply to all animals, it applies much more cogently to sexually reproducing ones, and it is possible to identify this variation as genetic only when some genetic analysis has been made. It thus forms a major source of the minor variation of animals, but a cryptic source to the taxonomist in most cases.

The processes are: *mutation* (of genes, which produces new features), *hybridization* (which introduces new genes into the species), *recombination* (which shuffles the gene expressions into new combinations), *ploidy* (in which diploid and haploid individuals may differ, or polyploids occur), and *chromosome aberrations* (acting much like mutations). These are not entirely distinct and may act in combination.

Environmental Variation

Although genetic variation is universal, and although the gene complement serves to channel and limit all other types of variation, by far the largest source of minor variation in most animals is the effect of environmental factors. They can act on almost any part of the body, at any time during its life, in any part of its range. They can cause temporary, cyclic, or permanent changes in the individual. These variations may be due to any of the following:

Climate, as distinct from seasonal change, may produce many variations within a species. The populations of *Rana pipiens,* extending from Canada to Panama, show many differences, apparently due primarily to climate working through the physiology of development.

Elevation and latitude may cause variation, such as size, within a species. Although the difference may be actually caused by some other factor such as temperature, it shows up clearly in relation to altitude or latitude.

Seasons, as cyclic phenomena, frequently induce changes that lead to spring forms and summer forms, or to cyclomorphosis-a succession of shapes due to a succession of seasons.

Background color is an environmental stimulus. Many animals respond to the color of their surroundings by changing their own color. The effect is generally to make them less conspicuous by blending into the background.

There are differences in ability to change color from species to species and group to group, but the interest here is in the differences in color between individuals of one species, or changes in one individual through time.

The only groups in which color changes commonly occur are the Cephalopoda, the Crustacea, and the cold-blooded vertebrates. They occur infrequently in the Hirudinea, Gastropoda, Insecta, and Echinoidea.

There are, of course, other types of color diversity in animal kinds; for example, genetic color phases, colors influenced by the food, or color influenced by the color of the material on which development takes place.

Density-Dependent Phenomena

The density of a population may directly or indirectly produce variation among the individuals. Some insects develop differently if grown under crowded conditions, even if food is plentiful. Many animals show differences when food is scarce or when population pressures force some into marginal habitats.

Food

As just mentioned, the amount of food may affect certain individuals. More obvious variation is caused by differences in the food utilized; for example, where two host-plant species are utilized or where prey is largely of different types for different individuals.

Host-Determined

Very similar to the last case is variation among parasites that utilize different hosts. The variation in parasitic insects may appear in size, proportions, cocoon color, and structural features such as presence of wings. The food of the host may affect the parasite, as shown in some parasitic wasps and some nematodes.

Parasite-Induced

Such parasites as gall-wasps are well known to evoke changes in the tissues of their plant hosts, and gall-like effects of parasitization are not unknown in animals. Not only do some nematodes produce galls in plants, but some cause gall-like alterations in parasitized ants. Microorganisms may also be considered parasites, and the diseases produced not only affect the individual during the course of the disease but may leave permanent effects.

If the disease occurs during larval stages, there may be drastic effects on development and the appearance of the adult.

Willful or Accidental Variation

Autotomy

A *crayfish* with one cheliped much smaller than the other may have suffered an accident to a cheliped and rid himself of it by autotomy, i.e. self-mutilation. While a new cheliped is being regenerated, there will be distinct difference from the usual appearance.

It is not certain that all autotomy should be classed as environmentally stimulated. The evisceration of sea cucumbers is in response to some outside stimulus, but the autotomy of the starfish may be due to internal stimuli. In any case, it may result in a four-armed starfish and a comet-star, through regeneration of both fragments.

Accidents

It would be difficult to define accidents, but any physical damage is likely to leave scars, if the damage is not fatal. If it occurs in larval or embryonic stages, it may have drastic effects on the structure of the adult. Some of the "monsters" or terata are produced by physical damage, although genetic factors may sometimes be involved.

Even damage to the egg may produce abnormal embryos and adults. The general subject of teratology, regardless of causes, is discussed further below. In some other *Crustacea*, if an eye is lost through accident, regeneration may produce not another eye but an antenna in its place. This is *heteromorphosis*, which leads to a variant abnormal condition.

Teratology

One of the kinds of diversity among the individuals of any species, frequently overlooked, is *teratology*. In the development of individual animals, it is not at all uncommon for disturbance in either the spatial or the temporal *synchronization* of the many processes to lead to abnormal organs or individuals.

In many animals, these deviations are difficult to detect, because no standard or norm is available. The gross "monsters" such as Siamese twins and two-headed snakes, as well as all the malformed foetuses, fall under this heading. The *exceptional* features which they show must be recognized as such by *taxonomists*, if they are not to be used as the basis for spurious groups erected for these non-recurrent forms.

Some living terata have presented features, such as two heads, nowhere else encountered in the animal kingdom. Insects with biramous antennae and double legs are among these. If the deviation affects only one member of a pair of structures, as it apparently usually does, the condition is likely to be readily recognized.

Many minor terata have been reported in animals such as insects, where the exoskeleton sometimes makes such features obvious. Without reference to the cause of the deformation, the following types of monstrosities do occur:

1. Giants.
2. Dwarfs.
3. Defects in any structure.
4. Embryonic irregularities:
   a. Incomplete development
   b. Non-synchronous development
   c. Abnormal cleavage.
5. Abnormal hermaphroditism.
6. Cyclops or siren.
7. Reversed organ position.
8. Siamese twins.
9. Two-headedness and other duplications.
10. Heteromorphosis.

Diversity of Individuals in Taxonomy

Taxonomists have always been concerned about "individual variation." What this term means and how to recognize the variation between individuals of one species has led to difficulties. It is no easier to identify this sort of diversity today, but at least its nature and causes are better understood.

If taxonomists are to segregate, name, and classify the existing species and if they are to do this on the basis of the attributes of the individuals, they must find the attributes which all corresponding members of a species have in common and they must avoid attributes which are lacking in a segment of the species.

They must recognize that most species consist of two sexes, of two or more developmental stages, and of large and small individuals; that some species also consist of several color phases, of diverse structural forms such as polyp and medusa, of several physically different castes, and of seasonal forms; and that in some species, the individuals appear very similar in most detectable ways, but in other species there is a wide range of difference between individuals in obvious features.

How to tell the variation within the species from the differences between species has always been the chief difficulty of taxonomy. The recognition of the hereditary nature of the ideal species characters does not solve this problem, inasmuch as some intraspecific variation is also hereditary and seems to he controlled by the same genetic mechanisms.

Theoretically, it is easy to make a distinction between those attributes that are shared by all members of a species and those that are found in only part of the members, but there is no simple way to distinguish these in practice. The comparative methods by which this is done are discussed in a later chapter.

THE DIVERSITY OF KINDS AND GROUPS

There is diversity of kinds, of groups of kinds, and of groups of groups, as one goes up in the hierarchy of taxa. Kinds are often diverse in the details of their features; groups of kinds are diverse in combinations of the details or in features thought to be less superficial; and groups of groups are diverse in major adaptations-in organ systems, in major diversities in body arrangement, developmentai patterns, etc.

The existence of a vast amount of group diversity has been recognized for centuries. In recent years, emphasis has frequently been put on the much smaller amount of unity or basic similarity among all animals. To emphasize that diversity is still the most obvious feature of animals, some of it is suggested in this chapter. Most of the diversity cited is at group levels fairly high in the hierarchy.

In contrast, species within a group would differ in less obvious ways: in proportions of parts, in the number of multiple structures, in coloration (pigment difference or arrangement), in specific protein molecule components, in slight behavioral differences, in definite but slight genetic differences, in slight differences in development, in different responses to environmental influences, in possession of different parasites, in use of different food, in dependence on different hosts, in occupation of different geographical areas, and so on.

All of these can be differences between species, but of course they can also be differences between populations or individuals within the species. If the differences are within the species, they are individual variation, discussed in the previous chapter.

How to distinguish which level a difference represents is the first problem to be solved in either classification or descriptive taxonomy. This problem will be discussed further in later chapters, but there is no easy solution or standard formula. Only the broadest possible knowledge of the organisms will serve to make the distinction, and this is usually applied through a series of refinements in successive monographic studies.

Limitations

There are limits to diversity, although the nature of the limiting factor is seldom understood. It is certain that the Second Law of Thermodynamics limits what evolution can produce. This is, of course, involved with the very nature of the molecules of protoplasm, as well as with the atomic structure and energy relations of matter itself.

On a much more visible scale, one can imagine many things that animals do not produce, such as three pairs of wings in insects, vertebrates with separate heads for feeding and a sensing-control center, or parasites requiring five successive hosts.

These things would not be any stranger than some of the things that do occur, such as the variable number of legs in Pycnogonida, the multiple-purpose life histories of some parasites, or the unique systems such as the Aristotle's lantern in Echinoidea. In the past, there may have been some things tried that are outside the limits appearing today. In fact some extinct groups do show unexplainable unique features.

If geologic time is long enough for all possible things to have been tried, given physical conditions then existing, we can assume the diversity that has existed is roughly what could exist. Paleontologists surely do not know all that has existed, very likely not a major part of it.

Universal Features

It has been stated that all metazoan animals are sufficiently alike for concepts that work in the Mammalia to work in any other group as well. Unfortunately this statement is clearly due to lack of familiarity with the diversity of invertebrates. Many groups lack the genetic effects of outbreeding, affecting the application of many evolutionary concepts.

In many groups, sex is determined in radically different ways. Development at all stages from fertilization on varies in many basic ways. Provisions for so basic a function as absorption of food by digestion are so different in Cestoda, Pogonophora, and Mammalia as to be similar only in the fact of exchange of metabolites with the environment.

There are metazoans without germ layers; there are some without separate cells (at least in parts of the body); there are ones that lack major marks of animals, such as locomotion, or possess major features of plants, such as production of carbohydrate skeletons; and there are ones in which there is virtually nothing that can be called behavior, not even coordinated reactions.

It is surely extremely risky to assume that *any* generalization based on higher vertebrates will apply even in principle to all animals, even all metazoans. If protozoans are considered to be animals, then nearly all rules are certain to break down.

Even to say that all are composed of protoplasm controlled by DNA systems is scarcely meaningful because of the known diversity in that group of molecules, and little generalization above that level is consistent with the known but sometimes forgotten diversity that exists.

THE EXTENT OF THE DIVERSITY

The presence of diversity in the animal kingdom is proverbial, but the extent of it is nowadays greatly understated. A catalog of all the diversity would be an encyclopedia of all zoology. It could not yet be written, because new diversity is still being discovered at a rate higher than generally realized.

The present generation has seen the discovery of a new phylum, discovery of living representatives of at least two classes thought to be long extinct, discovery of unknown organs in common kinds of birds, discovery of an entire level of diversity (biochemical) previously not detectable, and recognition of a variety of genetic mechanisms previously undreamed of.

Because the extent of this diversity is too often overlooked, and because it is the basic realm of study of taxonomy, it is thought to be worthwhile to illustrate it here. Examples of diversity have been chosen to illustrate the fact that the diversity is itself diverse-there are a wide range of features which themselves show a wide range of development or expression through the animal kingdom.

GENERAL FEATURES OF GROUP DIVERSITY

Textbooks of college zoology usually mention as few as 10 or as many as 20 phyla of animals, often with no indication that there are about this many more groups of animals that cannot be placed for sure in any of the 10 or 20. This is excused by reference to space limitations and the assumption that some groups are more important.

Even the recognition of 35 or 40 phyla does not acknowledge the diversity at this level. Evolutionists generally deny that any of the existing phyla arose directly from any other existing ones, which means that all the common-ancestor groups are not only extinct but unrecognized as fossils. Yet these groups must have existed, and there may have been quite a few of them.

It is just possible that they are not entirely unknown. In the more detailed paleontological works, there is frequent mention of unusual fossils which cannot be assigned to known phyla. Some of these are imperfectly known-not enough remains to tell whether they are different from living animals.

Others seem to be quite possibly the remnants of distinct groups. For example, conodonts present several features not duplicated in any living group. There is no real basis for assigning them to any phylum. The criconarids and hyolithids are conical or pyramidal shells of unique types, made by animals of unknown nature.

The peculiar fossil *Amiskwia* bears some resemblance to the Chaetognatha, but over a gap of 450,000,000 years, the differences leave some doubt as to the relationship. The little fossil cone shell *Matthevia,* which has the inner chamber divided into two by a thick transverse septum, gives little basis for assignment to any phylum. And there are many others.

Instead of assuming that there are only a limited number of phyla, it seems to be necessary to admit that minor groups and still unrecognized ones very likely occur or have occurred in considerable variety. It is unlikely that evolution produced the present diversity without many developments which eventually proved to be incapable of survival.

It may thus be expected that the number of recognizable phyla and classes will increase considerably, as the unique features of these isolated groups come to be recognized. A reasonable prediction would seem to be 50 phyla as a minimum.

In assessing the variety of the animal kingdom, or even in summarizing its aspects for beginning students, one of the most important facts is the diversity in size of the groups which occur. A group (perhaps a phylum or class) which consists of a few species in a genus or two is no less important biologically than another group at the same level in which the number of species now living is vastly greater.

In fact, for studying the diversity of animals the odd or peculiar groups, representing blind alleys or relicts or recent developments, are in many ways the most interesting ones.

Diversity in Group Size

Although most of the lesser-known groups are of small size, they do not of themselves show the diversity in size mentioned above. At every level in the classification, there is a wide range of actual size, as the following examples will illustrate. The phyla range in size, regardless of whose classification is chosen, from such a small homogeneous group as the Chaetognatha, with about 50 known species, to the Arthropoda, with over 800,000 known kinds.

Although the phylum Mollusca contains some 130,000 species, when these are divided into seven classes, they vary in size from the Monoplacophora with two living species (and a handful of fossil ones) to the relatively enormous class Gastropoda with its 80,000 or so living forms and thousands of fossil ones.

In the Arthropoda the classes Pauropoda and Symphyla with about 50 species together stand next to the Insecta with more than 700,000 species. At the level of order the mammalian Monotremata consists of three species, whereas there are some 3,000 species in the order Rodentia.

In the Insecta a recent monograph of the order Zoraptera includes 16 species, whereas the order Coleoptera contains about 300,000 kinds. At the family level the ratio can be as high as 50,000 to 1 within a single order. There is an isolated family of beetles (Platypsyllidae) consisting of a single species, and the family of the weevils (Curculionidae) contains 50,000 species and is still growing as many new ones are discovered. The final level in this series is that of the genus.

Great diversity in size exists, but some writers have suggested that all large genera should be broken up into smaller ones; for example, "There is every reason to believe that these giant genera will eventually be broken up into a number of smaller ones." This remark is based solely on ignorance of these large genera, because the specialists on some of them know that they are truly homogeneous and cannot even be divided into subgenera except on an arbitrary basis.

Some of these genera contain several thousand species, while many insect genera are known from only one species of isolated character. There is not a shred of uniformity in the size of the taxa at any level in the hierarchy of classification. Taxonomy is not concerned with the reasons for this diversity in size; it merely records the facts and tries to uncover patterns, uniformities, or discrepancies among them.

The processes that are believed to have produced the many kinds of animals (evolution) are not such as to lead us to expect any uniformity in the size of taxa. Instead, extinction due to various causes would almost necessarily lead to differences in size. It is only the extent of the extremes which might be unexpected.

Diversity in Breadth of Groups

Some groups of animals, even fairly large ones, are homogeneous, whereas some others are heterogeneous to a substantial degree. By homogeneous is meant consisting only of animals all very much alike in a large number of obvious features.

In contrast, some groups contain quite diverse subgroups having in common substantially less than all the obvious features. For example, the Pelecypoda or Bivalvia among the mollusks are almost all immediately recognizable to anyone familiar with a few of them.

The class Gastropoda, on the other hand, includes not only the readily recognized snails but also the land slugs, the sea slugs, the pteropods, the abalone, the limpets, and other forms of quite diverse appearance and structure.

In the Coelenterata, the Scyphozoa form a homogeneous unit, varying only in the details of a single basic pattern. The Hydrozoa, on the other hand, are extremely diverse. They include solitary polyps, solitary medusae, colonial polyps, and complex colonies of polypoid and medusoid members combined.

Considering the relatively simple structure of the organisms, the diversity in form within the Hydrozoa is extremely high. If the millepores, the stromatoporoids, and the graptolites are included, as is still a common practice, the intra-class diversity becomes much greater, probably greatly exceeding that of any other group of animals.

Two more or less comparable groups of annelid worms are the terrestrial earthworms (Oligochaeta) and the mostly marine Polychaeta. The first is a uniform group, doubtfully divisible into subgroups above the family level, whereas the Polychaeta consist of active swimming forms, as well as less active burrowing forms and sessile tube-dwelling forms. Most writers also include in the Polychaeta a very different sort of animal, the ectoparasitic Myzostomida. A general measure of the diversity within the various phyla of animals is provided by the number of classes recognized in each.

In one classification which includes 40 phyla, the 107 classes are distributed as follows:

Phyla of 1 class each	21	6 classes each	1
2 classes each	7	7 classes each	1
3 classes each	4	8 classes each	1
4 classes each	2	11 classes each	1
5 classes each	1	16 classes each	1

Thus, half the phyla consist of a single type of animal not divisible into classes, but a third of the phyla consist of three or more subgroups diverse enough to be listed as classes. The range of subgroups from one to sixteen represents the variation in internal diversity of the phyla. There is little correlation between this and the diversity in size of the phyla.

Although the largest phyla all consist of several classes, some of the single-class phyla are substantial in size and diverse at the ordinal and family levels (Nematoda and Graptozoa), as well as several of the two-class phyla (Bryozoa and Brachiopoda).

DIFFERENCES BETWEEN GROUPS

Differences between groups may be as great as the difference between unicellular and multicellular, between solitary and colonial, between presence or absence of a digestive system, or between having an exoskeleton over the body or being devoid even of an epidermis; they may be as slight as the number of serial organs, the presence of such a structure as a feather, or the position of the anus with respect to the tentacles.

Such differences do not automatically qualify to distinguish groups. Any pair of them can occur within one group at a level above the one in which they are distinctive. The range of features in which such differences can occur is too great to be tabulated here.

It can occur at any level of organization or activity, as illustrated in the following paragraphs.

Chemical Diversity

Some general biology books imply that there is great unity in the chemical basis of the different forms of life and groups of organisms. At the same time it is held that there is biochemical uniqueness in all kinds of organisms if not actually in all individuals. It is a trend of our times to emphasize the unity-the similarity.

This aspect is almost unique in being summarized in an elaborate ten-volume work entitled *Handbook o f Biological Data,* consisting of thousands of tables on many aspects of biochemistry. (It is seriously misnamed, inasmuch as it deals almost exclusively with biochemistry and physiology to the total exclusion of large aspects of biology.)

It would seem to be an easy task to summarize the diversity at the biochemical level from these numerous and elaborate tables. The biologist soon finds, however, that this is really a medical reference book in major part, with only occasional references to invertebrates, and even these are usually included as if in concession to those few who might notice the omission.

A few pieces of pertinent information can be gleaned from this source. There are some other publications of interest, particularly on insects, but no survey of the biochemistry of the Animal Kingdom is available. Such a work could not be other than sketchy, at best, because almost nothing is known of the biochemistry of many groups, and too often data are not comparable from group to group.

The present-day concepts of genetics require that some of the molecules of the genes be different in each kind of animal. The extent of the difference may be surmised in some cases, but the actual structure of any protein molecule of this sort is still not positively known.

Inasmuch as the instructions coded in the gene structure are translated into specific molecules, cells, and organs by enzyme systems, there must also be some differences in enzyme complement between different kinds. It is fairly certain that differences in molecular structure exist in all parts of all living things.

Cell Diversity

Cells illustrate well the dual viewpoint of unity and diversity. Basic cell types are found throughout the animal kingdom, but many unique cell types occur in almost every animal group, performing unique functions or variations of widespread functions. Nearly all animals have some amoeboid cells that are motile. They seem to be similar in structure in a wide variety of groups. There is diversity, however, with specialization in function: Some produce skeletons, some are phagocytic, some transport materials in the body, and some are capable of differentiation into other types for replacement. Amoeboid cells are among the less specialized cells of the animal body.

Nearly all groups of animals possess unique cells found nowhere else. For example, only Ctenophora possess colloblasts (lasso cells) and only fishes possess mormyomasts-the electroreceptors in the lateral lines.

Organ Diversity

In addition to such ubiquitous organs as mouths and glands, many groups have unique organs. Among these are the rhynchocoel or proboscis cavity of the Nemertinea, the corona of Rotifera, and the Aristotle's lantern of Echinoidea.

Diversity in Organ Systems

Almost any general zoology textbook will give a list of the organ systems of animals. The list will consist of the systems common to vertebrates, and there will be little mention of any diversity in different groups.

The list will probably closely parallel the list of basic functions or reactions of protoplasm-irritability, contractility, digestion, excretion, respiration, etc. It is of course true that most animals, vertebrate or invertebrate, do have sets of organs of similar sort for the performance of some of these functions, but the diversity among these is actually much greater than is usually stated.

There are even a few unique systems found only in one group and not usually mentioned. The following are examples: demanian system, Nematoda; probably an accessory reproductive system water vascular system, Echinodermata; for hydrostatic manipulation tracheal system, Arthropoda; for breathing air Malpighian tubule system, Arthropoda; for excretion lateral line system, fishes; composed of sense organs rectal respiratory tree system, Holothurioidea; for respiration.

In addition to these unique systems, there is substantial diversity among animal groups in the "standard" systems. In fact, uniformity throughout a major part of the kingdom is the exception rather than the rule.

Variety of Hard Parts

Most textbooks refer to various hard parts of animals, particularly the bones of vertebrates, the exoskeleton of arthropods, and the shells of mollusks. These do represent the three most common types of skeletal structures, but they are far from being all the hard parts produced by animals. There are also animals which produce tests, spicules, thecae, loricae, calyces, zooecia, jaws, cuticles, chitinous exoskeletons, external tubes, shells, coenecia, dermal ossicles, plates, and scales, fin-rays, beaks, feathers, hair, claws, teeth, hooves, antlers, and horns.

Hard parts may be secreted in four ways: First, on the outside of the body by the outer layer of tissue (epidermis) or by the surface layer of a protozoan cell. These include the tests of Foraminifera and other Protozoa, some of the coral of Coelenterata, cuticles in all animals, the zooecia of Bryozoa, the shells of Mollusca and Brachiopoda, the exoskeletons of Arthropoda and Vertebrata, and the dwelling tubes of Phoronida, Pogonophora, insect larvae, etc.

Second, hard parts may be secreted on the inside of the body by mesenchyme amoeboid cells (Porifera). Third, they may be secreted by the dermis or middle layer of the body wall-mesodermal in origin (Echinodermata and Vertebrata). And fourth, by connective tissue-also mesodermal in origin (Vertebrata).

The skeleton of many invertebrates and protozoans is external, a lifeless secretion, forming a hard covering over the body. The exceptions include the echinoderms and the sponges. The vertebrate skeleton is almost invariably cellular, composed either entirely of hardened cells or of cells and cell products.

These may be either epidermal, dermal, or mesenchymal in origin. Exoskeletons may be epidermal or dermal. Endoskeletal structures may be dermal or mesenchymal.

DIVERSITY IN REPRODUCTION

It is sometimes implied that animals typically reproduce by sexual means and their development from the fertilized ovum always follows much the same course. This is not merely an oversimplification, because sexual reproduction is by no means universal, and the details of development are extremely diverse.

There is little in common among all animals, except that part of the parent (or of both parents) goes to produce a new individual, and that mitosis is always involved in some manner. If sexual reproduction be defined as the production of new individuals by the union of sperm and egg from the two parents, then there are many animals in which sexual reproduction is not known to occur.

In fact, it may be that Sonneborn was correct in stating that not over half of the kinds of animals are produced by a bisexual process involving two parents. It is probable that non-bisexual processes (division, fragmentation, multiple fission, budding, sporulation, polyembryony, and parthenogenesis) produce a large majority of the individuals of all animals together.

At least nine forms of asexual reproduction occur in at least fourteen phyla of animals. At least fifteen forms of sexual reproduction occur, of which eleven are in the Protozoa.

Diversity in Development

The development of animals from the beginning of their separate existence until their death is generally assumed to include always an embryology-a period of egg cleavage, gastrulation, and embryo formation. This is, of course, a gross misconception. The individuals produced by six of the asexual methods develop without any of these stages.

Among those animals that do arise from an ovum, there is much diversity at several points: There may or may not be fertilization; the first cleavage plane may be meridional or equatorial or superficial; cleavage may result in any one of four types of blastulae; gastrulation may occur in any of nine ways; the three possible germ layers may be present in any of six combinations; the blastopore may become the mouth, the anus, or neither, or may never exist; mesoderm may form in any of six ways from either ectoderm or endoderm; any of four types of body cavities may occur; and larval stages in almost infinite variety may be present singly or in series in one life cycle.

Other Group Diversities

Few of the aspects of behavior have been cited above. There is diversity also in everything animals do. The study of comparative behavior is a relatively new field, but there is a wealth of diversity to be recorded. Comparative psychology would of course be included here, along with such features as consortism and constructions. Every kind of animal occupies a certain normal range, which it seldom or never escapes from.

A variety of factors account for these ranges, and kinds differ extremely in the size of the range, the limiting factors, the density of the occupation, the contact with similar kinds in other ranges, and so on. Although the ranges of animal kinds do usually fit into a general pattern over the entire earth, they vary without end in all aspects of distribution, as well as in the extent and means of their migrations, their capacity for transport by man or other means, and the changes they undergo through geologic time. A whole series of diversities are involved in this neglected aspect of comparative zoology.

THE DIVERSITY OF KINDS

All of the preceding examples illustrate primarily the diversity among groups, especially at high levels in the hierarchy. It is more difficult to illustrate the diversity at the level of species, partly because it is much more extensive. The kinds of *flies* may be distinguished by minute differences in the chaetotaxy (placement of bristles), the shape of cells between the wing veins, the slight differences in shape of antennal or leg segmeats, the proportions of any body sclerite or appendage, details of the genital armature, and arrangement of colors.

The kinds of *mammals* may be distinguished by pellage color, slight differences in bones including muscle scars and shapes, relative size of body parts, shape and color of teeth, and details of special hair arrangements. The kinds of *jellyfishes* may be distinguished by the position of buds, the length of the manubrium, the shape of the umbrella, the position of the gonads, the number and arrangement of nematocysts of each type, and the number and shape of the tentacles.

The kinds of *mites may* be distinguished by bristle arrangement, size and proportions of body parts, the details of genital armature, the shape and vestiture of mouthparts and other appendages, the details of the openings of the tracheae or air tubes, and the body markings. The kinds of *sporozoans* may be distinguished by the size of the sporozoites, the color of various spots, the presence of microscopic hairs, the number and size of glycogen granules, the size of the nucleus, the number of spores and their size groups, shape and extent of syzygy, the number of schizonts and their nuclei, the presence of a polar filament, and the location within host tissues.

In short, species in every group are distinguished by details within the general pattern of the group. That species do differ in such details is unquestioned after two hundred years of descriptive taxonomy. How to tell in advance what the details will be in any given group remains a secret, but in retrospect it is possible to generalize that they will be features that do distinguish species, usually the various expressions of some feature found in a group of related species.

Species are seldom distinguished by completely unique features, such as an organ known nowhere else. They are more likely to be distinguished by some detail of an organ, such as some difference in position or color.

A difference which is found to distinguish two species in one group may not serve to distinguish a third species. Features which yield useful distinctions in one group may be useless in another group. There is no way to define species characters or class characters in general, but it is possible to tell whether they are effective in any given case.

THE DIVERSITY OF TAXA

These examples may suggest the almost limitless variety of features among the groups of animals. Although most of the examples are cited at the class and species levels, they exist at all levels. Although the diversity seems to be without end, when one starts to tabulate the features of the different kinds of animals, there are very definite limits to most of the variety beyond which animals just do not go.

No insect ever has more than four wings, although there are three thoracic segments which could conceivably all have produced a pair of them. Apparently no animal is based on a grouping of three like parts around a central axis, although four, five, six, etc., are common, and bilaterality can be considered to be two such parts.

No animal is adapted to live its life continuously floating in the atmosphere, although this is conceivable in the same manner as floating in water. The diversity is also limited by universal occurrence of some features. Apparently all protoplasm consists basically of carbon-chain molecules. Respiration always utilizes oxygen and produces carbon dioxide as a waste product.

So far as known, all kinds pass hereditary determiners (genes) on to the next generation. And so on. But each of these very soon shows diversity if one carries the description a little farther, just as the sex of animals *is usually* determined by the genes but is *sometimes* determined by one of a variety of other mechanisms. The carbon-chain molecules are extremely diverse, as are the resulting structures and functions.

It is the presence of this diversity *and* the presence of uniformity within each kind that makes classification necessary and possible. The rest of taxonomy is largely the prelude to, or mechanical operation of, the classification system.

3

USE OF TAXONOMY

Classification is the grouping of like things. It is a part of the everyday life of every human being. A man classifies his neighbors as children, teen-agers, or adults; he classifies his food as meat, vegetables, fruit, or dairy products; he classifies the roads as smooth or bumpy; and he classifies his knowledge as science, art, or literature.

Every noun and adjective represents a classification of ideas or objects. Sometimes objects are classified directly, as in the classification yards of railroads, where freight cars are sorted out according to their destinations, or as in a kitchen, where dishes are stacked in a cupboard according to size or shape.

Sometimes things are classified according to features which can be detected with the senses, with the result that people can be classified into tall and short, or fat and thin, without pushing them into groups. Musical compositions can be classified, according to their patterns, as symphonies, songs, sonatas, operas, hymns, overtures, and so on, even though heard in no particular sequence.

Trees are classified as evergreen or deciduous, without transplanting them into physical groups. And one may classify ideas that have no physical existence or counterparts, such as democracy and tyranny. Furthermore, after these groups are made by classifying individual things-the freight cars, trees, and governments—the groups are frequently further classified into more-inclusive groups.

The very words for all the things of each kind cited above are examples of this. "Neighbors" is a group of people combining the groups "children," "teen-agers," and "adults." "Trees" is a group combining the groups "deciduous trees" and "evergreen trees."

STORAGE OF DATA

The grouping of ideas or objects under class names or words is a means of storing information, particularly the fact that they are alike in some way. The storage effect is at first in the mind of the grouper, but it may be communicated to others through oral or written language. The storage is done by use of a coding system of scientific names.

These names refer to the groupings and serve as a key to the information stored about them. If the classification is more elaborate than just a few groups at one level, its erection also serves a related function automatically. It shows the existence of groups and of groups within groups.

The very existence of the successive groups is new information, frequently of great value. The non-taxonomist does not normally take part in the synthesis of classification schemes. He does not normally describe species, write revisions, or study the nomenclatural problems. But if he deals with animals in any scientific way, he is almost sure to make use of the classifications of the taxonomists.

RECOVERY OF DATA

The use of a classification to recover the stored knowledge about a group is its major function. This is done by using the code names. Any name will lead a zoologist to all that is known about that species or group. It will also lead him to information about other species or groups and how they differ from the first. The name *Drosophila melanogaster will* lead any zoologist to knowledge of this species of animal by some of these steps: The genus name *Drosophila* can be looked up in a nomenclator, where it will be found to be a member of the family Drosophilidae, the order Diptera, the class Insecta, and the phylum Arthropoda.

Reference to these major groups in general books will show that there are certain special features characteristic of each. For example, the Arthropoda have jointed legs and a segmented sclerotic exoskeleton; the Insecta have only six legs but also tracheae and three body regions; the Diptera have hind wings replaced by halteres; and the Drosophilidae have aristate antennae, oral vibrissae, and certain wing vein features. All these things apply to *Drosophila melanogaster*.

Knowing the genus, through the first part of the specific name, has now led to knowledge of the family, the order, and so on. In the literature on these, obtainable from the bibliographies in the works already consulted, will be found: (1) the generic revisions or monographs that will provide information on the genus and this particular species,

(2) the references to any work on this species in the nontaxonomic fields of zoology, such as distribution, ecology, genetics, and embryology, and (3) the list of other names (synonyms) by which this species has at other times been called and under which other information about it is recorded.

When all of these leads have been run down, including all the other leads cited in these, all the known information about the species *Drosophila melanogaster will* have been assembled. In this particular example, the amount of data is enormous, because of the great interest in this species on the part of geneticists. Every possible aspect of the species is covered, and there are special works referring to it alone.

For most species of animals, there is no such large volume of information; nevertheless, most species have been reported on more than once, and it takes a determined search to un. cover all that has been discovered and recorded about any one of them. Classification also provides a means of referring to groups of kinds at one time.

Echinoidea refers in one word to all the hundreds of species of sea-urchins, heart-urchins, cake-urchins, and sand-dollars that exist. All that is publicly known about this group can be recovered from the literature. But also the position of Echinoidea in a formal classification indicates that it is, for example, one of the five existing classes in the phylum Echinodermata; that it is grouped with the classes Asteroidea,

Ophiuroidea, and Holothurioidea as the moreinclusive group Eleutherozoa; that it is itself made up of seven subgroups treated as orders. Its place in the Animal Kingdom is thus made clear, so far as it is known.

HIERARCHY OF GROUPS

Literally hundreds of facts about this species are thus shown merely by its place in the classification. It is obviously impossible to show a million species of animals in such a diagram. It is therefore customary to show only the placement of the one group at each level, in a descending scale of levels or categories, thus:

Phylum	Arthropoda
Class	Insecta
Order	Diptera
Family	Drosophilidae
Genus	*Drosophila*
Species	*Drosophila melaniogastcr*

It is taken for granted that each level contains more than just the one indicated subgroup. For example, there will usually be other orders

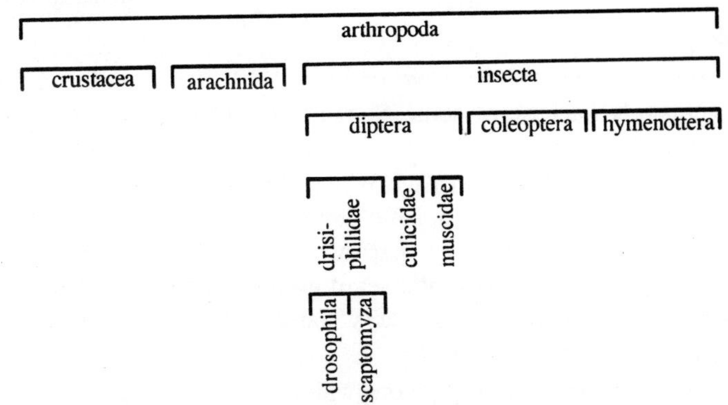

Figure 3.1: Hierarchy of Groups.

within the class and other families within the order. This descending sequence of levels or categories in the first column is a hierarchy. The sequence of groups in the second column is sometimes called a "classification" of the indicated species.

This is an unfortunate use of the word. It would be better to call it the hierarchy of groups of this species.

SPECIAL TERMS

All of these remarks take for granted an understanding of the words species, genus, group, hierarchy, and category. As there is some misunderstanding of these, even among professional taxonomists, it is necessary to define and discuss them.

There are two ordinary English words that are at the base of all taxonomy and classification. These are "kinds" and "groups." It has been known from ancient times that each sort of animal reproduces itself, producing others of the same sort.

These are kinds, the animals which can interbreed and produce more of the same kind (or produce more by asexual reproduction). A kind includes all the individuals that might have been produced as offspring of one pair.

Even before there was much knowledge of heredity and its mechanisms, it was obvious that kinds consisted of the animals that were or could have been related by being descendents of similar individuals. This is the same concept which is now called more technically species.

Groups also were recognized in ancient times. The many kinds which had their bodies covered with feathers were different from those covered with hair. Together these feathered kinds formed the group.

known as birds. The group could be large or small, inclusive or exclusive, natural or artificial. Any two or more kinds that are placed together figuratively because of some characteristic held by all of them arc a group.

The term is both general and specific, as it can be used effectively to refer to the group of aquatic animals with fins or to the group of kinds of birds we know as sparrows. Groups may consist of a set of kinds or they may consist of a set of groups. The groups that are called individually sparrows, woodpeckers, warblers, herons, etc., will altogether be the group called birds.

And the group of birds, along with the group of mammals, the group of reptiles, etc., will be the group called vertebrates. Thus, group is a noncommittal word, not specifying the number of its members or even whether they are individual kinds or groups of kinds. If the group is a taxonomic one, as in these examples, then the word *taxon* is a synonym of group. Taxon was first used by botanists and is now frequently used by zoological taxonomists.

In taxonomy, any group is automatically a taxonomic one. There seems to be no real need for any more technical word, so taxon is used in this book principally in the technical discussions of nomenclature. It is possible to arrange kinds (species), groups of kinds (taxa), and groups of groups (also taxa) in an ascending series of ever greater inclusiveness.

Several kinds are assembled to form a group, and several such groups into a more inclusive group. Then several of these more-inclusive-groups are assembled into a still-more-inclusivegroup. For example, see Figure elsewhere in this chapter.

This figure indicates that kind K, for example, belongs to group 3, to more-inclusive-group b, and to still-more-inclusive-group I. There are four levels of these groupings, and the levels are called *categories*. In this arbitrary case the categories are kind, group, more-inclusive-group, and still-more-inclusive-group.

This ascending scale is a *hierarchy*, which is a series of levels into which the groups can be arranged. In zoological classification, the levels in the hierarchy are named species, genus, family, order, class, phylum, and kingdom, from the least inclusive to the most inclusive. It is not correct to speak of some categories as larger than others, because a phylum might consist of a single species and thus be no larger.

The categories are properly described as higher or lower. The groups assigned to the categories, however, are not higher or lower. They are simply more or less inclusive, or can even be described as

kinds	groups	more-inclusive-groups	still-more-inclusive-groups
A B C	1	a	
E F	2		I
H I J K	3	b	
M N O	4		
Q R S	5	c	
U V	6		II
W X Y Z	7	d	

Figure 3.2: The grouping of groups.

larger or smaller, because they are at least potentially so. In a practical sense the first level above the kind (species) is the category genus. The groups placed at this level are called *genera* (singular, genus).

This use of identical names for the group and the category is the cause of considerable confusion and erroneous usage. There is no objective way to define genus, but each genus does consist of a group of species sharing certain features.

The genus is then the group of the species that show these characters that have been selected to set off this genus. Of course, this group like any other group, may consist of just one object. The next major level above the category genus is the category family. The groups of genera placed at this level are also called families.

Each is simply the group of genera possessing the features deemed to be appropriate to family rank. Above the family are in turn the order, the class, and the phylum levels. The groups of families are called orders; the groups of orders are called classes; and the groups of classes are called phyla.

In addition to these levels, which are almost universally used, there may be any number of additional levels inserted in between. Groups of families may be put at an intermediate level called superfamily; then the superfamily groups make up the orders.

Kingdom
Subkingdom
Phylum
Subphylum
Superclass
Class
Subclass
Superorder
Order
Suborder
Infraorder
Superfamily
Family
Subfamily
Tribe
Subtribe
Genus
Subgenus
(Species)

Figure 3.3: The usual categories of the zoological hierarchy.

Or the orders may be assembled into groups called subclasses, which in turn make up the classes. There are no direct limits to the number of categories (levels) that can he used, but the scale in Figure elsewhere in this chapter includes those most commonly seen.

There can be no definition of what a family is, or what a superclass is. It is either a level in the hierarchy, defined solely by its position in the series, or it is a group (taxon) placed at the family or superclass level and called a family or a superclass.

The only standard to determine the correct level for a group is the agreement of specialists. The group may be quite definite and understood by all, but its level may be subject to much difference of opinion.

It may appear in various classifications as a class, a subclass, an order, or even a phylum, according to the views of the classifier. It must be remembered that each of the categories potentially contains many groups of the next lower level. A class may consist of many orders, or the actual number of orders may be as low as one. The fact that a certain class contains just one order does not make the class and order levels identical, because the class potentially contains other orders as yet unknown.

For example, the phylum Phoronida consists of just two genera, probably belonging in a single family. It serves no purpose to recount that there is just one class, with one order, one suborder, and one family, because potentially the phylum could include other worms so different from *Phoronis* that they would be placed in a new class. And the same thing can happen at any other level. For this reason the basic categories of phylum, class, order, family, and genus are generally cited, even in groups consisting of only one or a few species.

4

TAXONOMY AS A SCIENCE

The matters dealt with under this heading are in large part the controversial aspects of systematics. Various interpretations have been advanced, but logical arguments have not always been presented for them. It is necessary to discuss some of these things only because there have been illogical but authoritative pronouncements repeatedly made about them, using two well-known rhetorical devices for persuading the unwary reader.

These are the repetition of catch phrases and the use of derogatory labels. Among these controversial matters is the scientific standing of taxonomy itself, the relation between taxonomy and phylogeny, the socalled "biological species concept," The New Systematics, the nature of natural classification, and the reality and objectivity of categories.

It is not possible to discuss these adequately here, but it is necessary to present some of the arguments for the assumptions made in this book as to the status of each of these problems.

It must be emphasized that this book is not intended to cover all of systematics. An attempt is made to deal with all aspects of taxonomy, but the other branches of systematics are more appropriately discussed under other headings. It is not intended to cover Evolution, Speciation, Phylogeny, Population Dynamics, or Genetics.

Much of what is sometimes called Biosystematics is omitted as belonging to one of the above fields. What has been called The New Systematics by American evolutionists is discussed only to the extent of showing that it has had little effect on taxonomy.

THE SCIENCE OF TAXONOMY

There is literally no end to definitions of the word "science." Whether or not any particular study is a science depends entirely on the definition adopted. It is pointless to carry on a discussion of such a matter, but it is possible to arrive at a better understanding of a field of knowledge by examining its basis, its methods, and its results.

There are several things to be said about science that are pertinent to systematics, or more especially to taxonomy. First of all, science is knowledge and it is the process which makes knowledge.

The knowledge is organized, and therefore a science is a system of organized knowledge. We can scarcely go wrong with the statement of Lenzen that: "The problem of empirical science is the acquisition and systematization of knowledge concerning the things and phenomena experienced in observation."

Inasmuch as the principal business of taxonomy is the discovery of the comparative facts of the kinds of organisms, and the principal business of classification is to provide a system in which these facts can be integrated, the part of systematics which includes both of these would appear to fit Lenzen's statement exactly. The field of taxonomy has been criticized as not being a science. This conclusion is wrong, even though there is some evidence to support it.

The amount of data to be collected and organized in taxonomy is so tremendous, and taxonomists have always been so far from completion of the work, that many of them have never accomplished much of the organizing but spend their lives accumulating the data. Some of them have even been relatively untrained in a scientific background and have operated much like stamp collectors or amateur naturalists. This type of work is, of course, not typical of taxonomy as a whole, even though it may have been much in evidence.

But even this work, as long as it produces new data even in small quantities, is entitled to the same recognition in science as any other activity that produces facts singly. There is no justification for declaring any experimental work to be unscientific merely because the experimenter published only the results of the experiment, leaving it to an Einstein or a Schrodinger to work out the implications and propose an explanation.

In taxonomy the conclusions drawn from the data are the assignments to species, genera, and phyla. These are always tentative assignments and therefore in the nature of hypotheses. All aspects of classification involve organization of knowledge, and the data of taxonomy are the basis of the classification. Even some taxonomists sometimes forget that their work is at the time a part of science only if it is fitted into the organized knowledge. As it was put by W. R. Thompson, "We must not expect to constitute a science of purely individual phenomena. The idea involves contradiction." And ". . . the science of the laboratory and museum deals with material properties and their temporal or spacial concatenations."

In the end we must agree with Popper that "what is to be called a 'science' and who is to be called a 'scientist' must always remain a matter of convention or decision."

THE BROADER TAXONOMY

From the very beginning of modern biological classification, from the time of Linnaeus, animals were classified principally on the basis of visible structural features. Various methods were devised for assessing the relative usefulness of different structures for this purpose, and occasionally other sorts of attributes were also employed.

It was found necessary to preserve specimens for later comparison, as verbal descriptions and even pictures were not always adequate. The only attributes that can be readily preserved are the structural ones, and it became nearly universal to rely on such structural characters in taxonomy. When other attributes seemed to offer additional material for comparisons, it was usually found that these were correlated with structural features.

This strengthened the taxonomists' view that structure is an effective key to most inherent attributes. After the publication of Darwin's works, it was expected that taxonomy would be greatly changed by the new ideas. Again, in the decade after 1938, the publications on The New Systematics led to expectation of another revolution in the basis of taxonomy.

Long after the publication of Darwin's *Origin o f Species,* astonishment was expressed at the fact that the classifications of the taxonomists were not much affected by the evolutionary ideas. More than twenty years after The New Systematics was announced, there is a great reticence to admit that the classifications of the taxonomists have again remained unchanged. Were the same factors responsible for these two unexpected developments?

The answer has been overlooked by the evolutionists of both periods, and a different revolution in taxonomy and classification has also been overlooked by them. It occurred in the two decades before The New

Systematics. In the third and fourth decades of the present century an important trend was started in the study of the largest "groups" of taxonomic subjects, the insects and the invertebrate fossils, and was felt in other groups as well.

As these two include over three-quarters of all known animals, the trend was of substantial importance. Unfortunately, it has seldom been referred to, because it was not immediately recognized as a successful trend and was pushed from the limelight by later developments. Beginning in the 1920's, an increasing number of professors taught that taxonomy and classification should not be based on a few key characters but on all available information of whatever sort.

This did not mean that equal weight was to be given to every feature, but that comparative and analytical methods should determine the usefulness of each fact. Not only was a much wider range of individual features to be used, but also data from new methods of study. Here was one of the major factors in the early growth of biometry, now grown into the vast field of biostatistics.

Here was acceptance of biological features on a wider scale than before. Here was wider recognition of the animal origin of fossils and the necessity of studying both the living forms *and* the fossil record to understand either one. This movement gained considerable momentum simply because it gave better results in taxonomy. Its earliest devotees did not happen to be widely influential or in positions of authority.

Their ideas produced superior monographs, helped to solve longstanding problems in "difficult" groups, and proved themselves against prejudice. The spread of these ideas seems to have continued in some aspects under the guise of the more publicized trends of the following decades, and it is likely that additional impetus was given by the discussions of the new ideas.

THE NEW SYSTEMATICS

In 1940 there was published in England a collection of essays and reports entitled *The New Systematics*. In it, several authors tried to assess the taxonomic work of the past and to suggest improved attitudes and methods for the future.

It was not claimed that there was any New Systematics in existence then or even that the old systematics was inadequate. The keynote was set by the editor, Julian S. Huxley, in the first two sentences, thus: "To hope for the new systematics is to imply no disrespect for the old. It has been largely the rapid progress made by classical taxonomy itself that has necessitated the introduction of new methods of analysis, new approaches to synthesis." At the same time the editor did introduce several concepts new to taxonomy, new in the sense that taxonomists had not accepted responsibility for them.

Chief among these was the need to discover the mechanisms of evolution. There is good reason to believe that the data of taxonomy will be important in solving the problems of evolution, but solving the problems of evolution is not the function of taxonomy.

The people who study the processes of evolution will be partly drawn from the ranks of the taxonomists, where their taxonomic training will be invaluable, but when working on evolutionary mechanisms they will be evolutionists or whatever they choose to call themselves.

The real taxonomists will still be busy with the overwhelming job of recording and systematizing the data on the myriads of kinds of animals. Subsequent books that took up the expression New Systematics were unanimous in applying the expression to the latter problem-the origin of the groups used by taxonomy in its classifications, particularly those called species.

This was largely a new field. It investigated mechanisms of speciation, rates, variability in populations, the genetic control of these, and other aspects of genetics and evolution. It made substantial advances in these fields, setting up what is in effect a new branch of biology that could well be called variation or the science of organic change.

Not content with developing a new field for investigation, the students of this changed use of the expression New Systematics sought to make the new discoveries the basis for major changes in the approach to classification of organisms. If this attempt had been based on sound arguments and valid premises, it might have resulted in a revolution in taxonomy.

Such a revolution has actually been claimed by the proponents, but there is much evidence that it was restricted almost entirely to the few who gave up the study of taxonomy for the study of speciation. *The New Systematics* did not claim to inaugurate a new era. Even the title was the subject of apology by the editor, who admitted it might better have been called *Modern Problems in Systematics.*

Before The New Systematics could be born, "the mass of new facts and ideas which the last two or three decades have hurled at us must be digested, correlated, and synthesized." " The editor might have gone further and included the mass of facts from the previous one hundred and eighty years, because taxonomy must always add all new facts to the sum of those previously discovered, keeping them all systematized and available. Within a few years, however, there were published other books that took up the idea of a New Systematics that would explain evolution.

In these it was reported that there had been a revolution in animal taxonomy, that The New Systematics had already displaced the old except in a few relatively unknown groups, and that the study of species formation and the factors of evolution had become the principal task of "modern" taxonomists. The idea that a revolution has recently occurred in taxonomy has received wide publicity among biologists.

There have been few attempts to determine whether there is any truth to the claim. No one can deny that there have been evolutionary studies by persons with taxonomic backgrounds, and there have also been ecological studies by such persons.

This does not make both ecology and evolution part of taxonomy. There may have been classifications that were widely different from those of thirty years ago, but if so they have been kept well hidden. There seems to be no serious doubt that most taxonomic work and most classification has been almost completely unaffected by the so-called great change.

One of the principal conclusions of *The New Systematics* (the book) was that taxonomy would do well to pay more attention to facts from the fields of cytology, genetics, ecology, physiology, and behavior. It did not state that taxonomy should *start* to give attention to these fields, because it recognized that attention was already being given.

It admitted the dual responsibility, that in each case the two fields must work together to increase knowledge, that, for example, genetics must make its data available in such a way that they can be useful to taxonomists just as taxonomy must assemble all its data into classifications that will be useful to geneticists.

There was nothing new in this to those who had been teaching for twenty years that taxonomists must use all available data. These men also taught that "the systematist may and should employ any means that are available in order to arrive at a knowledge of the biological facts, whether these means be found in morphological, anatomical, physiological, experimental, genetical, or even chemical studies".

A corollary of this is the stated need to study the importance or validity of each type of data for whatever purpose it is to be used. There have been few voices raised since 1940 in support of these ideas. The two outstanding ones are of botanists. Heslop-Harrison clearly expresses both the validity of orthodox taxonomy and the need for broader horizons.

"Many taxonomists," he says, "... hold to the legitimacy of the aims of orthodox taxonomy, and acknowledge the practical value of the existing taxonomic structure. . . . At the same time, the implications of the new work must be taken into account in bringing up to date taxonomic procedure and in framing, defining, and describing the units of orthodox taxonomy."

Among this new work he cites population structure, ecology, geographical variation, cytology, and genetics. It should be noted that Heslop-Harrison is not suggesting that taxonomists do the work on population structure, or ecology, or genetics. He claims only that taxonomists need to take into account the implications of work done by students of these fields.

This is exactly in line with the view of Ferris, but it is not the viewpoint of The New Systematics in its later form. Keck accepts a more direct goal of taxonomy to reflect phylogeny but recommends the same expansion of viewpoint to utilize more data from other fields than just "comparative morphology and geographic distribution."

The taxonomist should seek assistance also from genetics, anatomy, cytology, paleobotany, embryology, ecology, physiology, etc. He also cites as the tools of modern taxonomy of plants: field studies, pollen studies, parasitism, biochemistry, and cytogenetics. All of this applies equally to animal taxonomy.

It can be pointed out, however, that all these remarks stop short of the obvious generalization that the attributes or data useful to taxonomists in classifying organisms are all *comparative in nature.* At the time of recording they may not be stated as comparisons, but their value to taxonomy lies principally in eventual comparison with the corresponding data from other individuals or groups.

This generalization would not be of great moment if it did not lead to a further generalization, one that has been inherent in the teaching and taxonomic work of men like Ferris, Robson, and Turrill. Just as all taxonomic data must be fundamentally comparative, so *all data which are comparative* are of significance to taxonomy.

There is little basis for doubt that for most groups of animals comparative structure will remain of prime interest, but all other comparative data must be considered whenever available, and their bearing on taxonomic problems analyzed. If any justification is needed for the continued use of comparative structure as the prime factor in classification, it will be furnished by the continuing demonstration that data from genetics, ecology, parasitism, physiology, and behavior are usually and almost inevitably represented in structure at some level, so that they can be used indirectly in classification in the form of the correlated structure.

Of course, the correlation must be established in every possible case. Furthermore, since its presence strengthens the comparison and its absence weakens it, the correlation must be reported. Likewise, the nature and extent of the correlation must be analyzed. The final effect of most of these experimental or non-morphological attributes is thus to adjust and strengthen the morphological system. There is no limit to the advantages to taxonomy afforded by this all-encompassing approach.

It absorbs all comparative data of whatever nature and uses it to correct or bolster the classification previously erected. It can be extended indefinitely and always leads on to a closer agreement between the classification and the nature of the organisms. It can utilize any comparative data provided by the study of speciation or other evolution.

But the study of these fields is no more a part of taxonomy than is the cytogenetics and biochemistry that provide other data for its use. It is often overlooked that taxonomy makes no claim to the discovery of all the data it employs. The bacteriologists Lamanna and Mallette clearly state the situation, thus: "Whether there is conscious realization of the fact or not, all persons scientifically investigating organisms are making a contribution to the data of taxonomy.

In a very real sense the best taxonomy is a synthesis of all knowledge of biology." Realization of this situation has been slow, partly because of the gradualness of the accumulation and acceptance of the data from new fields and partly because of the obfuscation produced by recent verbose over-emphasis on one of the fields.

The expression "comparative zoology" is not often seen in publications, but it represents the entire legitimate field of modern animal taxonomy, just as it did earlier for classical taxonomy. In a major book on problems of systematics, entirely neglected by all the more recent writers on problems of species and taxonomy, written by Robson in 1928, there is this appropriate statement of the source of taxonomic data: "Every living organism exhibits a large number of attributes to which we give the name 'characters.'

Such 'characters' include every structure and property of the animal or plant, whether they be organs, cytological structure, physiological activities, habits or ecological relationships." The use of gross structural characters as keys to the differences of other nature is justified by Robson because of correlations demonstrated to exist. "If we thus are compelled to regard the sum total of an organism's attributes-metabolic, structural, habitudinal and reproductive-as the expression of its fundamental biochemical and biophysical constitution, it follows that the differences which we recognize as specific at the structural level must be likewise founded on more deeply seated differences."

It is now evident that in many fields there has been an increase in the acceptance of a broader base for taxonomy. There is more willingness to consider new techniques and new types of data. There is probably more open-mindedness about some aspects of taxonomy.

There is certainly more interest in taxonomic data on the part of biochemists and geneticists, who see the need for making their data available to taxonomy. There appears to be no basis for the claim that there has recently been a revolution in systematics.

There has been an increase in interest in many aspects of systematic theory and practice. The expression The New Systematics has been so consistently and persistently misused as a supposed switch to evolutionary interests that it is no longer of much use in its original meaning.

Nevertheless, there is continued improvement in training of taxonomists, in the breadth of data used in taxonomy, and in the use of taxonomic data in other fields.

CLASSIFICATION VS. POPULATION STUDIES

Several recent books have stated or implied that taxonomy, or classification, must be based on phylogeny. With this as a premise, it is argued that study of the evolutionary origin of species and other groups is not only part of taxonomy but the most important part. Based on this assumption, taxonomy becomes principally a means of recording data about populations, and much of the later New Systematics deals only with this aspect.

In these same books, species are defined as populations. Classification is said to group populations rather than individuals. Statistical methods are advocated which are applicable to populations but not to either species or individuals. The entire purpose, the methods, and the justification implied in these books are different from those of classical taxonomy. This view has been persuasively proclaimed.

It has appeal because much of modern biology is unquestionably concerned with populations. It is probably the fault of taxonomists that the relationship of classifying and identifying to populations is not recognized to be almost non-existent, because it is only the individuals and groups of individuals that can be grouped and categorized. Before a taxonomist can use knowledge of populations, he must complete some classification at the species level and above.

If he takes an interest in populations, it can only be after he has classified the group and identified the species. He can then distinguish subspecies or populations after the species are at least partly known. This will usually be the result of an evolutionary interest, not a taxonomic one. The well-trained taxonomist is likely to be the best-qualified zoologist for evolutionary studies, so it is not uncommon for him to do part of his research in this distinct field.

His interest in populations is usually not taxonomic but evolutionary. A claim has been made for the unifying effect of the Darwinian theory, as it attempts to account for the diversity of animals. Many zoologists look upon Darwin's work as the source of concepts which give meaning to classification. These same persons sometimes marvel that, as we can now see, the theory had practically no effect upon taxonomy.

It is impossible to tell by a man's taxonomic work whether he believed in evolution or even knew about it. Classifications have been practically unaffected by Darwin's theories or the later developments. This was actually inevitable, because taxonomy was and still is the study of the groups found among animals; it is not the study of how the groups came to be.

Any knowledge of this latter subject will be of great interest to taxonomists and will add to the data available to them, but this knowledge of mechanisms is not the goal of the study of taxonomy. In this book it is assumed that taxonomy is the study of individuals first, of groups of individuals second (including species), and of groups of groups third. It is agreed that the individuals are the product of heredity.

It is agreed that the species are the result of evolution (speciation), and it is admitted that the features held in common by the individuals are in part the result of common ancestry. All this is as important to him as the fact that the individuals are composed of systems of carbon-chain molecules organized into cells and organs. But neither the phylogeny nor the physiology is the immediate business of taxonomy.

It has more than enough to do in its proper classical role of making known the kinds of animals and the attributes in which they are alike or unlike.

AFTER *THE NEW SYSTEMATICS*

Although it was the first book to suggest the study of new attitudes and aspects of systematics, *The New Systematics* seems to be at the same time the last to recognize the nature of taxonomy. Books that followed in quick succession adopted the deprecatory epithet of The Old Systematics; they labeled the previous work as typological, nondimensional, meaningless, and inadequate.

By labeling The New Systematics as new, modern, objective, biological, and multidimensional it was implied that in all these ways the new approaches were better than the old. This would have been of little consequence if it had not been for the fact that these succeeding books failed to note the implications of the original essays and proceeded to change the emphasis from improvement in taxonomic method, philosophy, arid breadth to' concentration on the means by which evolution had produced the kinds taxonomists study.

For example, one of the early books stated that the systematist who studies the factors of evolution wants to find out how species originate, how they are related, and what this relationship means. This is probably true, but the implication that the working taxonomist is among those who have time to study the factors of evolution is certainly unjustified in the broad view.

This new subject, of interest to taxonomists, to be sure, is as distinct from taxonomy as genetics or ecology. Its data will have to be recorded and systematized by taxonomists, but this does not make the field a part of taxonomy. The original New Systematics had primarily the same implications for taxonomy as had the trend of the previous two decades described in a previous paragraph-to increase the breadth, soundness, accuracy, and usefulness of the classifications of organisms.

This worthy goal was soon forgotten in the changed emphasis placed on the expression The New Systematics. Perhaps this was inevitable, because one of the book's authors stated that such a thing as a New Systematics was impossible; another said that its major premises were unsound; and the editor's conclusions cited nothing in the way of radical new ideas or approaches but merely increases and improvements in programs and methods already being pursued.

Subsequent works used the expression for the quite different aspect of studying the origin of the groups to be classified. This complete change in the meaning of what has become a popular catch-phrase makes it difficult to discuss the original ideas or assess their impact on taxonomy.

The Old and the New in Taxonomy

One of the major features of recent articles by some of the zoological New Systematists, if not itself a trend in systematics, is the use of derogatory labels on the taxonomic work of those who still classify organisms on the basis of comparative data. The tone of this disparagement has become very caustic at times, using authority, ridicule, sarcasm, repetition, and other rhetorical devices in lieu of facts.

Not all the persons who have been quoted as supporting these views really do so, but effective rebuttal is seldom made. The New Systematics was ushered in by Huxley and his collaborators with a recounting of the needs of taxonomy, to correct its failures and to bring it abreast of the times, but without any claim that it had failed completely in its purpose.

It was in fact the very successes of taxonomy in making known nearly a million kinds of animals that necessitated the attempted re-evaluation and led to the suggestions for the future. Turrill remarked: "On the whole, taxonomists have every reason to be proud of the work they have accomplished since the time of Linnaeus by the use of descriptive and comparative morphological methods." Calman wrote that while new species are brought in almost every day: "What is very remarkable and significant, however, in this constant influx of novelties, is the rarity of the unexpected. . . . Seldom, very seldom indeed, do we come across a species for which there is not a place waiting in the accepted classification."

Reference is frequently made to the "difficult" groups, to *Rubus, Taraxacum, Crataegus,* and *Salix* in plants and to *Peromyscus, Cynips, Daphnia,* and *Artemia* among animals. The word confusion is frequently applied, and it would be possible for a non-specialist to get the idea that all taxonomists are confused and all taxonomy incomplete and inadequate.

To be sure, there are difficult genera in nearly all groups of animals. There are also some whole groups that are more difficult than the rest. Which ones might be cited as examples depends largely on what level of the classification is involved and on what we are thinking of as difficulties.

Of genera we may cite *Aimophila* (in the birds) and *Graphognathus* (in the weevils); of families, Muscidae (in the flies) ; of orders, Charadriiformes (in the birds) ; of subclasses, Branchiopoda (in the crustaceans); and of classes, Turbellaria (in the flatworms). In spite of these examples, and all the others that can be cited, any implication that the major work of taxonomy is meaningless, or confused, or incapable of producing the results for which it was designed, is unjustified.

Such an implication, when coupled, as it invariably is, with the use of derogatory labels, does no credit to the persons who claim that taxonomists must change their viewpoint and their approach to classification. Of the supposedly derogatory labels pinned onto classical taxonomy, the one most evident was Mayr's 1942 reference to "The Old Systematics" as contrasted with "The New Systematics." This was not the first time these expressions had been used, but it was the first time that full definitions were added that increased the potential effect of the word "old" and added other deprecations.

These definitions are quoted here in full, with bracketed numbers referring to the subsequent discussion paragraphs. "*The old systematics* is characterized by the central position of the species. No work, or very little, is done on infraspecific categories (subspecies) [1]. A purely morphological species definition is employed [2]. Many species are known from only single or at best a very few specimens [3]; the individual is therefore the basic taxonomic unit [4]. There is great interest in purely technical questions of nomenclature and 'types' [5]. The major problems are those of a cataloguer or bibliographer, rather than those of a biologist [6].

"*The new systematics* may be characterized as follows: The importance of the species as such is reduced, since most of the actual work is done with subdivisions of the species, such as subspecies and populations [1]. The purely morphological species definition has been replaced by a biological one, which takes ecological, geographical, genetic, and other factors into consideration [2]. The material available for generic revisions frequently amounts to many hundreds or even thousands of specimens, a number sufficient to permit a detailed study of the extent of individual variation [3]. The population or rather an adequate sample of it, the 'series' of the museum worker, has become the basic taxonomic unit [4]. The choosing of the correct name for the analyzed taxonomic unit no longer occupies the central position of all systematic work and is less often subject to argument between fellow workers [5]."

In what amount to formal definitions of the old and new systematics, we can only take these statements literally. A comparison of the two definitions discloses some strange contrasts.

[1]. It is simply not true that little work on subspecies is done in the classical taxonomy. The whole idea of subspecies was developed there. In appropriate groups a very satisfactory start had been made in determining the nature of the variation patterns in species.

It is only in such groups that any work of this sort has been done within The New Systematics, because in most classes of animals so little data are yet available that virtually nothing can be done with infraspecific variation or species structure.

[2]. The expression "a purely morphological species definition" is definitely a derogatory label. Even in Linnaeus' time more than structure was used, as shown by consistent recording *and consideration* of locality.

In this century it has been realized that many other features are correlated with structure, and structure has often been used as a guide to these other features-the easiest way to take them into account. Furthermore, whenever occasion demands, other data are used: hosts, parasites, life history, habits, physiology, breeding capabilities, ecological preferences, genetics, stratigraphic position, and others.

There has not been a major monograph in many years that can justly be called "purely morphological," and the best ones have been far from that, even without any overt acceptance of The New Systematics.

[3]. It would be very interesting to know how it is that the classical taxonomist in 1930 had only a single specimen or a very few to work with, in spite of all efforts to assemble as many as possible, whereas in 1950 he would have been able to obtain the whole population or at least an adequate sample of it.

This must be a blessing reserved for those who give the password "New Systematics." The truth is that the vast majority of animal species are still known from the few specimens obtained. Where specimens were plentiful, the older workers frequently gloried in the possession of a large series of some particular species.

There were some series studied as early as 1920 that had thousands of specimens from all parts of the known range. And every specimen was studied, as well as the range of variation. It is hard to see how a New Systematist can work with populations or series without ever looking at the individuals that compose them.

[4]. There seems to be some disagreement as to the basic unit used in systematics, as discussed elsewhere. Some taxonomists have always believed that they were classifying individuals first and then groups of individuals. It is hard to know what others think, but all taxonomic work familiar to the writer assumes individuals as the start-specimens are always present.

A taxonomist may assume that these specimens before him are part of a breeding population, but he usually does not see the population and has little data on it except what is derived from inferences on the individuals before him. The first level of classification, the groups of individuals, has usually been the one called the species level.

It differs from higher levels only in that the members of its groups are individuals rather than groups of individuals. This is not true if we employ subgroups within the species, as most speciationists and some taxonomists do. In practice, then, the level species is not different in nature from the level genus or the level order.

The claim that the species is reduced in importance in The New Systematics because of interest in subspecies confirms that the *species level* is no different from other levels. It can be made more or less important by changes in interest of workers.

[5]. There has always been interest in nomenclature. There will always be as long as zoologists hold it a necessity that they have distinctive names for the different kinds of organisms. There have doubtless been persons who acted as if the giving of names—their validation-was the goal of their work, but this does not justify the implication that all taxonomists considered the naming as anything but the labeling of the groups they recorded so that others might recognize them and use the recorded data.

Without names, there could be no classification. Without types, there could be no fixity of names. The New Systematics has done nothing at all to change this situation. It will do nothing in the future to change it so long as it is agreed to refer to the groups of animals by a formal system of names. Naturally, the nomenclature gradually comes to require less attention as a group becomes well known.

Thus the larger burden of nomenclature falls on the pioneers in each group. It is churlish to imply that this essential phase of the work is unimportant, and it is fatuous to imply that pioneering taxonomy is finished. There are still groups relatively untouched.

It seems obvious that this point of view is centered about the work on vertebrates, particularly that on birds. No doubt the taxonomic work at the nomenclatural level has been very nearly completed in this group, but the birds are no more than a hundredth part of the known animals, and a specialist's acquaintance with some of the invertebrate groups would give substantially different views on species, taxonomy, nomenclature, and other aspects of comparative zoology.

[6]. Because some taxonomists have done more than their share of cataloging and bibliography, some other taxonomists are in position to parasitize this work. With catalogs and bibliographies at hand, they can go on to other types of work, oftentimes giving no credit or thought to the labors that made possible their new outlooks.

It would be interesting to see how, without catalogs or bibliographic aids, a New Systematist would deal with a homogeneous subfamily of ten thousand species. Up to now such workers have been able to work in smaller and well-cataloged groups. It is hardly necessary to point out the illogical nature of all such sweeping derogatory statements.

They are not warranted by the facts but are confused with false implications. They would ordinarily be classed as propaganda-appearing to be what they are not and convincing by deceit if at all. They serve no useful purpose in science.

The reference in [2] to "*morphological*" came in some later works to be replaced by "typological." This also results in a derogatory implication when it is contrasted with the supposedly more scientific "biological."

Of far more importance than this derogatory implication, however, is the faulty thinking which makes possible its application to taxonomy and classification rather than to nomenclature. Typological, as applied to taxonomy, appears to refer to the study of types as representatives of the species.

There have no doubt been a few taxonomists who put so much weight on types that they seemed to build their whole knowledge from them, but this is an unreasonable conclusion in general. Even the most determined users of types had to study the available specimens before selecting the types; they made the selection on the basis of prior study of this series and of other species; they almost always knew something about the variation represented by the specimens.

The better workers, and nearly all workers in recent decades, used the types as name-bearers, as hitching-posts to settle points of name-application. The value of the type specimens for the purpose of name-bearing was so great that it provided basis for the misunderstanding so widespread among non-taxonomists that the types were alone considered in taxonomy.

This is far from the truth. The same idea in more sophisticated form is the basis for the derogatory use of "typological" for a taxonomic approach. It would be quite impossible to prove that there is any such thing as a typological taxonomy of substantial proportions, just as it would be impossible to prove that there is none at all.

The implication is unreasonable, however, unless evidence is presented to show that these are more than exceptional occurrences. The basis of taxonomy in general has never been types. It has usually been the specimens available to the taxonomist, one or many. Some have chosen their types to be middle-of-the-road in the variation pattern; some have chosen the types because of sex, condition, source, ownership, or other circumstance.

Some have chosen many types for each species, having a variety of purposes in mind. But the only direct purpose served by most types is to show to what the name is to be applied. This gives us a type-founded nomenclature; it does not give us a typological taxonomy.

The Opposing V iew

So much discussion of the ideas of a few persons on what taxonomy should concern itself with might lead to a belief that the latter-day interpretations of The New Systematics are the only ones held or put into print. They are certainly not the only ones held, but the aggressive and illogical attacks that have met some publications have deterred many from expressing their views in print.

The correspondence of the writer as an officer of the Society of Systematic Zoology for sixteen years shows that many taxonomists are troubled by the implications of the new ideas and many are definitely not in agreement with them. It is often overlooked that there have been some who expressed these views in print.

First of all, there are those with philosophical and logical training who see the fallacies of the claims of objectivity, reality, greater importance, more naturalness, phylogenetic basis, and so on. Unfortunately, none of these have effectively argued their case. Not that their presentation has been unsound, but it has not reached and interested enough taxonomists to be effective.

First among these was Gilmour in *The New Systematics* itself. His views of the nature of natural and phylogenetic classifications were accepted by the editor, J. S. Huxley, and are substantially those argued in the chapter else where in this book.

These views of Gilmour were misconstrued by one later writer, who uses the appropriate term "*phenotypic species* concept" but misquotes Gilmour in several ways, implying that his conclusions lead to the fall of all science. This is not justified.

That writer's views were based on an assumption made early in his paper but not labeled as such: that systematists accepted a new labor, after the evolution theories appeared, of arranging the groups of animals so as to reflect the actual course of evolution. With this assumption, some of the conclusions would follow logically.

There is evidence that ideas of this sort were talked about in the post-Darwinian days, but it is hard to find any classifications of that period that were changed because of these ideas. The *working* taxonomist did not and could not take them into direct account. Several evolutionists have admitted that there was no great change in the classifications, and one searches in vain for examples of classifications that were changed. Next there are Woodger and Gregg, supported in the abstract by all the non-biological authors of books on logic. The evidence in these books, bearing on "natural" classification and on the nature of categories and groups, is overwhelming.

Their thesis is that rigorous use of language is essential to clarity, and in the case of these words dual meanings cause much of the difficulty. These biological philosophers believe that the ordinary language of science, merely an extension of the language of the everyday world, is not sufficiently precise to serve the purposes of a complex field such as taxonomy and the methodology of taxonomy.

Even if taxonomists are not prepared to adopt their symbolic language to obtain the maximum rigor, they must make every possible effort to obtain clarity and mutual understanding in their language. Too often, apparent differences of opinion can be shown to be merely differences in the use of words.

It is not necessary to go to philosophers to get backing for the importance of rigor in language. In the introduction to Roget's *Thesaurus* there appears the following very pertinent passage:

"It is of the utmost consequence that strict accuracy should regulate our use of language, and that every one should acquire the power and the habit of expressing his thoughts with perspicuity and correctness. Few, indeed, can appreciate the real extent and importance of that influence which language has always exercised on human affairs, or can be aware how often these are determined by causes much slighter than are apparent to a superficial observer. False logic, disguised under specious phraseology, too often gains the assent of the unthinking multitude, disseminating far and wide the seeds of prejudice and error. Truisms pass current, and wear the semblance of profound wisdom, when dressed up in the tinsel garb of antithetical phrases, or set off by an imposing pomp of paradox. By a confused jargon of involved and mystical sentences, the imagination is easily inveigled into a transcendental region of clouds, and the understanding beguiled into the belief that it is acquiring knowledge and approaching truth. A misapplied or misapprehended term is sufficient to give rise to fierce and interminable disputes; a misnomer has turned the tide of popular opinion; a verbal sophism has decided a party question; an artful watchword, thrown among combustible materials, has kindled the flame of deadly warfare, and changed the destiny of an empire."

Taxonomists have insisted on exact and clear terminology in description of organisms, in the terms used for structures and situations, and in the names used for the groups. It is strange they have not insisted on similar clarity in the expressions used for the ideas involved in discussing the basis of taxonomy, the concepts, theories, problems, and other aspects of methodology.

As Gregg puts it, taxonomists are frequently guilty of ambiguity of reference as well as ambiguity of meaning. A number of other writers have examined one or more aspects of The New Systematics and denied the validity of the so-called modern view of it. Many more have ignored the claims entirely and simply continued to use the idea of species distinguished by characteristics that are primarily structural simply because structure is the most easily investigated aspect of most organisms.

Virtually all monographers have tacitly followed this method. It would be a serious error to leave this subject without reference to W. R. Thompson. His book and papers listed in the bibliography contribute substantially to these discussions, with major emphasis on logical arguments and justification of assumptions. His writings abound in worthwhile clarifications, viewpoints, and critiques.

The Taxonomy of Today

If the statements of the New Systematists were correct, taxonomy today would be very different from the taxonomy of a few years ago. Most work would now be done on subdivisions of species, since the latter would be mostly known; structural features would be largely replaced by ecological, genetic, and geographical data; for generic revisions hundreds or even thousands of specimens would be available, instead of only one or a few; the population would have become the basic taxonomic unit; and names would be no longer timeconsuming.

Many taxonomists will recognize that these so-called changes are actually descriptive of the current work in only a very small segment of the animal kingdom-the higher vertebrates and a genus or two among other groups.

Elsewhere, what little data of new types are available are welcome but are insignificant compared to the comparative data that has always been the basis of the taxonomy. In most groups of animals the supposed great change in practice simply has not occurred. Most taxonomists who continue to do taxonomic work are still doing it in almost exactly the same way as before.

Many of them do have a better understanding of broad biological concepts and theories and improved methods, but no one has given them any better way to classify animals or any reason to expect a better way to appear. It is a little strange that while the New Systematists claim a great change in taxonomy, they also see great confusion in taxonomy.

It does not seem to occur to them that the supposed change and the confusion could be cause and effect instead of effect and cause. It is possible to deny that there has been any widespread change, but it would be difficult to deny that there is confusion. Fortunately, the working taxonomist has often been untouched by the confusion, which has seemed to trouble mainly the New Systematists.

Actually, it is exceedingly difficult to find a piece of taxonomic work that is different in basic approach from the best work of a few decades ago. For the second time in a hundred years, taxonomy has been left substantially unchanged by a new concept heralded as cataclysmic.

A few biologists have recently attempted to force taxonomists to abandon the methods and concepts that have been the basis of its successes. They have insisted that the taxonomists *must* study the origins of the kinds of animals they have been studying. This so-called "modern" approach is firmly entrenched in the sense that it is being actively proclaimed, and giving results that justify the labor.

These results are not part of taxonomy, although they should interest taxonomists; they are a part of a new science of speciation. Recent publications show that only a few taxonomists have really accepted the views of the speciationists as they apply to *taxonomy* to the extent of weighing the evidence presented.

Certainly many taxonomists have been passive or completely aloof. Others have been actively opposed to certain implications, and this group is larger than is usually realized. Those taxonomists who have accepted the recent statements have seldom given any evidence that they have themselves examined the arguments, the logic, and the conclusions and are willing to say that they actively agree in the implications.

There is no reason to suppose that the casual quoter of the new ideas sees all their implications and accepts them all. It is certain that the implications have not all been brought out for him to examine at leisure, and there is good evidence for believing that a few important implications have not been faced even by the proponents.

The preceding paragraphs are believed to show that the application of speciation ideas to taxonomy has not been universally accepted or even widely practiced, that the arguments purporting to show that these ideas must be adopted by taxonomists are far from conclusive and in fact often illogical and unfounded, that the purpose of taxonomy is to classify animals and our knowledge about them rather than to illuminate their evolution, and that current use of language falls far short of adequacy for discussion of the methodology of taxonomy.

It is specifically not intended to deny evolution or that species have had histories (phylogenies), or even that the phylogenies are somehow related to the present nature of the species; nor the importance of the study of speciation, populations, genetics, evolution, or any other biological subject; nor the desirability of finding and using data from all fields of biology in our classifications.

There is nothing but language and acceptances 2 standing in the way of recognition of the real goals and uses of classification. If taxonomists can make the language adequately rigorous and free from rhetorical obfuscations, it should be possible for them to deal with the acceptances on the basis of fact and logic. If one refuses to consider semantics and epistemology in discussions of methodology, one can expect no end to the "problems" of taxonomy.

5

SPECIES AND SUBSPECIES

Although species and subspecies are linked together in nomenclatural problems, and in the informal speech of taxonomists, they seem to be taxa of substantially different nature. They are, in fact, more different from each other than species are from genera.

There is some possibility that subspecies are not taxa at all but merely concepts. Some of the ways in which taxonomists deal with species and subspecies involve identical actions and procedures. In this chapter these species and subspecies will be discussed separately, with occasional references to their similarities and differences.

SPECIES

It is possible to make an elaborate problem of the question "What is a species?" In biology in general this may be necessary, as there are many ways of looking at the manner in which animals occur in nature. In taxonomy, however, it is neither necessary nor appropriate, because taxonomic species are simple and easy to work with.

This is not the same thing as saying that they are objective or easily defined or simple to discover, for they are none of these. It may be partly because of the subjectivity and lack of definition that taxonomists have been able to build up a functioning system of species and groups of species, flexible enough to represent growing knowledge yet accurate enough to be effective.

There is an apparent paradox in the statement that species, which cannot be defined, can be classified. This is due entirely to the mixture of two meanings of the word species. It is not possible to define what a species is, or what species are, in general. They are the taxa placed at the species level, but there is no real definition in this statement. Species in this conceptual sense cannot be classified either.

Just as a chemist probably could not rigidly define just what is "a chemical" and what is not, so the taxonomist cannot define what is a species and what is not. The chemist, however, *can* define each one of the chemicals known to him and can distinguish them, and the taxonomist *can* define each species known to him. Thus, definition, which is frequently thought of as a necessity in science, is really a necessity only at certain levels.

It is not necessary to be able to define rigidly such words as zoology, psychology, and so on, but it is necessary to define some of the units which are employed. Taxonomy has no difficulty in doing this, even though the actual understanding of these individual units is constantly increasing. Different species are different "kinds" of animals. The members of each kind are not always alike, but we gradually learn which differences distinguish kinds and which differences merely distinguish some of the individuals within a kind.

When somewhat different individuals live together normally, it is assumed that they are the same kind. When somewhat different individuals develop from one batch of eggs or in one litter, it is recognized that their differences are those between children of one family. The young are generally somewhat different from their parents, but they are still not different species.

If there are two parents, they may be different in one or more ways, and these differences too are recognized as not showing difference in kind (species). There are many of these differences between individuals within a species; for example, differences due to nutrition; malformation in development; mutilation, accidental or otherwise; environmental conditions; or dominance and recessiveness of genes.

In some circumstances little variety is to be noted among the individuals of a species, but the possibilities listed above generally produce a very substantial variety if all individuals are considered. There is no objective way to tell whether a difference is merely a variation within a species or actually a distinction between two species. It is the basis of good taxonomy that the taxonomist develops the ability to recognize the value of most differences.

When he errs, a later reviser with more relevant knowledge corrects his error. This continuous correction not only serves to perfect the system but constantly improves the accuracy of the alert taxonomist in making his judgments. This is the very essence of taxonomic work. In modern terms, a species consists of all the individuals with a common inheritance back to the point where the ancestors differed in enough features to be considered a distinct species.

There are immense philosophical difficulties in the way of translation of this into taxonomic discrimination, but these philosophical difficulties do not generally prevent the taxonomist from making judgments which yield a useful set of species that can be described and distinguished by differential features. These are the species of the taxonomist; they are not necessarily the species of the geneticist or the evolutionist.

Some taxonomists, including all those whose opinions are known to the writer, believe that when the species are well enough known and biological concepts in general are sufficiently well understood, the species of the taxonomist will coincide with those of the geneticist. At the present time, however, the species definitions of the geneticist and those of the evolutionist are almost completely unusable by the taxonomist.

Species in Taxonomy

Formal taxonomy deals only with the species of the taxonomist. These may be called taxonomic species, a term not overworked but nevertheless highly appropriate. The possible relationship between this kind of species and the kinds used by evolutionists, ecologists, and others is suggested in the next section (*Nontaxonomic* species) and discussed in other chapter of this book.

In this taxonomic sense, a species consists of all the specimens which are, or would be, considered by a particular taxonomist to be members of a single kind as shown by the evidence or the assumption that they are as alike as their offspring or their hereditary relatives within a few generations.

When there is no evidence of the hereditary relationship, the taxonomist will rely on distinctions that have been found to be effective in segregating species among other animals.

Most of this book is concerned with species. Virtually all aspects of taxonomic theory and practice involve them, either directly, as groups, or as specimens. These aspects are not re-discussed in the present chapter, but certain other points relating to species are cited briefly. The non-taxonomic usages of this term are then cited for the purpose of distinguishing them from the taxonomic uses.

Terms Descriptive of Species

Some of the terms employing the word species are descriptive of the species of the taxonomist, whereas many others are used to refer to evolutionary or ecological ideas. The latter are cited in a later section, and the former are discussed briefly here.

Cryptic species are ones which are hidden, whose distinctive features are not evident under the usual procedures. Not usually a technical term.

Sibling species—a term applied to pairs or groups of very similar and closely related species. In practice this term can be applied only to similar species, when it becomes a synonym for cryptic species. When applied to closely related species (in a phylogenetic sense) it becomes a hypothetical situation, which cannot be dealt with in taxonomy but can be useful in speculations on evolution. (See non-taxonomic sibling species, below.)

Physiological species are those distinguished by activities but not readily by structural features. There is no real distinction, as structure is always involved at some level. These are also cryptic species.

Sympatric species are ones normally occupying the same geographical area. *Allopatric species* are ones normally inhabiting completely different areas. *Continental species* are those that live on the large land masses, as distinct from the insular species.

Insular species are those living on isolated islands which owe their fauna to dispersal methods other than overland migration. This isolation affords opportunity for study of immigration, speciation, etc.

Cosmopolitan Species

This expression is used for species that occur widely over the earth, in all major regions. The Greek base of this word implies universality. No species occurs everywhere in the world because none can live on land and in deep water alike. This term is meaningless if used carelessly or taken too literally.

Tropicopolitan Species

Literally, a citizen of the tropics. This ill-formed word is used to mean found throughout the tropics. (Also called *pantropical species.)*

Montane species are those found only at higher elevations on mountain ranges, isolated by the surrounding lowlands.

Morpho-geographical species are those of the ordinary taxonomist, from Linnaeus to modern times. Although data other than "morphology" and geography have been increasingly used in recent years, these still remain the basic species of taxonomy.

Typification of Species

In modern taxonomic practice, all species (and subspecies) must have type specimens. In some cases the type may never have been selected or labeled, or the type specimen may have been lost. A proposal *of* a species without a type, or at least a specimen that *could be* the type, would not be accepted in taxonomy, and the taxon could not receive a name acceptable in zoological nomenclature. This has been a basic rule in taxonomy for more than a century.

Types are used in a variety of ways. These may be either taxonomic or nomenclatural in purpose. They include the following:

(1) In early knowledge of a species the type is usually the chief source of unchallengeable characters of the species. It will not show all the characters of the species, but it will show some which can be expected to appear on all comparable specimens of the species.

(2) It continues to show, for every sort of diversity, one point that does unequivocally occur within that species. Every feature of the type falls within the variation range of the species.

(3) It serves as a check on the accuracy of the published descriptions and their completeness.

(4) It provides an anchor for the name, indicating the point in the diversity to which that name is forever attached.

Each type thus serves as basis for description, as a standard for identification, and as name-bearer. It is evident that these uses are not entirely distinct. It is impossible to separate a species from the characters of its members or the names applied to it. It will be noted that these functions of types do not include "showing what the species is," or "showing the limits of the species," or being the "basis for the definition of species."

No taxonomist believes that the type can do these things. It is surprising, therefore, that some recent writers have felt it necessary to deny at length that a type can serve all these purposes. Taxonomists use the type as the primary basis for the original description.

To the description of the type is properly added the range of features of the other known specimens thought to be part of the species. In the course of time, data accumulate until a monographer can more fully describe the species-all the specimens believed to belong to the same specific taxon as the type.

Taxonomists do not use the type as basis for *definition* of the species. No specimen can possibly show limits of variation or the variety of forms assumed within the species. No taxonomists attempt such an obvious misuse of types. Simpson lists the three supposed functions of a type: Basis for the description and definition of species, standard of comparison, and vehicle for a name. He states categorically that "No one specimen can possibly fulfil them all properly."

This is true, but only because of the inclusion of the word species. No specimen of any sort can ever serve for description of a species, which always includes variation of several sorts among individuals. Taxonomists have not tried to describe the species from the type. They describe the type as one specimen that unequivocally belongs to that species.

As taxonomists have usually proceeded, the type thus can be used for description, for comparison, and for anchoring the name. Types are universally used in all these ways, except where the specimens are consistently fragmentary. The fragments are inadequate for description of even one individual animal; they fail in comparison unless correspon-ding fragments happen to be available; and they even fail as name-bearers if later specimens cannot be identified with the type because of lack of correspondence of the fragments.

It is thus primarily among vertebrate fossils that any difficulty of this sort occurs. Although Linnaeus did not use types in the modern sense, the need for them arose gradually and has resulted in continual refinement of the concept. Whether they are called types or not, the specimens on which a species was based will inevitably be used to settle questions of ambiguity in description, of mixed species in the original lot, and as a source for data not recorded by the original describer.

Simpson, in denying the effectiveness of types for all non-nomencl-atural purposes, has suggested the term *hypodigm* for "all the specimens personally known to [the taxonomist] at that time, considered by him to be unequivocal members of the taxon. . . ." This hypodigm, rather than a type, would be the basis of the species.

This would be satisfactory at that time, but when later authors learn more about the supposed species, this hypodigm will be of little use to them in separating the mixed data. The word is acceptable as denoting the entire understanding of a species (or group) by a taxonomist at a particular time, but it cannot replace the type in subsequent study.

The hypodigm might possibly include more than one species, both for the original describer of the species and for subsequent classifiers. The type cannot be composite by definition, although there can be errors in association of fragments from several individuals.

As a concept the hypodigm always exists, the sum of all that is known by a taxonomist about what he deems to be one species. As something that a later worker can refer to, or use, there is no such thing as a conceptual hypodigm of an earlier author. Simpson did not use the term as a concept but to refer to the specimens themselves.

This specimenhypodigm is therefore of little taxonomic value to future students and is no different from the expression "original series." Simpson also argues that only populations can be classified and that therefore a single specimen is not so useful as the sample of the population. The difficulty here is that "population" is an abstract term; a congregation of animals is not necessarily a population but frequently a mixture of several populations.

The taxonomist is interested in species. The only animal that can be positively known to belong to a given species is the one specimen on which the species was based. All others are merely *identified* with it, believed to be the same species, even believed to be part of the same population. (This statement is actually inapplicable to asexually reproducing animals, where the members of a clone still physically connected are certainly the same. At the extreme in sexual animals, there is no real assurance of identity even in litter-mates or parent-offspring sets, because hybridization is always a possibility and usually cannot be excluded in practice.)

In connection with typification and the hypodigm there should be noted another viewpoint forcibly expressed by Simpson. He considers the hypodigm, the original specimens, to be a sample from which the taxonomist draws inferences as to the variation in the entire population.

One judges whether a specimen belongs to a particular species not by comparison with any one specimen (type) but on whether it falls within the limits of variation that have been inferred from the hypodigm. The inferences are probably derived by statistical procedures. He even claims that if only one specimen is known, inferences are drawn from it, and these inferences are the basis for comparison and identification.

It seems unnecessary to challenge the logic of these statements because they simply do not apply to taxonomy. Populations are indispensable to the evolutionist. They are unquestionably features of species occurrence, because the term merely describes the manner in which animals are known to occur. But populations are not generally important to the taxonomist.

He is not usually interested in statistical probabilities, but in actual situations. He can describe specimens, and he can group them in species.

He may eventually be able to verify this grouping by various biological evidence. He can group the species in a classification. Populations do exist, but they are part of a different approach to animals. Populations do not represent levels in the taxonomic hierarchy, nor units of classification, nor anything that the taxonomist is likely to know sufficiently well to use in taxonomic work.

Typology

For at least a century and a half taxonomists have made use of the device of typifying a concept with a selected specimen or an included subconcept. These "types" have been in use for species, for groups of species, and for subdivisions of species.

The types serve a variety of purposes and have been indispensable in taxonomy. In recent years evolutionists have introduced the idea that the use of types is what is called typology. Typology and neo-typology have come to be terms of derogation, used by evolutionists to emphasize the supposed unscientific nature of taxonomy.

For example, the basic concept of typology is described by Simpson: "Every natural group of organisms, hence every taxon in classification, has an invariant, generalized or idealized pattern shared by all members of the group." The taxonomists would agree with Simpson that the concept he describes is not a useful one in taxonomy or evolution, but they would challenge him to show that this is really how types have been used.

In Hansen we read that "The Linnaean type concept led taxonomists up a blind alley and is no longer accepted; the idea that drove it out is that of biological evolution." It is not certain that it is correct to label the type concept of the last hundred years as "the Linnaean type concept," but the fact is that in the decades after Darwin there was no change in the use of types by taxonomists in general.

Hansen further states that "evolutionary theory .. . destroyed the type concept . . . , for the central idea of evolution is change, which is the antithesis of static types." In the first place the type concept has not been destroyed but is in daily use by virtually all taxonomists.

It is, furthermore, completely false to imply that there is anything static in the taxonomic use of types. As pointed out by Muesebeck, "Around this (type) there needs to be built the species concept . .. ," and this species is not static; it encompasses much diversity not shown by the type and may change in time.

The typology of the evolutionists is not the type concept of taxonomy, whether we think of pre-Darwinian or post-Darwinian times, or of current practice.

Non-Taxonomic Species

As new branches of biology have become interested in aspects of animal existence, they have frequently used the species of the taxonomist in conceptual framework quite different from the subjective and continually corrected system he employs.

Some of these uses are based on facts of the nature of the animals, and some are based on hypotheses of the history of the species, or the capabilities of the animals. By grouping these uses under the heading Non-taxonomic Species; it is not intended to imply that none of them are of interest to the taxonomist or relevant to his work.

It is not intended to give rigorous definitions of each of these kinds of species. It is enough for our purpose to point out that these are, in general, within the purview of biologists other than taxonomists-that when a taxonomist says species, he probably is not referring to any of these but rather to what Davis and Heywood refer to as the morphologica-lgeographical species, herein called the taxonomic species.

Among these formal and informal terms or expressions there are some that relate to some feature of the species, some that represent hypothetical conditions, others that are not formal terms but mere adjectival expressions, and still others that serve only to reflect un favorably on certain workers.

Genetical species are groups of interbreeding populations, which are reproductively isolated from each other. They are thus the same as biological species.

Biological species are usually defined as groups of actually or potentially interbreeding natural populations, which are reproductively isolated from other such groups. This gives theoretical groups, which can seldom be distinguished in practice.

As Simpson has pointed out, *all* definitions of animal species give us *biological* species; he therefore prefers the name genetical species for this and cites also biospecies. (It should be noted that populations do not interbreed, only individual animals.)

Biospecies (see Biological and Genetical Species).

Agamospecies are ones consisting of uniparental organisms. They may produce gametes but there is no fertilization. Such a distinction cannot really be made, because fertilization may be facultative, and many animals can reproduce either uniparentally or biparentally either as species or individuals.

Sibling species—a term applied to "pairs or groups of very similar and closely related species." When applied to "closely related species" (in a phylogenetic sense), this expression refers to hypothetical species; these cannot be dealt with in taxonomy, but can be useful in speculations on evolution. (Compare under taxonomic species.)

Polytypic species are those which consist of two or more subspecies. This is the original definition of Huxley; according to later writers this usage "has now been almost universally adopted." Nevertheless, there have been many uses of this term to cover variable species in which no subspecies have been explicitly recognized, where the populations differ among themselves but insufficiently to be recognized as subspecies, in the opinion of the reviser.

The term *polymorphic species* has also been used in these same ways, but the term polymorphism is used in such diverse ways in biology that it would be best avoided as a general modifier of the word species. *Monotypic* species consist of a single subspecies. This and the preceding would be considered taxonomic concepts if subspecies were considered to be taxa.

Evolutionary species are lineages (ancestral-descendant sequences of populations) evolving separately from each other and with their own unitary evolutionary roles and tendencies.

Transient species are the ones existing contemporaneously, as a cross section of the lineages of evolutionary species.

Successional species are temporally successive species in a single lineage.

Paleospecies (see Successional Species).

Paleontological species have no representatives now living, all known examples being fossils.

Panmictic species are those in which a single interbreeding population occurs. Therefore these are the theoretical counterparts of monotypic species, theoretical because panmixia can only be postulated.

Philopatric species are ones which show no tendency to extend their range. (Again, this is a hybrid term, formed from two languages.)

Incipient species are geographical subspecies or other segregates, which, it is presumed or postulated, will become isolated and then be distinct species.

Morphospecies are ones "established by morphological similarity regardless of other considerations" (Simpson). They are not genetic groups but groups of like objects. (These include the "form species" and "paraspecies," following.)

Form species are groups of fossil objects not identifiable as any particular biological species, such as fragments or isolated parts.

Paraspecies are the parataxa at the species level. (See Parataxa, below.)

Non-Dimensional Species

The taxonomic species have been described as lacking dimensions of space and time. With this as a premise, they are called non-dimensional, applicable only to non-evolving animals, and therefore not biologically acceptable. In reality both space and time are present in the use of taxonomic species, but only a short segment of time (the span of a few generations) is available for consideration.

This expression serves only to derogate the real basis of taxonomy; it is used only by the speciationists who attempt to force taxonomy into evolutionary studies.

SUBSPECIES

Much has been written in recent decades about subspecies and their use in taxonomy. There are strong feelings that they are usable, useful, and desirable. There are also strong feelings that they are not really relevant to taxonomy and are an unnecessary encumbrance to classification and nomenclature.

Subspecies are widely used by zoologists who work with vertebrates, perhaps consistently used. They have been used in many invertebrate groups but in most of them only occasionally. In work with invertebrates, in fact, the concept of subspecies often merges into that of varieties, with no uniform basis for discrimination.

The problem of terms discussed above for species applies in considerable part also to subspecies. There is a level in the taxonomic hierarchy in which are placed groups of animals (taxa) called subspecies. The level is the category subspecies; the taxa are the subspecies taxa. The term thus refers both to a level in the hierarchy and to the taxa placed at that level.

The principal theoretical question to be asked about subspecies is seldom discussed and has not been answered effectively. It is this: Are the segregates called subspecies actually of the same nature as the taxa of species level and above? If this question cannot be answered in the affirmative, there will be serious doubt as to the relevance of subspecies in taxonomy.

Definition

Recent definitions of subspecies are in agreement on the two basic features: (1) a distinct geographical area is occupied, and (2) there are structural features partially setting off the subspecies. Other ideas included in some definitions are that it consists of local populations, that it is set off also by ecological features, and that its distinctive features will hold for about 75% of the specimens but not necessarily for all of them.

A recent definition by Mayr incorporates most of these ideas: "A subspecies is an aggregate of local populations of a species, inhabiting a geographical subdivision of the range of the species, and differing taxonomically from other populations of the species." This emphasizes the population nature of the subspecies and also the fact that the distinctive features need not be "morphological" but must be "taxonomic."

It should be noted here that the subspecies cannot be known until the species is known. Only after the limits of the species are set, for that moment, can the variants be seen to represent what might be called subspecies. Some definitions of subspecies imply that they are "incipient species" or at least populations that are nearing specific status.

It is certainly theoretically possible for a subspecies to become isolated and evolve into a distinct species, but the ordinary subspecies is distinguished by its present features and distribution only, not by its future possibilities. In pointing this out, Simpson states that subspecies are taxa of a markedly different kind than species.

Taxonomic Nature

It is sometimes assumed that there is no basic difference between subspecific and specific characters, either morphologically or in mode of inheritance. It is taken to follow from these presumed facts that there is therefore no conceptual difference between species and subspecies. It seems to have been forgotten that these are not the only ways in which species and subspecies can differ.

In nearly all definitions, species can be distinguished because of gaps in the variation of their features. Subspecies as usually defined cannot be so distinguished, except in some percentage of cases, a figure often placed at 75%. Both species and subspecies consist of the same basic materials, the individuals, but there is a complete break between species and subspecies conceptually in the distinctness of the former and the overlapping of the latter.

The entire taxonomic hierarchic system of zoological classification is based on the fact that species and other taxa are presented to us as distinguishable entities. The individuals can be identified with one species or another in practice. Whether or not this is theoretically to be expected among evolving organisms is not relevant-the system is based on the assumption that it can be done, and the elaborate classification now in use is evidence that it has been done successfully in the eyes of most practicing taxonomists. But this system may not be capable of classifying taxa that are not distinct-that are therefore not really taxa.

It was noted by Borgmeier that while two species are essentially different (in the features taken to be specific), two races or subspecies are essentially alike "because they agree in all basic structures and are linked together genetically." Because not all species form subspecies, this level is not one of universal significance as is the species level. Borgmeier concludes that it is only a partial subcategory of the species level.

It was stated as long ago as 1940 that "there are relatively few good' species that are not actually composed of groups of `subspecies'." This was, of course, an extreme overstatement, as the structure of the vast majority of species had never been (and still have not been) examined for this purpose. The statement may apply in the bird and mammal groups, and there is little doubt that there will be an increasing number of cases discovered in other groups. Nevertheless, this does not justify the enunciation of a new law of nature.

Hubbell concluded that "population analysis below the species level is too complex to be bound by formal taxonomic and nomenclatorial rules. . . ." He proposed six "precepts" which serve to summarize his views of subspecies: "(1) Clinal variation is variation of characters in populations, not of populations. (2) Clines in themselves therefore cannot be taxonomic units. (3) In a population showing only a stepped cline in a single character or in a group of correlated characters it is feasible and may be convenient to treat the segments between steps as subspecies. (4) In populations in which clinal change is gradual or in which two or more non-coincident clines exist it is inadvisable to try to separate subspecies. (5) In general, infraspecific variation is best treated by description, graphic presentation, and non-technical names. . . . (6) Nothing should ever be named for the sake of naming it, but only in order that something may be said about it."

In the large recent literature on subspecies in taxonomy, it is evident that nomenclature is a major factor in the controversy that has arisen. Many papers that seem to be addressed to the problems of subspecies turn out to be concerned almost exclusively with the question of whether such segregates should be named.

This is unfortunate, because the decision on whether or how to name any biological objects should not affect discussions of whether there is something biologically worthwhile to be recorded about them.

The problems involved here are (1) whether there is in nature enough diversity within some species to be usefully studied; (2) if so, whether this diversity can be treated in the taxonomic system; and (3) if so, whether the segregates can or should be named in the formal system of nomenclature. The first question is generally answered in the affirmative.

The second question has scarcely ever been faced; it is the crux of the present problem and is here believed to be likely to be eventually answered in the negative. The third question has clouded the second and is answered either negatively or affirmatively according to the experience of the speakers.

The Rules of Nomenclature have for a half-century permitted such naming. It is possible to look on subspecies as pseudotaxa. A taxon is a classificatory unit of any rank, but it is also a group of individuals. If the group cannot be circumscribed, at least in practice, it can scarcely be classified.

It is doubtful if subspecies are ever classified in the same manner as species. They are populations recognized within the species, not groups of individuals assembled to produce a taxon. They are thus not classified and so are not taxa.

Pseudotaxa would thus be segregates of a taxon which appear to be subordinate taxa but in reality cannot be segregated and so cannot be classified. They are thus false taxa from a taxonomic point of view. They may, however, be acceptable isolates in the eyes of other zoologists.

In any case they may be of much interest to taxonomists even if they cannot be dealt with as taxa are. It seems quite likely that the study of subspecies is the aspect through which taxonomy became involved in recent decades with population studies. The subspecies are populations, presumably ones with a certain amount of unity.

This cannot be said of species, which are (potentially, at least) groups of populations, and which are by definition fully set off from other such groups of populations by the features which are therefore called taxonomic (or specific). These general conclusions have resulted in there being few references to subspecies in this book. Their treatment and use is often part of other aspects of systematics.

References to recent discussions of subspecies, their problems, and their misuse are given in the Bibliography. Their names have been regulated by all modern codes of nomenclature, and this aspect is dealt with in Part VI of this book.

Other Subdivisions of Species

From the very beginning of formal taxonomy, it was recognized that some species include groups of individuals that can be readily distinguished. The basis of the distinction was varied, but the cause was usually unknown. Some individuals were of a different color, had larger body parts, or differed in other features to a lesser degree than was elsewhere accepted as of specific value.

As knowledge of animals increased, it was recognized that some of these variations were geographically isolated. These were often called *races,* but in later years such geographical segregates became universally known as ***subspecies.*** Where there were color differences, the term *color* fornrwas often used.

Sometimes ***phase*** or ***color phase*** was used for this also. In a few cases, such as butterflies, specimens so rare as often to be unique were termed *transition forms,* supposedly intermediate between two species or subspecies (but not hybrids). Similarly, single specimens with unusual features, sometimes probably teratological, have been termed *aberrations.*

Specimens or groups of specimens have also been described as *forms (f ormae), Rassenkreise, Formenkreise, natios,* and *colonies.* Other terms, such as *blastovariations, morphae, mutations,* and *variants,* have been used, both in zoology and botany, but they are not always intended as formal taxonomic categories.

They have had little use in animal taxonomy and have no standing in the system of nomenclature. There is no reason why any taxonomist should not use any idea or term which he finds useful, whether or not it has been widely adopted. He will have a responsibility to define and use it consistently.

But none of the possible levels below species are to be named within the system of nomenclature, except subspecies. An example of an elaborate system of terms for minute segregates within a species was published in 1938 by Bright and Leeds. In recording the aberrations in color pattern of a certain species of blue butterfly (Lycaenidae) these writers use seven hundred and thirty-seven names for the aberrations of this one species, and they also propose a system of terms for identifying similar aberrations in other species.

These names do not enter into zoological nomenclature. They were evidently found useful to these writers in publishing the results of their study of the variability of these insects.

Parataxa

When the material (specimens) with which a taxonomist works is

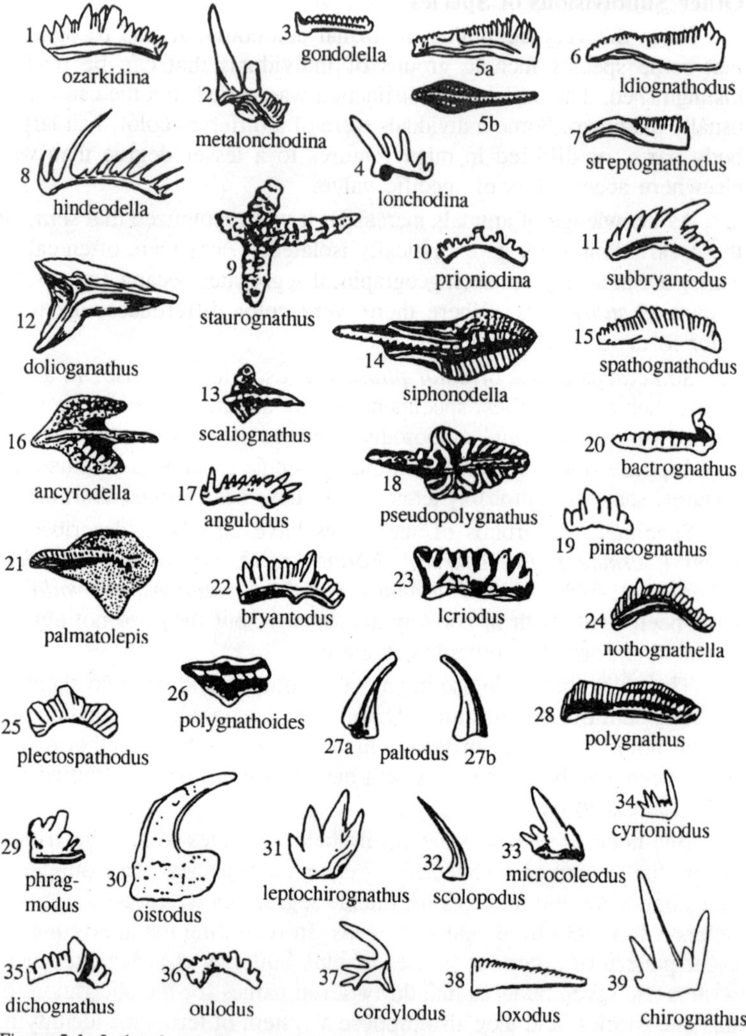

Figure 5.1: Isolated conodonts, jaw-like structures known only as fossils and produced by animals of unknown nature. These can be identified and correlated from stratum to stratum. They have been named as genera and species.

fragmentary, it may consist solely of isolated parts of animals -parts not now and not likely to be identifiable to species because in the various species they were too much alike.

If these fragments are of use in stratigraphic correlation even without specific identification, there arises a need for names to supplement the system of specific names, so that the fragments can be referred to even when their species cannot be determined. Paleontologists have sometimes named these fragments as if they were genera and species, in the usual manner.

If, later on, the fragments are associated with other parts of the animal which can be identified with species, there is a conflict of names. Furthermore, the fragment-species may include objects that actually belong to several species, so that synonymy will not suffice to show the situation. To circumvent this problem, it has been proposed to name the fragments as *parataxa* under separate rules of paWtaxal nomenclature.

The following paragraphs are taken from a preliminary draft of such a proposal, by R. C. Moore and P. C. Sylvester-Bradley, with their kind permission. "Discrete parts of various kinds of animals, chiefly skeletal parts, occur commonly in nature; more especially they are represented by abundant fossils in sedimentary strata of all geological ages from Cambrian to Recent.

Examples are isolated coccoliths; spicules of sponges, octocorals, and holothurians; ossicles of erinoids, cystoids, blastoids, echinoids, and asterozoans; annelid jaws (scolecodonts) ; radular elements and opercula of gastropods and cephalopods (aptychi) ; and the abundant fossils of unknown zoological affinities called conodonts.

A large majority, if not all, of these bodies are usefully classifiable within the groups to which they belong, even though the genera and species of animals from which they were derived is almost universally unknown. Such discrete fragments of animals constitute a special category of zoological entities which, though classifiable in varying degrees of detail and precision, offers critical problems in nomenclature.

"There is little need for the classification and nomenclature of fragments when whole specimens of animals are available for study. This applies to virtually all work by neozoologists on living animals and may be accepted also for most work by paleozoologists on extinct animals because the fossils on which many thousand taxa have been recognized and named are judged adequate for discrimination of various genera and species of whole animals.

In addition, there are multitudinous dissociated fragments of animals which are far from sufficient for identification of the whole animals that produced them and yet these are so distinctive in themselves as to have great usefulness for identifying the sedimentary strata containing them. These fragmentary palæontological materials are indispensable for

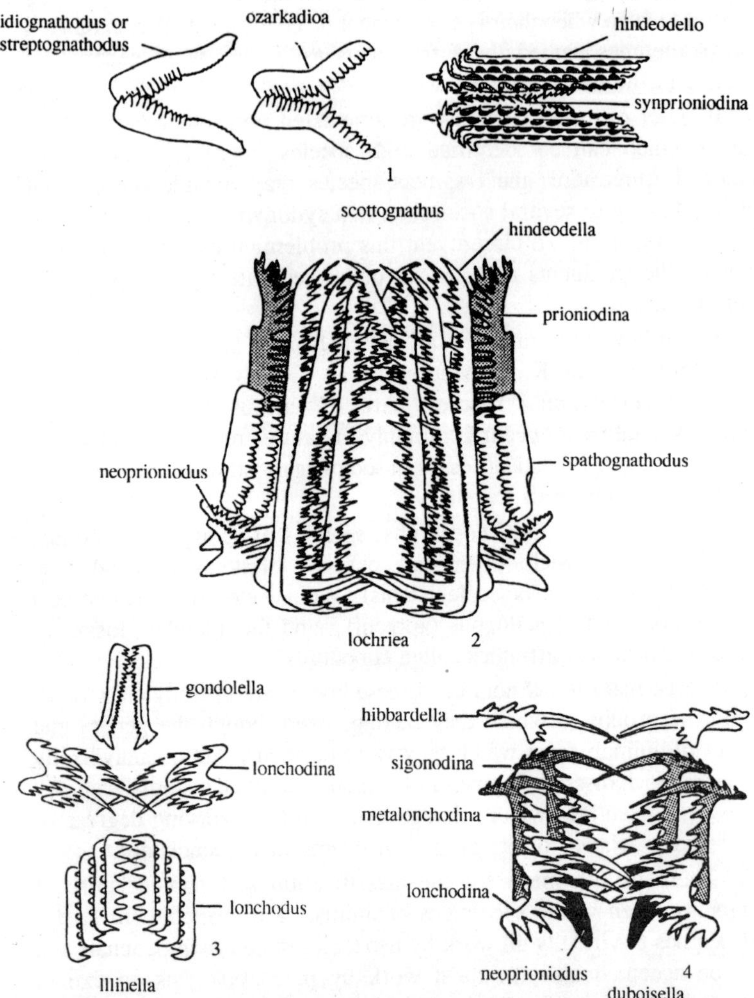

Figure 5.2: Conodont assemblages containing some of the same forms as shown in Figure 5.1. Because each assemblage evidently came from an individual, each is now believed to represent a species, and the isolated objects in Figure 5.1 are now thought to represent something less than species, a level called parataxa.

correlations of many rock formations in the earth's crust and for aid in establishing a trustworthy geochronology of the post-Precambrian part of geological time.

However, in order to make use of such fragments, they must be classified, named, described, figured, and recorded as to occurrence.

When this is done, many prove to be invaluable. For example, the dissociated fossils called conodonts have been demonstrated to constitute the. only reliable means for determining correlations and relative geological age of various strata containing these fragments.

Othe? highly fragmental remains of animals, especially echinoderms are similarly useful, but so far have been little studied because no satisfactory means of naming them in accordance with zoological rules has been available. When suitable procedure is provided for applying names to discrete animal fragments without reference to the whole-animal species which they represent, this will encourage greatly the study of such fragments, making them useful in stratigraphical palaeontology:

"The taxonomic arrangement adopted in by far the greater majority of fossils studied is exactly comparable to that which would have been proposed if whole animals had been available for study. In many cases, if a fragmental specimen is at first inadequate for the identification of the whole animal from which it was derived, evidence may accumulate later which will establish its identity.

In these cases the normal operation of Art. 27 of the Regles (which states that the Law of Priority applies when any part of an animal is named before the animal itself) takes care of the nomenclatural situation. In a certain number of cases, however, the stratigraphical importance of the fragments far transcends their importance as biological entities.

In these cases a dual nomenclature has grown up, one providing names for the fraginents, the other for the whole animals. Such dual systems are contrary to the present provisions of the Regles, but they have great utilitarian value and are currently employed in the taxonomy of conodonts . . . , ammonoid aptychi . . . , holothurian spicules . . . , and, to a somewhat lesser extent, in a number of other groups.

This application seeks to regularize the establishment of certain of these dual systems by the establishment of parataxa as a special category for the classification and nomenclature of the specified fragments. In a sense a parataxon is a taxonomic category, but, as Professor Chester Bradley has pointed out to us, in a zoologically more important sense it is outside of taxonomy.

The study of parataxa might even be termed 'parataxonomy.' Zoological taxonomy is a single system based on natural relationships into which, with varying degree of success, all animals can be fitted. It is just because fragments of the type here described cannot be fitted into that system that parataxa are called for.

It might be argued that if these names cannot be applied in ordinary taxonomy, then they are better ignored; to this there is the very forceful counter argument that it would be most confusing to have the same name applied to both ordinary taxa and to parataxa. Such homonymy must be avoided.

The regulations we here recommend therefore suggest that for all purposes except those of the Law of Homonymy, parataxa should be regarded as not coordinate with corresponding whole animal taxa. To this extent they may be ignored by the taxonomist who is only concerned with zoological taxonomy."

This proposal by paleontologists at the London Congress was rejected as far as the rules of nomenclature are concerned. Parataxa as such cannot be named within the system of binominal nomenclature. They can be named as species, genera, etc., if they are assumed to be such taxa.

The names already introduced will presumably be treated as if they are specific and generic names. Paleontologists will have to resort to other means for distinguishing these "taxa" from actual species and genera based on identifiable specimens.

It has sometimes been suggested that this problem exists also in parasitology, where certain larval forms are found that cannot be identified to species. At this level, the problem would be nearly universal, as unassociated stages or fragments can be found in all groups of animals.

The unusual feature among the particular fossils concerned is the stratigraphic need for names. This same need has been claimed in parasitology, but parasitologists are by no means agreed that the use of parataxa is a reasonable solution in their field.

6

IDENTIFICATION

Identification has been called the utilitarian side of t2xonomy. Classification stores the facts known about kinds of animals, but identification enables us to retrieve the appropriate facts from the system to be associated with some. specimen at hand.

Thus, identification is better described as the recovery side of taxonomy. Identification refers to the association of specimens with the correct name for the species, which means association through the name with other specimens of that species.

It presupposes that classification has already distinguished the species of the group and that names have been applied to them. In taxonomic practice there is often no sharp distinction between identification and classification, as the latter always involves the former and the former may lead to extension and improvement of the latter.

There are comparatively few groups of animals in which there is no background of classification. It is thus usually possible to undertake to identify specimens by reference to what has already been published.

In some groups, the percentage of previously ynknown species is high, so that attempts at identification, in the strict sense, fail, because there is nothing with which to identify many of the specimens. In these cases, further description and classification is necessary, so that the unknown or "new" species are added to the recorded classification.

There is no quick and easy road to identification in any group. Even if an identification is as certain today as is humanly possible, it may be quite wrong tomorrow, when someone discovers and publishes a fact hitherto unavailable. There is no substitute for experience. No one should ever expect to make a publishable identification of an isolated individual or population in a group in which he has had no previous experience. The safest identifications are usually those made by a specialist in the group at the time he is identifying many specimens of many species and thus obtains a view of the group as a whole, as well as of its parts.

BACKGROUND EXPERIENCE

In order to make useful identifications in most groups of animals it is necessary to have experience of several sorts. This experience includes knowledge of taxonomic methods in general, the features and terms for them employed in the particular group, the usual study techniques, the identification literature on the group, and the natural history and comparative zoology of the group.

Familiarity with Taxonomic Methods and Resources

Identification involves a working knowledge of all the other subjects that are part of taxonomy, or even of zoology. It is not possible to identify a particular organism with a particular group without an understanding of how the classification was made and what its limitations are.

It is necessary to be experienced in taxonomic characters and terms in the particular group, as well as in the techniques used to preserve the specimens. There must be an understanding of the state of the knowledge of the group and the extent and availability of the literature about it, together with a considerable knowledge of the biology of the group of animals.

If this sounds as if identification of dependable accuracy can be made in most groups only by a specialist with long experience with those particular animals, the point has been successfully made. The point applies, however, primarily to genera, species, and subspecies. Useful identification to group can often be made by the ncn-specialist, by carrying the identification down the hierarchy only so far as the technical requirements or difficulties permit.

The concepts of taxonomy and classification are discussed elsewhere in this book. It is here assumed that theestudent is able to work with the ideas of species, genera, homology, similarity, and so on, to extract pertinent features from descriptions, and to handle the aspects of identification represented by the following paragraphs.

Taxonomic Characters of the Group

Nearly all taxonomy is highly technical and specialized. The characteristics used in distinguishing or grouping birds are so different from those used for nematodes that even a detailed knowledge of one would be of no help in making identifications in the other. Even within a single phylum, the differences between classes or orders may be great.

In some groups of insects wing venation is extremely important as a taxonomic feature, but in others venation is seldom mentioned, while in still others wings are absent. In the Coelenterata all the Scyphozoa have the medusa form and are classified on features of the medusa. Anthozoa all have the polyp form and are classified on features of the polyp.

The Hydrozoa, on the other hand, exist as either polyp or medusa and also in other forms called polypoid and medusoid; they may have both polyp and medusa forms in one life cycle; consequently, they cannot be classified on the basis of the features of any one body form. It is, therefore, essential for a person undertaking to identify specimens in a group to have a general knowledge of the nature of the animals and the features that have in the past been used for identification of them.

Special Terms in the Group

Along with the specialized nature of the study on many groups, there have grown up special terminologies for the features used in classification and identification. In order to use the identification literature, a student must have a familiarity with these terms.

In a recent monograph of the Bryozoa there is a list of three hundred and sixty-one special terms necessary to describe the species, and the special terms used in describing insects have been the subject of several large glossaries.

Glossaries of the terms in particular groups are not uncommon, but they usually appear as an appendix to a monograph or general book and are difficult to find. Some of the reference books for definitions of the specialized terms are listed here.

Study Techniques Currently Employed

From the early days of taxonomy to the present time there has been a continual change or evolution in the methods of study. Better microscopes provide better visual observation; special media permit the making of microscope slide mounts that are more revealing and permanent, and better storage methods permit direct comparison over a longer period of time.

In some groups the workers actively seek out new techniques. In other groups change comes very slowly, perhaps because the old techniques are still giving satisfactory results. It is possible to argue the advantages and disadvantages of both the old and the new methods of taxonomic study. Here we are only concerned with the fact that the methods in use at any period have a considerable effect on the taxonomic work produced in that period.

The study of fleas and lice was never very effective until the invention of suitable slide-mount techniques; and the customary ways of studying pinned insects proved to be inadequate to solve the problems of the malaria mosquitoes in southern Europe until the taxonomists began to study the eggs. In order to understand the taxonomic work in some groups it is necessary to know the study methods and their limitations.

The Literature of the Group

There is a large accumulation of separate publications on most groups of animals. These publications range from short papers in obscure journals or pamphlets to large books and monographs. They are available in widely varying degrees. Few groups are so well cataloged that all pertinent literature can be readily discovered.

Most non-specialist identifications are made from the literature, especially from the less technical types of publications. Consequently, it is often necessary to know the general reference literature which will lead one to the specific works appropriate for the problem at hand.

One of the few ways for a beginner to get a start in identifying specimens in a certain group of animals is to use the books which cover (sometimes incompletely or superficially) all groups or at least a wide segment of the kingdom. From these books can be obtained clues to the more technical and restricted works. Some of these general works are listed in a later paragraph.

Familiarity with the Animals

The actual mechanics of identifying animals is so different in the various groups that it benefits us little to cite any of the details in a general book. A student must learn by working with the particular group, seeing how older work has been done and what facilities are available.

Although it was previously stated that a detailed knowledge of one group will help little in making *identifications* in another group, it is nevertheless true that detailed experience in one group will make it much easier to study a second group. The number of kinds of animals now known is so great, the diversity among them covers such a tremendous range, and the terminologies in use for describing this diversity are so specialized, that no one can expect to make sound identifications in an unfamiliar group of animals.

The problems are very different in widely separated groups of animals. Furthermore, familiarity with the group must be considerable if the group consists of animals with few clear distinctions, has a disorganized literature, requires elaborate preparation of specimens, or has been the scene of contradicting or highly personal monographing. What it means to be familiar with a group in this sense is suggested under several headings below.

Natural History

The most obvious sort of familiarity with a group of animals is to know how and where its members live. The old term natural history is nowadays sometimes replaced by ecology, but the latter is much more formal, implying technical studies of animals under various conditions. Natural history still covers the study of the animals as they are seen in natural surroundings by an interested person.

This aspect of knowledge can be of great help in identification, but it is probably of less direct value than the other aspects of knowledge of the group. What the taxonomist does need to know is where the animal lives, in association with what plants and other animals, in how large aggregations or populations, with what habits and reactions, with what seasonal or cyclic changes in these, and in general all there is to know about its life.

Life Cycle and Developmental Forms

Nearly all formal identification is restricted to adult animals. This does not mean that it is not necessary to make identifications of immature forms of species but merely that this occupies a minor place, especially with respect to the identification literature.

It often happens that so far as a given book is concerned only adults can be identified, and this makes it necessary to be able to recognize the developmental stage of any specimen-whether it is adult or larval. In most sexually reproducing animals, there is little difficulty in recognizing the first normal developmental stage-the egg-and the embryonic stage produced by the early cleavages of the egg.

In viviparous animals the foetus or late embryo also is not difficult to recognize, because of our general familiarity with the appearance of unborn or unhatched animals. But in the vast majority of kinds of animals there are stages in the life cycle which are so different from the adults that they cannot be identified, except through use of special methods designed for such larval forms. The variety of these developmental forms is suggested in a later chapter.

It is here necessary only to recognize the immature forms as such, and to use the special means to identify them. In many groups of animals, it is not possible to identify male and female by the same key or the same features. Here again it is neces*sary* to be able to recognize the sex of the specimen. It is quite common to make identification keys that apply only to one sex.

Comparative Zoology

It is strange how seldom the literature refers to the fact that the data in all aspects of taxonomy are comparative in nature. Taxonomy has always compared structures, colors, shapes, and sizes. As data became available on physiology, biochemistry, ecology, behavior, distribution, etc., the more alert taxonomists utilized these also, insofar as they were comparative and the procedures of these disciplines could be adapted.

In most groups of animals the standard morphological data have been gradually augmented during the present century by data of other types. It is often not within the capacities of taxonomists to gather these data themselves. They can use it only when it is supplied by specialists in the fields concerned.

For example, few taxonomists have the training or the facilities to collect biochemical data about their animals. If the information is made available to them by biochemists or serologists, they generally welcome it and use it to whatever extent is practicable. Whether from biochemistry or serology or from any other field, all data that are comparative are of importance to taxonomy.

The various types of comparative data are discussed in a later chapter. Here we are interested primarily in the data useful in identification. In general, these are the ones used in classification, with one major class of exceptions. Identification frequently depends even more heavily on the fact that many attributes are correlated; for example, that an animal's metabolism, development, and behavior are almost certain to vary in a pattern parallel to some of its external structural features.

Inasmuch as classification should already have established these correlations, any of the correlated characters can be used for identification. In this way it has been bound that the different species of birds have distinctive songs. These species can be identified by the song alone, even when the bird itself is unseen.

Methods of Identification

Assuming that the inquiring person has enough of the foregoing background knowledge to proceed with identification, there are only a few ways he can proceed. If a collection of examples of all the pertinent species is available, he can compare his specimens directly with one after another until he finds the match to it.

This method may be one of the most accurate available for zoological work, but it can also lead to serious error. If specimens are not available for comparison, it may be possible to obtain the help of someone familiar with the group. A taxonomist who specializes on this group is probably the best source of accurate identifications, and this is an excellent way to start building a reference collection by means of which future identifications can be made.

Even when a reference collection is available, the major source of identifications is the literature. This may be the basic descriptions of the species, later monographs or revisions, or keys specially made for the purpose.

Direct Comparison

Theoretically all identifications are made either by direct comparison of specimens or by comparison of specimens with published statements about the group. In only a few groups of animals has it become possible to identify most species by memory, but even here the reference books are in the background. Identification by direct comparison is practically limited to preserved specimens in museums.

In large museums it may be one of the most important means of identification. Familiarity with the classification of the group is still required, but the use of literature is eliminated or reduced. In practice, direct comparison of specimens may suffice for identification in any situation where identified specimens are available for the comparison.

If a herpetologist is studying the frogs of an area and has preserved and identified examples of the five species known to occur there, he can probably make on-the-spot identifications by direct comparisons. This can be done only so long as he doesn't encounter a sixth species, one that has strayed into the area or was previously undetected there. It is this possibility which makes identification by direct comparison alone less than certain.

Only a person familiar with the group will be able to tell the meaning of the difference that will usually appear. Only experience will enable one to judge if the specimen at hand does or does not agree sufficiently closely with any of the comparative specimens to be safely identified with that species.

Identification from Literature

In associating a specimen with the species to which it belongs, the basic act necessary, if the original specimens of the species are not available for comparison, is to compare it with the published descriptions of the species. In a group of any great size, this would be a very tedious task, involving hundreds or thousands of comparisons.

Therefore, it is necessary to narrow the field-to skip over the great bulk of the species which are not closely similar to the specimen at hand. This elimination can be accomplished in some cases by the quick scanning of pictures to eliminate the subgroups that are obviously not appropriate. More effective elimination is possible if there are keys to the group.

Keys

A key is a tabular device that presents alternatives referring to features of the specimens. By comparing the specimen feature by feature with the key couplets, one gradually eliminates all the nonagreeing subgroups and arrives at the only one which agrees. For example:

Key to Writing Instruments

1.	Using ink	2
	Using lead	3
2.	Using a sharp nib for spreading the ink	*ordinary pen*
	Using a minute ball to spread the ink	***ball-point pen***
3.	Wooden body holding a fixed lead	***ordinary pencil***
	Metal body with movable lead	***mechanical pencil***

If one held an unknown type of writing instrument to identify with this key, he would compare it with couplet 1. If it used lead, that line would tell him to pass to couplet 3. Comparing the instrument with couplet 3, if it had fixed lead in a wooden body, the line would tell him that it is an *ordinary pencil*. The instrument has now been identified as an ordinary pencil by use of the key.

It could happen that the unknown instrument uses neither ink nor lead but instead writes with a waxy crayon material. If so, it could not be identified in this key. If the key was complete when written, it included all known kinds of writing instruments, so it would mean that the crayon is a new species. A new key would be made to include it, thus:

1.	Consisting of waxy crayon wrapped in paper	*crayon*
	Not as above	2
2.	Using ink	(pens) 3

Using lead (pencils) 4
3. Using a sharp nib for spreading the ink *ordinary pen*
Using a minute ball to spread the ink *ball-point pen*
4. Wooden body holding a fixed lead *ordinary pencil*
Metal body with movable lead *mechanical pencil*

It could be, again, that during wartime metal shortages, some manufacturers would make a mechanical pencil with movable lead but enclosed in wood. This instrument could not be certainly identified in these keys. There would be ambiguity as to whether one should put importance on the body material or the movability of the lead.

These illustrate two of the common faults of keys: (1) not covering the item being identified, and (2) variability of the item with resulting ambiguity in the key.

Other faults include: (3) a key designed for adult animals may not work for young ones, but the identifier may not know which stage he has before him; (4) a character in a key may apply only to individuals of one sex, but the identifier may have only the other sex or may not know which he has; (5) a key couplet may work well for most examples of an unknown but may fail when an unusual one appears; for example, dwarfs, terata, or hybrids.

Keys are made for several purposes that are somewhat distinct. *First,* there are general keys that are intended to place the specimen in the major group to which it belongs. Such a key should work for all variations, both sexes, and even immature forms. It is intended to put the identifier on the track of the more specific literature that he needs. This it does by giving him the name of the phylum, class, or order, by means of which he can pass on to more specialized keys.

A second sort of key might have been prepared by specialists in a group for professional use by non-taxonomists. Field manuals for the identification of parasites or pests of great importance may contain very effective keys of highly artificial nature.

They may serve their temporary purpose adequately, but they do not satisfy the taxonomist in his own work because they were not designed to convey much information.

For example, two parasites might be adequately and promptly distinguished by the fact that one shriveled up at once when placed in 95% alcohol, whereas the other parasite maintained its size and shape. This would be an effective key character for public health workers, but the taxonomic parasitologist would wish to use a feature of more objective nature, very likely something that could be seen in already preserved specimens.

The third sort of key is one that would be drawn up by a taxonomist for his own use and the use of his colleagues in this specialty. Here, the first characters in the key would usually be the ones thought to divide the included group of forms into the most important subgroups.

It would doubtless use much more technical terms than the previous two, and it would assume an intimate knowledge of the animals on the part of the identifier.

In some groups of vertebrates, such as the birds, the keys may have been simplified to such an extent that they would fall into our first type. The species are so well known and so few in number that they can be adequately identified without technical keys.

In the large phyla, and most invertebrates, it has been found nearly impossible to make good keys to species capable of use by a non-specialist. Sometimes it is even difficult to make such keys to genera or even families.

Pictures

In a few groups of animals, nearly all the species can be identified from pictures of them, especially if the pictures are assembled in atlases that show all the forms. In most parts of the world the mammals and birds can be identified from colored pictures; the butterflies of the world have been illustrated in color to such an extent that most can be identified; and in parts of the world some of the mollusks can be readily identified by colored pictures of their shells.

In the rest of the animal kingdom, the use of pictures is limited principally to verification of decisions made from keys and descriptions, but they are very useful for this.

Descriptions

Identification of a specimen with a named species depends on finding that the specimen is identical in pertinent features with the original specimens of that species. In the absence of direct physical comparison, usually not possible in practice, the last resort is to compare the specimen with the published description of the original specimens and the later descriptions of monographers.

Very often this is the ultimate source of a specialist's identification. It must be recognized, however, that a great deal of unseen background also goes into this process. There will be detailed familiarity with these animals and the descriptive works of the author of the species. There will be an expert's knowledge of the pitfalls connected with the use of descriptions and the application of names.

It cannot be emphasized too firmly that in most groups of animals it is impossible to make publishable or dependable identifications of species by routine use of non-specialized books or comparisons. A large part of the extant records involve doubtful identifications and are to this extent worthless.

By Specialists

Probably the safest single procedure to obtain correct identifications is to solicit the help of a specialist in the group, particularly one who has recently monographed the species of the world. Such a specialist has the maximum of knowledge and experience of the group, and he will be able to make positive identifications better than someone using literature or even identified specimens.

It should not be supposed, however, that a specialist can always make such identifications at a glance. In many cases the specialist is aware of so many unseen problems that he will require careful study of even routine specimens. There are groups in which adequate identifications can be made with little difficulty, but these are exceptional.

It is very common to send specimens for identification to a specialist in the group; however, there are certain matters of manners and professional ethics involved:

(1) Specimens should never be sent without prior permission.

(2) Identifications should never be requested without allowing all the time the identifier needs for the work. After all, he has other responsibilities and interests, and he does not generally owe any such service to you. In case of real emergency, a full statement of the need will probably educe cooperation.

(3) Inasmuch as most identifications are made without remuneration, it is courteous and sometimes expected that the enquirer allow the identifier to keep the specimen or part of the series. This is a slight recompense for his time. If the enquirer is himself trying to build up a reference collection, he may reasonably ask to have examples returned whenever possible. He will often find that the identifier can supply him with examples from other lots that will be at least as useful to him.'

(4) Always be sure that specimens sent for identification are properly prepared, preserved, and packed. It is a discourtesy to ask a busy specialist to examine inadequate material.

(5) Never seek a specialist's time for sorting of miscellaneous material. Sort the specimens carefully to species, and keep together all the examples taken at one time.

(6) Give the specialist all possible information about the specimens. Where, when, and by whom they were collected, together with the weather, ecology, parasites, or any other known information.

(7) Send as many examples as possible, as the variation within the series will be of interest and value to the identifier.

It is not intended as a reflection on any specialist to point out that even here the results are not entirely free of the possibility of error. Even a specialist is human; he may underrate the importance of these specimens, he may make a slip-of-the-pen in writing down the name, he may even be ignorant of some new discovery yr other factor that would influence his study, or he may even be careless. Finding the appropriate specialist is not easy. A museum or zoology department may be able to provide a start. A directory of such specialists was published by the Society of Systematic Zoology in 1961.

7

NATURE OF CLASSIFICATION

Classification is grouping. The groups are known as taxa. A group of groups (also a taxon) is more inclusive than one of its included groups and is said to be at a higher or more-inclusive level. The level is the category. A system of levels or categories is a hierarchy.

The groups themselves, the taxa, are the principal result of classifying. With more than a million kinds of organisms known, it is necessary to group them into classes to be able to deal with so many. This grouping into classes is really the only purpose of classification, although the taxa will be useful in a variety of ways. The first level of grouping involves specimens.

It is known that many individuals belong to a single kind, having many features in common and being able to interbreed freely. These kinds are known by the term species. Species are of importance in other fields than taxonomy, and the use of these groups may be different in the other fields.

It therefore happens that there is a difference of opinion as to what constitutes a species, either in practice or in theory. Misunderstandings have arisen and continue to cause difficulties between fields. The higher levels of grouping are not so much subject to controversy.

The theoretical views may not correspond closely to practice, but reasonable use of these groupings is possible. The practical aspects of classifying have been discussed in other chapter of this book. Some theoretical aspects are discussed below.

CLASSIFYING SPECIES AND GROUPS

Confusion of Terms

Before the ideas of grouping and categorizing can be usefully discussed, it is necessary to define and distinguish four words that must be employed in this connection. These words are concepts, groups, categories, and species. A *concept* is an idea in the mind of a person. It results from sense impressions and imagination. It is the mental picture "seen" at the time and remembered.

It exists only in the mind of the one individual, for there is no direct way to communicate concepts. By converting the concept into a statement, verbal or pictorial, one can induce another person to form a concept from the statement.

In the case of concrete concepts, those representing objects, it is sometimes possible to compare two concepts by comparing the statements about them with the objects and reach a degree of certainty that the two concepts represent the same thing. In the case of abstract concepts, those representing classes of objects, hypothetical objects, and transient phenomena, there is no way to compare the concepts of two individuals, no way to be sure that they are the same.

The nearest approach to assurance is by defining the terms used in the statement by reference to other concept-statements previously agreed upon. All language is based on such definition. It is unlikely that any two individuals have exactly the same concept or idea which they associate with any given term. Their ideas are always colored by their past experience.

It is therefore ineffectual to speak of a concept held by many persons, such as "the biological species concept." We can only study the statements made about the concept, and it is possible for many persons to express agreement with the statements.

Unless each statement is completely free of ambiguities, however, there can be no assurance that the individuals are agreeing to the same thing, because they in turn agree only to the new concept they have formed from the statement, and any ambiguities will lead to different ideas of what the statement means.

This use of the term concept in place of such a term as definition serves to obscure the nature and source of the information or ideas under discussion and to prevent logical treatment of the statements. Inasmuch as concepts can be known to others only through the statements made about them, the statement becomes the thing that is important whenever concepts are involved in science, because there can be no science without communication.

It must therefore be understood that when the word *concept is* used in a general sense, the actual object of reference is the *statement* derived from the concept. Only the statement can be examined; only the statement can be judged as to accuracy, truth, or agreement with other statements. An obvious misuse of the term concept occurs in the recent statement that certain concepts are *valid* and that two concepts are not *invalidated by* the existence of an intermediate concept.

This shows lack of understanding of what concepts are. There is no such thing as an invalid concept. A statement about the concept may be contrary to fact, but every concept exists in some mind and cannot be described as valid or invalid, true or false, philosophical or practical. When the concept is described in words, the description can be labeled as inadequate, if one wishes to do so. *Groups*, by which we mean groups of objects or groups of groups, are not at all like concepts.

They may arise from concepts, from sense impressions, but they can be entirely definite if the features setting them apart are clear-cut. The groups may be of any size; they may be founded on intrinsic features or extrinsic decisions. Groups of objects will be equally definite to all persons, but groups of groups will be recognizable only if their definitions are unambiguous. For example, the words which have been assembled into this sentence form a group that is entirely definite. Any person can recognize the group and its limits.

On the other hand, if one suggests two groups of dogs, the large dogs and the small dogs, no one will be certain where to draw the line between the two. The former group (the sentence) is objective, the latter ones are subjective, simply because of the nature of the distinctions. *Categories* are levels in a hierarchy, to which are assigned groups. They are almost exactly comparable to a set of shelves. Any given group under consideration may be placed on any one of the shelves (categories).

The place of the shelf or level in the hierarchy is definite, the group may or may not be definite, and the placing of it on the shelf is entirely definite and unequivocal. The shelf (level or category) is part of a series, the hierarchy, which is originally indefinite in the sense that it is the result of choice, but once the choices have been made and the levels determined, the hierarchy becomes entirely rigid and definable.

In order to use the categories there must be a name for each one, and it is accepted procedure to call them species, genus, family, etc. But these names are also applied to the groups placed in the levels. A group placed in the family level is called a family. This leads readily to misunderstanding when it is not clear whether the word family refers to a particular family group or to the level at which such family groups are placed.

The species level seems to hold the most interest for many taxonomists. Many have attempted to define the group which should be placed at the level called species, but these attempts have not met with obvious success. This seems to have been the result of failure to consider the nature of the various things represented by the word species.

These four terms are frequently used without definition and with meanings that seem to vary with the ciicumstances. They are very often ambiguous. In any discussion of the confusion of language in taxonomy, it is therefore necessary to distinguish clearly what meaning is being attached to them.

They will be used here with the following meanings, and the usages of certain other writers will be contrasted with these: *Concept*, the idea produced in the mind of an individual by sense impressions and imagination; *group,* the limited set of objects or sets segregated on any basis by any individual; *category,* one of the levels in the hierarchy, to which the groups may be assigned; *species, (1)* one of the groups, the one placed in the category called the species level (a species group); (2) the category or level at which the species groups are placed (the species level).

Groups and Categories

The entire concept of classification is based upon the fact that objects or ideas can be assembled into groups, the groups into more-inclusive groups, and the more-inclusive groups into still-more-inclusive groups. When there are many groups on several levels involved, groups, larger groups, and still larger groups, we may recognize a similarity in level between certain groups, so that some of the groupings are placed in the level of larger groups and some in the level of still larger groups.

This is the process known as categorizing; the different levels are each a category. The categories are higher or lower depending solely upon whether they are made up of objects, or groups of objects, or groups of groups. There is no real connection between the groups and the categories. Categorizing is one of the basic methods of thinking. Bruner et al. point out that judgment, memory, problem-solving, inventive thinking, esthetics, perception, and concept formation all involve categorizing. The development of formal categories is tantamount to science.

But there is no separate existence to any category; each is purely an invention of the mind intended to give order and accessibility to the objects of classification. The objects classified may be real or conceptual. One can classify anything that can be represented by a substantive (a noun, or a gerund). The groups, whether of objects or of concepts, can always be given reality or objectivity by definition.

The categories cannot have reality or objectivity. Among biological taxonomists there has been constant use of the term category. Examination of these uses shows that in many, if not most, cases the word is misleadingly applied. Reference is sometimes made to the level in a scheme but more often to the groups that are put at this level. For example, among recent writers we find these remarks:

(1) "Systematic categories are . . . based on an enumeration and evaluation of morphological resemblances." The author is referring here to objects or groups, which *can* resemble each other, not to categories which cannot.

(2) "Some of the major categories are useful, as, for example, the fusulinids and the graptolites." These, of course, are animal groups, not categories.

(3) "The discovery of that category of animals that we call the mammals." Obviously, the mammals are a group, not a category.

(4) "The evolution of higher taxonomic categories. . . ." It is impossible for *a category* to evolve, but few biologists would fail to believe that *groups* have evolved in some way.

(5) "The higher systematic categories are formed by uniting lower categories that share certain characters." Categories are not made up of subordinate categories, which cannot be united; they are simply individual levels. The group which is placed at any given level is made up of subordinate groups (or of objects). The latter have characters (or attributes), but the categories have only the relative attribute of being higher or lower in the system than some other category. This same book also says that "a family may be defined as a systematic category . . . which is separated from other families by a decided gap." A family, in actuality, is a group of genera

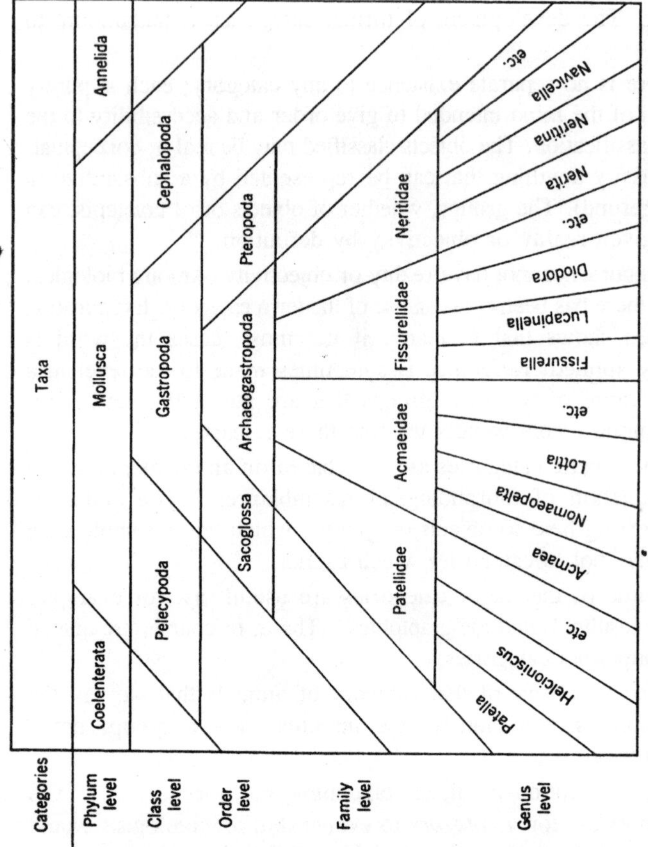

Figure 7.1: A classification of part of the phylum Mollusca to illustrate the difference between taxa (groups) and categories (levels) of the hierarchy. The arrangement of categories is fixed by convention; the placing of any group at a certain level is a matter of individual opinion, as Sacoglossa, for example, may be thought to be better placed at either a higher or a lower level.

which has been placed at the level in the hierarchy which is called the category family. And again, ". . . the taxonomic characters are a consequence of the categories." Obviously they are a consequence of the grouping, if we wish to make such a statement.

(6) "Because of the ambiguity 'Phyllopoda' is best not used in systematic nomenclature to designate a definite taxonomic category." This name represents a group of animals, in the opinion of someone, but no category is represented by such a name. The category would be Order, or Suborder, or some other, according to the terminology applied to categories in zoological classification. Again this writer says, ". . . there are many major taxonomic categories that are confined to

salt water. . . ." Of course, no category from phylum to subsubspecies can be considered to be restricted to salt water, whereas there are many large *groups* that are so confined.

(7) "Genera are grouped into somewhat larger categories, however, and these in turn into still larger groups." Here the false usage is practically admitted, since category is equated with group. Nevertheless, there are no such things as larger categories, only levels that are higher in the system. The groups put at the higher levels usually will be larger than those in the lower levels, but not necessarily so.

(8) A paleontologist writes: "The recognition of species, genera, and higher systematic categories depends on real or assumed discontinuity of the distribution of certain definable morphologic features." Again, of course, groups are meant, as categories have no foundation in morphological or other features but only"in the system we adopt for arranging the groups on the basis of *their* features.

(9) "There is extremely little disagreement in well-worked taxonomic groups as to the limit of the species. . . . Such agreement is utterly lacking as regards the higher categories. . . ." Categories do not have limits at all, and it is doubtful if there is any noticeable disagreement about categories, whether order is higher or lower than class, or whether the level between class and family shall be called phalanx or order. The real disagreement applies only to the groups to be placed in each level. A few years later the same author writes: "They (sibling species) are found in nearly all systematic categories, although they seem to be decidedly more frequent in some than in others." Sibling species are particular groups of organisms. By definition they are placed in the level we call the species level.

These same groups exist in the genera to which the species are assigned and in the orders to which the genera are assigned. Obviously they exist in every group of whatever size that includes them. Each one exists at each higher level, so that there are exactly as many sibling species at the phylum level as there are at the specific or generic levels. They cannot be more frequent in one category than in another, although they may be more frequent in one group of animals.

Such examples could be extended indefinitely, for it is a rare biology book that has escaped this error. There are doubtless persons who would claim that such a large number of writers cannot be wrong, yet this is clearly the case, because these writers have failed to distinguish between two things that are different in nature.

It would be possible to go on using the word category as a synonym of group, but this would only necessitate use of a new term for the level in the scheme. There are a few taxonomists who have clearly distinguished between categories and groups as used in zoological classification.

One is Simpson, who makes the distinction explicitly and then uses the words in their proper meaning. He states: "The framework of classification is to equate . . . groups of animals with the categories of the hierarchy Also: "All categories above the species have in common that they may include groups discontinuous ... between themselves."

Although he does not directly discuss the distinction between categories and groups, it is clear that the categorical hierarchy is an arbitrary arrangement and that the groups, as natural as they can be made, are assigned to the categories by the taxonomists. Another writer who makes this distinction very clearly is Gregg.

In discussing the loose usage of such terms as "objective reality" and "exist," Gregg has occasion to emphasize the difference between membership in a class (group) and the relation of a part to a whole. He points out that an organism can be a member of several taxonomic groups but cannot be a member of any taxonomic category.

For example, a fruit fly may be a member of the groups *Drosophila,* Diptera, and Arthropoda. On the other hand, the group Drosophilidae not only can be a member of other groups, such as Diptera, Insecta, and Animalia, but can also be a member of one taxonomic category, that of Family.

This category family is not included in any other category; it is simply a level chosen and named at an arbitrary place in a series of levels. Things are not classified into categories but into groups. It makes no difference what things are being classified. When a taxonomist sets out to classify groups, he does not classify them into categories either but into more-inclusive groups.

Only when he has groups, more-inclusive groups, and still-more-inclusive groups can he make use of the hierarchical levels which are called categories. He does this by assigning each group to some level, the more-inclusive groups to the higher levels. It also makes no difference what basis he uses for the grouping-the hierarchical system is not dependent on the nature of the groups.

In most of the examples cited above, it is evident now that the writers use the expression "the category genus" (for example) as equivalent to "the groups placed in the categorical level called the genus level."

If this were always clear to the casual reader, there might be no serious objection to the looseness of the phraseology. However, it is sometimes claimed that categories have certain attributes at one level and not at another. If this claim is made the basis for further argumentation, it becomes of real importance to know that the groups but not the categories can be so described.

When coupled with several other terminological obfuscations, this becomes a real hindrance to communication.

Reality and Objectivity of Categories

The misapplication of a word may not be a serious thing in ordinary language, although there is bound to be misunderstanding. Perhaps no harm would result even in science if no conclusions were drawn from the statement. In the case of the term category, however, there has been continuing obfuscation of a very important problem because of the failure to distinguish between categories and groups.

This problem is the profound difference of opinion that appears to exist over the question of the reality of the category species and the other categories. There has been widespread reference to the greater objectivity or reality of the "category" species. The only justification that is possible for these statements is the fact that there is a possibility that species *groups* can be more objectively delimited than other groups.

There is ample evidence that in practice most species are in fact no more objective than genera or classes-they are all based on gaps in the variation of evolving animals. But the known mechanisms of evolution seem to justify the belief that species in certain groups of animals can be based on the attribute of interbreeding capacities, which is not available at lower or higher levels in the hierarchy.

It has sometimes been assumed that, because this is possible in certain groups, it must be generally true. The fallacy of this is shown by Sonneborn (discussed in the next section). Although a category, which is a concept, can have no reality, the groups placed at that level may have reality regardless of what the level is, from subspecies to kingdom. If any group is defined upon attributes which are real and exclusive, it will have real existence if it consists of actual individual objects with material existence. This of course does not mean that all groups of whatever size or placed at whatever level are equally real or objective.

They vary according to their individual basis as defined. It may well be that *individual* species can be more objectively defined than *individual* orders, but this does not mean that the *concept* species is more objective than the *concept* order, or that the *category* species is more objective than the *category* order.

Dobzhansky and others have stated that species are more natural than the groups in other levels. This may be true, depending on what is meant by natural. It is probably not possible to become aware of the whole nature of a species, although many facets of its nature can be known.

But one can delimit the various species in such a way that the resulting groups conform to the nature-so-far-as-known most completely. Dobzhansky's statement was in the form that "the category of species is more natural than other categories . . ." and this can have significance only if he means "the groups placed in the category species" and "the groups placed in other categories."

The man who has given the closest study to the use of language in taxonomy is unquestionably Woodger. His conclusion on the reality of species and absence of reality at other levels is summed up thus: "[There is] no justification for distinguishing between species and other taxonomic sets.

As abstract entities they are, so to speak, all in the same boat; they sink or swim together." But if one is speaking of evolutionary species and genera, "there is again no justification for distinguishing species as real from genera as unreal. . . . Only if we regard species exclusively in the evolutionary sense and genera exclusively in the taxonomic sense, can we say that species are real and genera unreal, and then only if we wish to deny the existence of abstract entities. But this is clearly an unsatisfactory mode of comparison.

The taxonomic system "and the evolutionary phylogenetic scheme are quite different things doing quite different jobs and only confusion will result from identifying or mixing them." The maintenance of a clear distinction between groups and categories would eliminate the arguments over "reality" of species. It would leave open the question of whether the groups at one level can be made more objective than those at other levels, so that the speciationists could argue logically the case for species. Up to now the argument has been clouded by the misuse of the word category and also by the indistinguishability of the two meanings of the word speciesthe speciationists' concepts of the individual groups of interbreeding individuals, and the taxonomists' concepts of groups of individuals isolated from other such groups by gaps in the variation of attributes.

Phylogeny as basis of classification. It has many times been stated that it is the aim of taxonomists to detect evolution at work, and of classification to reflect phylogeny, which is the history of the evolutionary changes. These statements have great appeal and will find general assent on the part of many modern biologists.

Nevertheless, no one has taken the trouble to present a justification for the statements, except to say that the apparent arguments against these ideals are not really pertinent. Why they are not pertinent is always left to the imagination of the reader.

The claim of a recognizable phylogenetic basis for taxonomy and classification is left without justification apparently because no real argument is possible. No single fact of phylogeny is definitely known for any species in nature. All are based on assumptions of varying validity.

In order to base a classification on phylogeny, one would have to know the pertinent facts of the phylogeny of every species to be included in the classification, and there is no likelihood that this level of knowledge will ever be attained. Mayr et al. deny that this is so: "Since it is the avowed aim of a modern classification to reflect phylogeny, one might assume that classifications could not be attempted until phylogenies are clearly and unequivocally established.

This is not the case." There follows as the only proof of this denial, "Many of our existing classifications are actually pragmatic and based on the degree of similarity, regardless of whether they reflect blood relationship or not. Such a system may occasionally be more useful than a strictly phylogenetic system."

This seems to be an argument against his claim and certainly does not support it at all, as there is no proof that any of these pragmatic classifications actually do reflect phylogeny. The examples which follow this argument compare classifications labeled as "practical" with ones labeled as "phylogenetic" and lead to the conclusion that the former is not more useful than the latter. It seems to have escaped notice that these classifications are all based on the facts known at the time the classification was made, and that the so-called phylogenetic classifications cited are different only because their authors had available additional information, not because their basis is truly phylogenetic.

It is not quite correct to say that there have been no arguments given to support these claims of phylogenetic basis. Mayr gives two, as follows: "(1) it [the phylogenetic system] is the only known system that has a sound theoretical basis . . . ; and (2) it has the practical advantage of combining forms . . . that have the greatest number of characters in common." These statements are not only inconclusive but irrelevant.

No usable basis whatever is available for the phylogenetic system other than *inferences from the same data* that are used *directly* in the so-called practical system. The phylogenetic system not only does not have a "sound theoretical basis" but would always be identical with one of the possible "practical" classifications of the same material, and so never has a distinct existence.

As to the practical advantage claimed, this is exactly the advantage demonstrated by Gilmour many years before for the practical classification. In fact, this is the whole basis for practical classification. The maximum correlation of attributes enables us to make the largest number of inferences about the things classified.

It is true that many classifiers have not had access to all possible data on attributes and have furthermore failed to use as many correlations as they might, but these failures do not in any way affect the theoretical potential of this system. Neither is there any distinct basis shown on which a phylogenetic system might be based, nor is there anything shown that might helpfully be obtained from such a system which cannot be obtained from what these writers call the practical system.

Here is a major case of the obfuscation that can result from deprecatory labels. Since all biologists must be concerned with evolution, and since evolution inevitably produces phylogenies, any system ostensibly based on phylogeny has great appeal. The usual name given to these is natural classification.

All other systems are then labeled artificial or practical, usually with the implication that they are unscientific. It is not clear what meaning is herein given to the word "natural," unless it means reflecting nature or the true nature of the subjects. If a natural classification could be based on proven phylogenies, then it probably would reflect nature substantially. It surely would reflect the *phylogenetic* nature of its subjects.

It would not necessarily reflect the ontogenetic nature of these subjects, their biochemical nature, their psychological nature, or any other of their natures. Such a system would in fact be based on correlation of phylogenetic attributes. The true alternative to this is not an artificial system, however that term is used, but a system frankly based on *all available attributes* of whatever nature.

No classification has been proposed that utilized all possible attributes, but at any stage in the development of the classification of a group, the best system was the one that used knowledge of the largest number of attributes. This is also a natural system; it is based on the nature of the subjects, all the natures that are known.

It happens to be a useful natural system at the present time, because it uses available data; the phylogenetic system is not at the present time a useful natural system because *independent* phylogenetic data are not available for its basis. It is possible to have an unnatural system, one not related to any aspect of the nature of the subjects. For example, one can classify objects on the basis of who collected or owned them.

This is actually done in some museums by keeping separate the collections of various individuals or expeditions. These groupings are related to something other than the nature of the subjects. But classifications of this sort have never figured in the arguments over natural and artificial systems. There simply have been no unnatural systems, just as there have been no phylogenetic systems.

Simpson gives the most reasonable and complete discussion of phylogenetic classification of any recent writer. He denies categorically that a classification does or can express phylogeny, and he describes the "primary purpose of a classification" as "simply to provide a convenient, practical means by which zoologists may know what they are talking about and others may find out."

Many of his readers seem to have overlooked these forthright statements, preferring to take note of a later sentence that seems to contradict the first: "The basis of this system is phylogenetic, as has been strongly emphasized here, and this means that the groups to be recognized in classification should be as nearly as possible valid phylogenetic entities and that the criteria of definition are to have phylogenetic implications... .

These same readers fail to note the implication of still another statement: "Phylogeny must itself be determined before classification can be based on it." This is the very thing denied by Mayr et al., but it is the most important point that can be made. As a paleontologist, working with sequences of forms that are interpreted as giving data on phylogeny, Simpson apparently believes that there *are* phylogenies known, although he admits that none is perfectly known and universally accepted in detail. In fact, for it to be possible to claim that there are phylogenies known, one would have to define a phylogeny as the *supposed* or *postulated* history of the species.

If it is defined as the actual history, surely there are none that could qualify. The use of a hypothetical phylogeny as basis for classification leaves us with the likelihood that every student will suppose a different phylogeny and thus produce a different classification. Agreeing to the facts of structure and occurrence of fossils does not necessarily lead to agreement on the phylogeny, as witness the repeated changes in the "phylogenies" of such animals as horses.

On the other hand, in a system based on correlation of attributes, agreement on the appropriate attributes very nearly insures similar results in classification. Grant claims that: "A system of classification of the biological species must be judged, not on the basis of convenience, but according to whether it represents accurately or inaccurately the realities of nature." There may be argument over what realities are to be represented, but it is hard to picture a classification that substantially represents the realities in nature without being highly practical as well.

If it really represents nature, it will permit us to draw important generalizations from the data, and this is the purpose of all classification, as pointed out by Gilmour. The idea that classification must show the phylogenetic relationships of animals is the one referred to by Pearl, when he denies the common view that the evolution theory *must* have an effect on taxonomy.

It simply has not had the expected effect, although many aspects of evolutionary study have contributed to the advance of taxonomy and have contributed some data of importance in classifications. But the fact that we concede that evolution has taken place and that therefore at least some animals are related by descent to some others does not force us to use genealogical relationships as the basis of our classifications.

And although this has frequently been stated to be a logical necessity, which it is not, there have been almost no cases in which a classification has actually been proposed on the basis of a pre-established phylogeny.

Even the outstanding recent apparent exception to this proves to be based primarily on comparative data previously assembled and analyzed, with both the phylogeny and the classification based on these comparative data. This is, in fact, an inevitable situation in the present state of our knowledge of phylogeny.

It was truly said of classification that "its value lies solely in the aid which it can give in the understanding and the interpreting of the facts which it reveals." And one of its points of aid is in supplying inferences and data on which we can base the speculations about phylogeny.

It was Ferris who wrote this, and he recognized that the more data there are available for the classification, the more aid it will give us in various applications. The aim thus should be to make the classification "display in the most advantageous and most nearly correct manner the facts that have been discovered." This will include all facts of whatever nature, even phylogenetic.

The classifications now in use are all "natural" in the only useful meaning of that word. They can be made more and more useful, and will be, by incorporation of new data whenever such become sufficiently available. This includes even phylogenetic data, but at present there are no useful data of this sort, because the correlations obtainable from the phylogenetic inferences that are obtained from other data have already been utilized in the system under the guise of structure, distribution, ecology, physiology, etc.

Any attempt to distinguish between phylogenetic and artificial systems will do nothing but confuse the true nature of natural classification that reflects the maximum amount of all the natures of the subjects. Such confusion would delay the improvement of the useful natural classifications, still based largely on structure but increasingly on data from all other fields of biology.

It is greatly to be hoped that taxonomists will not be so attached to the "acceptance" represented by the phylogenetic basis of classification that they will fail to recognize its true position as just one of the possible natural systems, one at present completely unattainable, and one not yet demonstrated to be even theoretically superior to any other.

Taxonomists need not fear that they will lose anything by recognizing this state of affairs. They will actually gain several important things: (1) freedom from the confusion of believing in and aiming at an unattainable goal; (2) a practically as well as theoretically justifiable basis for their important scientific work; and (3) a start toward the recognition that rigor in language is a factor of tremendous importance in a field as complicated as taxonomy.

Language should be our servant. We must not allow it to be our master, overpowering us by means of the notions attached uncritically to words.

SPECIES

There have been a large number of publications in recent years dealing with the subject of species. The newer branches of zoology have had to deal with the kinds of the taxonomists, but their chief interest is in other problems than how to distinguish the kinds that exist.

The ecologist may want to know how kinds affect each other and what this effect means to the biota as a whole; the geneticist may want to know how the kinds reproduce themselves and maintain their identity, and how they can change; the evolutionist may want to know how the changes are accepted or rejected, how one kind changes into something different, and how the known kinds came to exist; and the phylogenist may want to know the course of the changes, the ancestry of each kind and group.

All of these are worthy biological questions. Each of these scientists looks at the kinds from the viewpoint of his questions. He sees in the idea of distinct kinds what his questions lead him to look for. The result is a series of different viewpoints about the basis and nature of the assemblages we call kinds.

Nearly all recent discussions of the word species, or the concepts behind the word, relate to its use in these modern fields. Two things have been clearly brought out-that the usages are related in the basic nature of living things and that the needs of the various fields of study are so diverse that there is no imminent likelihood that the several concepts can be directly correlated on the level of the definition of terms.

The taxonomist is still very largely concerned with kinds. He is interested in what is discovered by the geneticist about mechanisms of change, and so on, and in the speculations of the phylogenists and evolutionists as to the course of the successive changes, but as a taxonomist he works exclusively with the distinguishing of the kinds and the grouping of them.

He deals with animals, not genes; with life histories, not phylogenies; with the relative stability of today, not the probable changes in prehistoric time. Some of the evolutionists have made strenuous efforts to unite the taxonomic and the phylogenetic concepts of kinds. Perhaps it would be more accurate to say that they have tried to force taxonomists to use their evolutionary kind in taxonomy.

This has been a wasted effort, because taxonomy continues to distinguish and group kinds by their attributes, using the evolutionary ideas only to temper their judgment. There is at present no possibility that taxonomists can use directly the theoretical bases of kinds that are so helpful to the geneticist and the evolutionist, because he has a tremendous system, based entirely on direct features of the organisms, that cannot be mixed with the new concepts.

The Nature of Species

In *The New Systematics* Hogben remarks that "we need not prolong a barren controversy about the various definitions of species." Later writers apparently disagree as to whether the subject is barren, because much additional material has been written. If agreement on a definition of species, or on what the basis of species is to be, is taken as the criterion, the more recent discussions have been as barren as the old.

It would seem that this was inevitable, because the arguers have never settled the preliminary problem of what it is the argument is designed to settle. A major symposium on The Species Problem did not even attempt to define the problem or the issues.

No one can hope to get anywhere in a discussion of any subject unless he takes the trouble to distinguish between the multiple meanings of key words. "Species" is such a word; its meanings are several and rather distinct, including these: (1) "Species" without any article would usually be plural and mean the various populations of organisms which are recognized by some means. These populations are groups of individuals. (2) "A species" would refer to one of the populations or groups. (3) "The species" would sometimes be singular but collective and denote the general concept covering all the groups which are known as species. (It would also sometimes be plural and have the same meaning as (1).) (4) "The level of species" or "the category species" refers to the hierarchical level chosen for these populations or groups.

The first of these refers to group of individuals, groups which may have reality, objectivity, importance, or a definite relationship to nature, if so defined and distinguished. The second refers to one of the same groups and thus has the same reality and basis.

The third as a plural is the same as the first, but as a singular it refers only to the idea of groups which fit the prescribed conception. There is nothing objective or real about this idea; it has no relationship to the nature of organisms or to the nature of the groups. (It doubtless does have a relationship to the mind and to the sense-impressions which gave rise to it.)

The fourth is a man-made thing, or more properly a man-selected position. It has a definite relationship to the other categories in the hierarchy, but it bears no relationship to nature. It is not objective, natural, or significant in itself. As part of the hierarchy it has the significance given to it by the act of placing it between two other categories. There are other meanings than these of the word species. Apparently, however, most meanings will fall into one of the two types illustrated by (1) and (2) or by (3) and (4).

If one now goes back to examine some of the statements about species, to see how this distinction applies to them, some interesting things appear. There will be the constant misuse of the word category for group, which will have to be taken into account. In 1941, one writer stated that "the category of species is more `natural' than other categories used by systematists."

If he really meant categories, his statement would be wrong, because the categories are all exactly alike in their nature and are all completely artificial. If he means the actual groups or populations, as the context shows he does, then he is correct if the particular species (plural) referred to are ones which are delimited on natural grounds.

There is no question that the concepts of breeding populations and gene pools sometimes enable one to fix the groups at one level more clearly than at any other so far as these features are concerned, and the groups which correspond with such concepts may then be said to be more natural, objective, and significant.

In 1942, it was stated that "species are real and objective units, because the delimitation of each species is definite...." Here the individual groups are obviously intended, and the statement is correct if the qualification about the definite delimitation is true. In 1953, the same author wrote, ". . . the species occupies a unique position in the taxonomic hierarchy."

Here there can be no question that reference is made to the level known as the species level, the level to which species are assigned. The basis for the statement is given thus: "Essentially there are three kinds of categories: 1. The species. 2. Groups of populations within species. . . . 3. Groupings of species. . . ." This is the same as saying that the species level is unique because it occurs between the next lower level and the next higher level. In this case, of course, the imputation of greater reality or significance to one level in the hierarchy is unjustified. The level has no reality. This can be ascribed only to the groups placed in it.

In 1953, another zoologist wrote, "The species, with its included subdivisions, is a different sort of group from those above it." Here the references to subdivisions and group make it seem that "the species" refers to "a species." If so, he is right if the species in question is based on some natural phenomena that are different from those used for the groups at higher levels.

On the other hand, the category species cannot have subdivisions; it consists of groups that consist of subgroups clear down to individuals, but the level is fixed and indivisible. In another example, in 1957, it is stated that "an objectively defined species concept is available to take its place" (the place of the typological species concept). This apparent imputation of objectivity to a concept is false by definition.

Apparently what may have been meant and what might have been true is that there is new interest in objectively defined individual groups that can be placed at the level in the hierarchy called the species level. This writer claims that the species of the typological concept can be defined only subjectively. The only thing objective about the new species concept is the ,delimitation of the groups placed in it. But on this basis the groups of the older concept are on exactly the same foundation as those of the new concept, *provided* that the same basis is used in delimiting the groups.

If the newer groupings are based on more clearly definable features, then the new groups may be more objective to that extent, regardless of whether they are species or families. Part of the confusion over species is due to the fact that some persons believe that they are classifying actual animals into groups having like attributes, whereas others believe that they are classifying species produced by evolution.

The taxonomist is called upon to record the structures, behavior, distribution, and other relations of groups of individuals. He finds that correlations between these things are useful and meaningful. The phylogenist is called upon to interpret the probable evolution of groups. He is little concerned with individuals and their attributes but more with the ranges of characteristics and the factors that cause groups to remain separate. Each of these specialists has called certain of his groups species, but they may have in common only this name.

The concept which the taxonomist calls by the name species is based on data gathered from individual organisms by means of his senses and used for the business of taxonomy, which is discovery and systematization of data. The concept which the phylogenist calls by the name species is based on data drawn from populations by means of inferences and used for the business of phylogeny, which is the deduction of the past history of the group.

Nothing whatever is gained by denying the existence of these two very different concepts. No solution has been attained by the alternative scheme of claiming the existence of many other concepts of species, which turn out to be mere variants of these.

No end to the arguments over species concepts can be reached until it is recognized that at the present time there is no way to correlate the species composed of individuals having attributes with the species composed of populations supposedly phylogenetically related. To accept the one is not to deny the other.

They both exist; they both serve useful purposes; but they are not necessarily correlated. At the present time zoologists can deal with each separately, but cannot yet combine them into a single concept in practice. This leaves two things represented by a single term. Misunderstanding and confusion are inevitable.

Taxonomy may again be forced to surrender and abandon an established term (species) to a new group of zoologists who use it for a more recent concept, as has happened also in the case of the term genotype. Such an unreasonable eventuality might actually be necessary in order to counter the illogical arguments of the speciationists that the species are not properly understood by the scientists who discovered and distinguished a million of them.

Sonneborn recognizes this difficulty (see below), and so do others, but their voices are lost in the chorus that considers semantics a part of philosophy and therefore of no value. A little attention to semantics would prevent a substantial waste of time, energy, and ink by making clear the lack of a common ground for argument.

Outbreeding Data

It has been argued above that there is no such thing as *a biological species concept* or *a typological species concept*. There cannot be, in a general sense, because it is not possible to assure that the same concept is held in the minds of many people. These terms should be replaced by less ambiguous ones.

Concept can be replaced with definition, which is what is intended anyway, but this still leaves two ambiguous words in each term. The only kind of species that can be defined is the group of individuals, either those sharing certain attributes or those that can interbreed. So species can be replaced with group or species group.

Biological refers to data drawn from the fields of biology. There have simply been no species that were not based on biological considerations. Typological denotes a type-centered approach which simply does not exist in practice.

What is left is a *species-group* definition, which may be based on few or many characters, features from one field or all possible fields, features related to ancestry, structure, or function. There is simply no other way in which the species of classification can be defined.

One can define the species level in the hierarchy by its assigned position. Species can be defined as interbreeding populations in nature if their breeding capabilities are known. Taxonomists can define species as groups of specimens agreeing in pertinent attributes.

Phylogenists can define in very indefinite terms phylogenetic species, but they cannot define individual species of this sort. No one can define any general species concept supposed to be held by more than one person. In discussions of the so-called biological species definition, it is often found necessary to note that in most forms this definition can be applied only in sexual animals.

Since sexuality is widespread among animals, it is assumed that the biological species can be recognized throughout the kingdom, except for a few exceptional groups. A closer look at this idea reveals that if the interbreeding of sexual animals is to be taken as the criterion of species, there must be available either one of two things: (1) knowledge of the breeding capacities of all the forms whose species status is to be established, or (2) substantial evidence that inferences can safely be drawn from species in which it is known to ones in which it is not.

There must be either direct information or reasonable inferences for all species. The number of times in which actual interbreeding capabilities are known between two populations is so small compared to those in which it is unknown, that the percentage is virtually zero. This leaves inferences from these few cases as the only evidence that could be used in actual determinations of species status.

There is some evidence to show that inferences can reasonably be made over fairly large groups. There is also evidence to show that in most phyla of animals there are unexpected exceptions which make it impossible to draw such inferences safely.

These exceptions include not only the many forms of asexual reproduction, but also the ones in which parthenogenesis and self-fertilization occur. A list of the dozens of groups of animals in which asexual processes occur would show them to be too numerous to be passed off as "exceptions" or "in the minority."

Sonneborn has estimated that it will eventually turn out that bisexual forms do not outnumber the asexual and unisexual ones. This view will appear extreme to some zoologists, especially to those principally familiar with vertebrate groups. Nevertheless, the list should serve to show that asexual individuals are sufficiently widespread that they *must* be taken into account.

All of this is not the main point of interest to taxonomists. Whether species are sexual or asexual, inbreeding or outbreeding, is not the whole picture in taxonomy. If taxonomists are to make use of a species concept that is based on outbreeding, they must be able to determine that outbreeding *can* occur.

They must be able to do this in at least some cases in every group and in all cases if the groups are to be defined on this basis. This is the crux of the matter: Can they deternine, in all forms that they wish to classify, that crossbreeding can or cannot occur between the individuals?

The groups in which they cannot do so include at least the following: All those in which binary fission is the rule; all those in which sexes do not exist; all those in which parthenogenesis occurs; all those in which there is obligate self-fertilization; all those in which budding, gemmulation, sporulation, or dichotomous autotomy occur; all those in which we find it impossible to perform breeding experiments; and all those known to us only by fossil remains.

There is no question that these include a majority of the materials on which taxonomists work. In fact, they probably include more than 90% of all organisms. This is the reason why the breeding population can never be the actual unit of classification, why the ability to produce fertile offspring cannot be the actual basis for classification among animals in general.

Furthermore, classification, if it is to take account of all available data, must deal with individuals who do not breed or at any given moment are not part of a breeding group. Here are those castes of social insects which have no reproductive function, the non-breeding stages of forms with polymorphic life histories, and the individuals which simply do not breed because of lack of opportunity, malformation, malfunction, or other factors.

These are all living animals; they cannot be omitted from our classifications. The argument that these have no effect on the future of the species, no place in evolution, is true, but it has no bearing on the need to recognize their existence and place them appropriately in the classification. The natural system based on all known attributes is quite capable of dealing with these forms.

The phylogenetic system refuses to deal with them, usually claiming that individuals are not the units classified. When species or breeding populations are the objects classified, these "exceptional" individuals are not troublesome because they are either ignored or blanketed into the population on the basis of non-breeding attributes.

Here the choice is between two procedures: first, sidestepping the problem by ignoring many individuals along with the data that pertain to them; and, second, recognizing that a system based on individuals incorporates all forms of them along with their important contribution of data. Taxonomy has everything to gain and nothing to lose in frankly accepting the system which it has in fact always used.

The "Species Problem"

The species of the speciationist's biological species concept are based on what he calls a "biological" definition. Taxonomists are not supposed to ask the meaning here of the word biological but to accept the fact that it is more important, meaningful, and useful in the study of evolution than something called typological or morphological.

The biological species is based on breeding populations, barriers to the spread of genes, and mechanisms for the control of mutations. The evolutionists seem to be convinced that this concept is useful to them, in fact indispensable. The taxonomist on the other hand rarely finds himself in possession of data on breeding populations, barriers, or genetic mechanisms in sufficient quantity to be directly useful in classifying animals.

There can be no question that he does not have these data in sufficient quantity to make them *the* basis of a classification on a large scale. Because of this, the taxonomist is forced to use other data. Since the classifications upon which he must build are all based on such other data, he finds this no hardship at all. As a result he uses a concept of species based on correlation of attributes, principally structural ones.

He is convinced that such a concept is essential to his work of classification. Speciationists emphasize the evolutionary importance of species. The importance of species to the taxonomist is also great, in some opinions far greater. Keck gives the main argument for keeping the concept for taxonomy: "From the utilitarian point of view the retention of the taxonomic concept of species is extremely important, for its replacement by a new category on a different basis would play havoc over a big segment of biological literature."

He further warns against continued employment of species as a basic evolutionary unit in place of breeding population or some other unit. It is evident that the classical method of taxonomy, the use of species based on comparative data, has produced the present-day classification which proves itself every day in practice.

The so-called "modern" method of the speciationists has produced much valuable data about evolutionary mechanisms and pathways, but it has produced no species or classifications useful for the recording and systematization of knowledge.

The Biological Species Concept

It is not appropriate for anyone to use the expression "biological species concept" in reference to a particular way of defining the term species. The use of this expression suggests that a definition is used that involves aspects of the biology of organisms not used in some other definition that is not called biological.

This distinction does not exist. Everyone seems to agree that there are species in nature, or at least that there are now gaps in the continuum produced by evolution, and gaps between the end products of the branches even when the branches are unbroken.

Taxonomists have studied or recorded a tremendous variety of features of organisms, all of them biological features and including all known types of biological features. It is impossible for there to be anything more appropriately called "biological."

8

Descriptive Taxonomy

Whether taxonomy be defined broadly or narrowly, there are several activities included in its scope. In the broadest sense, taxonomy includes all the procedures of systematizing. In the usual restricted sense, taxonomy includes the segregation, description, and naming of species and genera, the cataloging and identification of specimens, and the publication of the data, descriptions, and names.

The term is thus still too broad to be the subject of a chapter in this book, and it is therefore dealt with in several chapters on the various aspects of taxonomy. The describing of species and genera has occupied a large part of the time of taxonomists from before Linnaeus. It is the principal means of making known the kinds of animals and their distinctive features.

New species are described to make their existence known to other students, and species already known may be redescribed at later dates when more information becomes available about them. Every revisionary and monographic study describes or redescribes the genera and species included.

Description, in one form or other, is one of the essential steps in the taxonomic system, Description is not the very first step taken by a taxonomist. The steps may vary according to the circumstances under which he becomes interested in a certain group of animals. Oftentimes, the sequence of events is as follows:

When a group of animals interests a student so much that he

decides to do taxonomic work upon it, his first inclination is to collect, to amass examples of the available kinds, to preserve them in the accustomed way, and to use this collection in his studies.

Next he will try to identify these species, to establish their identity with previously known species. If they are previously known species, this will supply him with the scientific name for each one. If any prove to be unknown species, they will stand in his collection as "new species." This identifying will acquaint him with some of the recent literature on the group, or a museum where there is an identified collection. He will now become interested in all the literature of the group, back to 1758 if necessary.

He may well take to collecting this literature almost as interestedly as he does the specimens themselves. The complexity of the literature and the multiplicity of Latin names therein will very likely start him cataloging. This may take the form of cards which represent the detailed facts from the literature, to be rearranged into whatever pattern serves to help the taxonomist understand the various species and all that is known about them.

A good job of cataloging requires an adequate search for pertinent literature and an adequate analysis of that literature. By now he should have such a command of previous work that he can make certain of his identifications, but he will want to check these further by comparing them with the opinions of other people.

The literature may contain many such opinions, but he will want to study specimens in museums and obtain named specimens from other sources, such as by exchange, purchase, or borrowing. If he has made the most of all opportunities so far, he is now in a position to begin a serious study of this group.

By study, at this point, we do not mean taxonomy. Now is the time for him to study the named species before him-those specimens available, the descriptive data in publications, and the natural history of the group in every aspect that is known or can be observed. He must learn how the sexes differ, the forms assumed in the life history, the seasonal or environmental forms produced, and the castes that occur.

He must know how the animals live, with what other organisms they are associated, how they perform the various functions of living, and how they reproduce their kind. He *must* find out how individuals of one species vary and how the species are similar to and different from each other.

The word student was used above for this beginning taxonomist. It is a most appropriate word, because his work so far has been largely study-of specimens, of literature, of life histories, and of variations. The studying does not end here but goes on through all the taxonomic work he will do. The most successful and respected taxonomists can still appropriately he called students of the animals on which they specialize.

The study never ceases. It should include the investigation of new ways to compare the animals, new methods of extracting information from the specimens, and new methods of collecting, preserving, and examining them. It should seek to apply new discoveries made in other aspects of biology to his own work. It should always strive to increase the general background knowledge and to broaden the perspective with which the specimens or species are examined.

If the student now has the background knowledge, has assembled an adequate collection and an adequate library, if he has learned the characters (or features) by means of which this group can be classified, and if he is prepared to avoid the special pitfalls of this group as well as those common to many groups, he is now ready to undertake descriptive taxonomy-the public discrimination and description of the species. Some people would say that he must also learn what a species is and how one can be recognized in practice.

Inasmuch as there has never been effective agreement upon either of these points, it must be concluded that he will have to rely on his knowledge of past work, of modern concepts, and of the nature of the animals concerned. The actual description is the simplest part of this sequence. By observation of specimens, measurement, tabulation of data, statistical analysis, and so on, he will determine the features of each species and record them in words, figures, drawings, or photographs.

His description may be composite or it may be taken entirely from one specimen. If the species described has a name already, this will serve to connect the new description with the older literature and labeled specimens. If the species does not have a name (a new species), the taxonomist is in for an even more rigorous series of steps-this time ones forced upon him by the opinion of world taxonomists.

He must propose a name for this new species-one acceptable to the taxonomic world as expressed in the rules of zoological nomenclature then in force. The steps involve the selection, spelling, and publication of the new name; they need not be itemized here. The application of any acceptable scientific name to a species serves at least two purposes. It provides a label for referring to the species, and it shows the opinion of the namer as to the genus to which this particular species belongs.

A description, or a series of descriptions, may be useful to a student in his further studies, but to be part of science in fact they must be communicated to others. This is accomplished principally by publication, which involves both printing and distribution. (The forms and requirements of publication are described in later sections.) In a sense the work of the taxonomist ends here. To be sure, he does not stop studying the animals.

He does not stop identifying, naming, or classifying. But most of these steps are now repetitions of steps already described. The exact order given here is not always followed, and at every step there may be deviations, skips, or additional steps. These ten steps have really covered only the study and description of one species. A much larger task of the taxonomist is the revision of groups of species. This involves the same steps in even more comparative manner.

It also involves more bibliographic work and the preparation of keys for identification of the groups and species. Here descriptive taxonomy merges into classification. Among these eleven steps, there are a number of problems, some obvious and some hidden, but all posing difficulties for the beginning student or even for the expert. Some are discussed below, in order to make clear the nature of these problems and suggest some of the things that individual taxonomists may do to avoid the difficulties.

OBSERVATION OF FEATURES

All taxonomy and, indeed, all biology begins with observation of the features of individual organisms. These features are sometimes referred to as characters. Some of the implications of this latter word make it unsuitable in a discussion of generalities, because the "characters" used in taxonomy must not be restricted to any one type of feature.

All of the aspects mentioned in the other chatpern of this book, Comparative Data, and any other comparative data ever discovered, must be included here. Observation can be accomplished with the aid of any of the usual senses, but by far the largest number are observed with the aid of the eyes. Many others are detected by instruments with results that are again visual.

Even the results of experiments must be observed. In most ordinary taxonomy individuals, either living or dead, are directly observed visually. The features deemed to be worthy of description are then recorded as a written description or graphically in pictures. At this point it is of primary importance to observe everything—the usual taxonomic features, any unusual features of possible taxonomic value, and any features of the biology of the animals. Not everything that is observed is worthy of recording, or at least of publishing. The important thing is to see all possible features so that *the most appropriate ones* can be used and *no necessary ones* are missed.

What is worthy of recording is an almost entirely subjective thing, varying from group to group. In a general way, it is proper to record the type of information found in earlier work to be useful in the particular group *and* such additional and perhaps unusual features as the observer thinks may prove useful in the future.

The indiscriminate recording of all features has sometimes been advocated, but it defeats its own purpose. The volume of data alone would obscure the effective items; the person best qualified to judge the usefulness of the different data in taxonomy would abrogate his role of making this distinction; and the literature of descriptive taxonomy, already voluminous, would become completely overpowering.

It should be pointed out, however, that the use of only the customary procedures for observing, and the recording of only the customary data, will never make more than a minimum contribution to knowledge. It is always important to add to the useful techniques, to record new types of data that can lead to superior discriminations, and to clarify earlier work by more exacting study of the customary features.

Preparation of Material

The observation of the features of the specimens generally requires some preparation of the specimens for study. This may be the skinning of mammals, the pickling of fishes, or the pinning of insects, but it is oftentimes also the preparation of microscope slides, the spreading of insect wings, the relaxation of insects for dissection of genitalia, the cleaning away of the matrix rock from fossils, the staining of translucent features, and so on.

Effective preparation is essential to good taxonomic work, especially at the descriptive level. "The important thing in the preparation of material for study is not the following of any particular set method, but rather the treatment of material in such a way that the structures which it is necessary to employ in systematic work (that is, those structures, regardless of size or obscurity, which the study of comparative morphology shows to be significant for such purposes) shall be rendered clearly visible".

If one reads here for the word structures, all features that can be examined, he will have a most appropriate rule for all preparation of specimens for descriptive work. It was Chamberlin's belief that the searching out of new methods of observation was of critical importance. Only through gradual improvement in methods can taxonomy improve its results.

One example may be appropriate here. A few years ago Dr. Adam Boving, beetle larva specialist at the U.S. Department of Agriculture, was studying the tiny almost colorless grubs of the family Anobiidae. He laboriously dissected to examine musculature, because external features were insufficient for his purposes.

Then a non-biologist equipped his microscope with polarizing lenses, and he found that he could see with the polarized light most of the surface muscles without dissection, and in other cases muscle fibers and bands were much more clearly discernible. Thereby a real advance was made in the study of these animals as well as a better classification of them.

The Series or Sample

There have been many statements in recent years about the importance of samples and sampling techniques in taxonomy. In classification, where species are being grouped and distinguished, samples of the species, or representatives of some sort, must be used. In descriptive taxonomy, it is seldom that sampling is necessary or desirable, especially in isolated descriptions at the species level.

The "series" of the taxonomist is not a sample in the statistical sense. It simply consists of all the available specimens. These are usually a few individuals, collected at isolated times and places, and perhaps a few larger collections or lots each containing a number of specimens taken together at one time and place.

If the species is common, these collections will themselves sometimes be samples of what was present at that place. Rarely it will be a carefully selected statistically unbiased sample, but more often it will simply be the specimens obtainable at that moment in that place, biased by the collector's interests, by the method of collection, and by other factors.

The use of such a mixed series, specimens from many places taken at different times by different people using different collecting methods, can have disadvantages, but frequently the advantages outweigh them. The most effective feature of such use is that it tends to eliminate the effects of the bias of any individual sample. In many cases it is superior statistically to any single intentional "sampling."

In the description of a new species, the series of specimens before the taxonomist usually consists of a few specimens taken at one time in one place, either because this is the only time the species has been seen or because it exists nowhere else.

The series available will vary from this minimum up to an extensive collection from many places, available because the new species is being isolated from a previously known but composite species, in which the mixture of species was undetected. In the former case, it may be that little will be known about the species beyond what the few specimens show.

In the latter case, there may be a great deal of information about the new species, including what the specimens show but also including its biology, its bionomics, and its relation to human welfare. Those who assume that taxonomy is nowadays concerned with populations and not types will also feel that there must be a large enough series to make possible the drawing of inferences as to the total variation in the population from which the specimens came, but in most groups of animals the majority of new species are still described from a very few specimens-solely because that is all that are available.

Even in revisionary work, it is generally true that many of the included species are so rare as to be available in very limited numbers, often in no single series of statistically useful size. Formal, studied inference as to the variation in a real but unseen population is almost never undertaken in a direct sense in taxonomy. It may be more important in population dynamics and evolutionary studies.

Taxonomic Characters

A great deal of taxonomic work is based on observation, comparison, tabulation, and analysis of features of individual animals. These features may be positive or negative, involving presence or absence of structures, qualitative or quantitative, and structural, functional, behavioral, or developmental. The features are aspects of the comparative data described in an earlier chapter.

In any kind of data each animal has certain features which can be isolated, described, and dealt with. These features are the pool from which the characters used in taxonomy and classification are drawn. A taxonomic character has been defined as any attribute of an organism by which it differs from an organism belonging to a different taxonomic group.

An important point is made here that taxonomic characters are possessed only by organisms, that is, individuals. In the sense of structural and physiological features, groups such as species and genera do not have characters. The features which we ascribe to such groups (such as generic characters) are merely the features which all included comparable individuals have in common.

Few taxonomic characters are shared by all members of a species. Immature specimens, damaged specimens, the wrong sex, may not show the features of the ones chosen for description. A character is thus a feature shown by all appropriate specimens at appropriate times.

Few taxonomic characters are absolutely restricted to the species at hand. They do not have to be exclusive to be characters. They will, however, be useful characters only if they occur in a pattern that enables the taxonomist to use them.

Characters that are completely distinctive in one species or group are called *diagnostic characters*. They are the features which have been particularly chosen because they are sufficient to distinguish The individuals or taxa concerned from all other such individuals or taxa. They are always taxonomic characters, but not all taxonomic characters would serve well as diagnostic characters.

A description will usually list many characteristics that are at least partially distinctive, but only the most distinctive and stable of these would be singled out for a diagnosis. In some discussions of taxonomic characters it is assumed that evolutionary history is involved in the features used in taxonomy. Although such features certainly did have an evolutionary history, the history is never known as a fact.

It is not the phylogenetic nature of the features that makes them useful in taxonomy but their comparative nature-their stability, distribution, and clear-cut delimitation. The extended discussion under this heading in Mayr, Linsley and Usinger deals primarily with the kinds of taxonomic data and the phylogenetic aspects of characters.

Selection of Characters

The means actually used in making the choice of what characters to use in classifying species has been discussed briefly in other chatper of this book. Similar methods are used in the selection of characters for discrimination of species. It is not hard to see what is required of the characters-that they be universal in the appropriate part of the species and that they be distinctive for this species.

It is quite a different matter to state how they may be selected to produce these results. There is no question that the selection is largely subjective, but this does not mean that it need be arbitrary or based on guesses. It will be based on the accumulated experience of the taxonomist, especially his knowledge of the literature. The latter will recall to him what characters have previously been used, and which of these have proven to be effective and which have not. His knowledge of the animals and their life will enable him to judge what new characters are suitable and what new techniques may yield helpful new characters.

The taxonomist will thus observe many characters of the animals. He will intuitively or statistically evaluate the effectiveness of each character with reference to several things: (1) its stability within the species or group, (2) its distinctiveness in separating one group from the others, (3) its availability on the specimens which will have to be classified or identified, and (4) its comparability with the descriptions and classifications already published on this group.

None of these factors can be neglected with safety. Preliminary surveys of the features of the specimens may be helpful and so may statistical or graphic analysis of variability.

Good Characters

Obviously selection is aimed at finding the most effective characters. Some taxonomists may believe that this means the ones that show the real genetic relationships between the species. Others may think it means the maximum correlation of attributes. Still others may think it means merely that the results give the most satisfaction in identifying, classifying, and other taxonomic work. Whatever the views on this, the characters thought to be most satisfactory are called *good characters*. They are simply the ones that produce the desired results.

There are, however, a few attributes that can be ascribed to good characters in general: (1) They are not subject to wide variation among the known specimens, (2) they do not show a high intrinsic genetic variability, (3) they are not readily modified by the environment, (4) they are consistently expressed, (5) they are available in the specimens which must be used, (6) they are visible with reasonable procedures, and (7) they can be effectively recorded. Of these the ones representing the inherent nature of the animals, (1)-(4), are the most important, but failure to consider the others can seriously affect subsequent use of the characters.

Measurements

An integral part of most description is the citation of pertinent measurements. These may be the dimensions of the whole animal, the dimensions of certain parts, ratios of any two dimensions, body or organ weights, or other numerical or mensural data. In most groups of animals, some measurements are considered to be desirable or necessary. In some cases, elaborate measurements and ratios may be necessary.

There is, however, no reason to use either measurements or ratios unless these add to the usefulness of the description.

Five criteria of good numerical observations are listed by Simpson, Roe, and Lewontin thus: "they should be logical, related to a definite problem, adequate, well delimited, and comparable and standardized."

STATISTICAL CHARACTERS

It is customary to consider statistical analysis to be a major part of taxonomy. It certainly occupies an increasingly important place in many branches of biology. However, in the description of taxa, which means the description of the features of individuals or of groups of like individuals, there is little place for statistics as such.

Numerical data will often be useful, but it is not usually possible to deal statistically with the features of one specimen or with any features held in common by a group of individuals. The place where statistics becomes useful is in the study of populations. In spite of some published statements that taxonomy deals basically with populations, it is easy to see that almost all descriptive taxonomy deals solely with individuals and with groups of individuals which hold the pertinent features in common. The statistical characters used extensively in the study of microorganisms are numerals representing growth rates, reactions of cultures to experimental treatment, population or culture features, etc.

These are true statistical characters of populations. They do not represent features of individuals. Although at some levels animal taxonomy can employ such characters under special circumstances, they are not usually available. They are not among the features that are herein described as comparative, because taxonomy does not usually compare populations. Many characters of animals can he converted into numbers, ratios, proportions, etc. These are sometimes supposed to be statistical in nature. However, real taxonomy does not normally result from statistical manipulation of such figures, no matter how useful they may be elsewhere in biology. Some taxonomic uses of statistics are discussed in other chapter of this book.

Description

The word description is applied to two slightly different things. In dealing with species, the published statement of its features is called a description. This may be long or short, detailed or general, verbal or pictorial, but its purpose is to convey to others the features of this species (or specimen) that are deemed to be of interest in further study.

Some workers think that all observable details should be described, and they sometimes produce descriptions that occupy many pages apiece.

Other workers feel that economy and even usefulness demand that they restrict themselves to what seem to them to be the useful characters. No one has ever produced a really complete description, even in the cases in which an entire book has been devoted to one species, and taxonomic practice generally expects a carefully selective description that will permit detailed comparison with the descriptions of the other species in the genus.

In reality there is no such thing as a description of a species. The species is merely the sum of the individuals. The actual features described are therefore the features of the individuals available. No two specimens are ever exactly alike, so a description may include the range of variation of each character, analysis of the statistical frequencies, and comparison of these with the geographical distribution of the species so far as known.

There is another purpose for describing; according to convention, a new species can be named only if it is described, but the nature or extent of the description is not specified. It is best to fulfil this legal requirement by preparing the best possible (that is, the most useful) description, so that both purposes are served at one time.

The taxonomic purpose of the description is to enable subsequent workers to recognize the group described. There have been attempts to restrict the word description to a particular aspect of recording data-the general features as opposed to the comparative features that distinguish the taxon from other taxa.

This seems to yield no useful distinction, because any adjective is descriptive and no one ever knows for sure what characters do in fact distinguish all forms of the two species effectively in the light of later discoveries. No one would attempt to write a description without prior experience. In determining that a species is new, or assembling material for a revisionary study, a general familiarity with the characters and descriptive problems in this group must be gained before starting on the work of writing the new description.

This advance knowledge of descriptive characters has both good and bad aspects. It is helpful to have all descriptions in a group comparable in style, characters, and descriptive terminology, so that they can be compared. But it is unfortunate if following the old format prevents the taxonomist from seeing and recording new kinds of characters not previously utilized.

The word *description is* often taken to mean all the material published together about that species. This may include any or all of the following, depending in part on whether or not the species is new:

The name of the species

The author of the name

The date of publication of the name

N. sp. or New species (if appropriate)

Reference to illustrations Synonymy

Diagnosis (a condensed statement of distinctive characters)

Description (a more detailed exposition of characters)

Measurements

Type locality

Distinguishing features (in case a formal diagnosis is not given)

Specimens examined

Collector

Location (in what collection)

Other localities represented by the specimens

Types and their location (in what museum)

Collector

Geologic occurrence

Discussion of variability among the specimens

Remarks on any of above, on habitat, habits, or other

List of material examined

In the case of a genus, the description may and should include most of the following items:

Name of the genus

Author of the name

Date of publication of the name

N. gen. or New genus (if appropriate)

Synonymy

Subgenera

Genotype, name of species

Manner of fixation

Date of fixation

Name of person designating

Synonymy of this species

Original genus

Genotypes of all synonyms and subgenera

Distinguishing characters of the genus

Diagnosis (a condensed statement of distinctive characters)

Key

Notes on relationships

Included species (in addition to the genotype)

Notes on history of genus Source of material

A formal style is desirable in describing species or groups, but the style should not interfere with the presentation of relevant information. A final paragraph of Remarks can always serve to include any information that doesn't fit in the formal arrangement. It should never be assumed that *any* information will be of no value, as later workers may recognize a value not obvious to the describer. Of course, there are practical limits to the descriptive material.

In the description itself there should be a definite sequence of features, preferably the same ones used by other workers. In insects, for example, this might be color, general appearance, head, antennae, mouthparts, eyes, thorax, wings, legs, abdomen, and genitalia.

This sequence makes it much easier to compare descriptions and to find out if a certain feature is described. Measurements and counts should be used whenever appropriate. Illustrations may be more useful than words, but poor figures may be worse than none. In many groups photographs are of little value in description.

They cannot compare with careful drawings of diagnostic characters or features, in most cases, although they may be effective in showing posture, habitat, or natural appearance.

Some individual points worth considering are the following:

1. Uniformity of style in presentation.
2. Comparison directly with similar species.
3. Record absence of features as well as presence.
4. Excessively long descriptions may obscure the important points.
5. Very brief descriptions may omit needed characters.
6. Telegraphic, concise wording, however, does save space.
7. Italicize key words, or otherwise emphasize them.
8. Where analyses of variations were made, include summaries.
9. Try to describe so that the species can be understood by a person who does not have specimens at hand, or by an inexperienced person.

10. Try to improve on previous descriptions in the group, in accuracy, use fulness, breadth, and depth.

Graphic Descriptions

Verbal descriptions are not the only means of recording the features of specimens or populations. The use of graphic representations is increasing in importance and in some groups is of greater utility than words. Some technical journals have rules requiring the illustration of all new species.

The rules of nomenclature have always accepted a "figure" of a specimen in lieu of a verbal description, although, regrettably, the new Code is not clear on this point. There are, however, illustrations that leave much to be desired, or are simply downright useless. There is a tendency to believe that "the camera cannot lie"; but photographs *can* distort, *can* overemphasize, and *can* reproduce so poorly as to be ineffective.

There are many taxonomists who believe that photographs are seldom as useful as good drawings. The case for the use of drawings is well made in the valuable but out-of-print book *The Principles of Systematic Entomology,* by *G. F. Ferris*. In the chapter entitled Entomological Drafting, which is equally applicable to animals of other kinds, Ferris makes these comments:

"No purely verbal description, with the hampering limitations that are inevitably associated with it, can thus form a satisfactory substitute for the (described) object. It is possible to describe a simple geometrical figure in terms of words, but as these figures become more complex the difficulty is enormously increased.

How much more difficult will it be then to describe an insect with its complex spatial relations of parts, its structures of varying form, its variety of curves, its various axes, its different planes, its wealth of detail! The task is one for which words are an unsuitable tool.

There remains but one other way by which this ideal may be approached, and that is by means o f some sort o f pictorial or graphic presentation."

Sometimes the illustrating of taxonomic material is referred to as art-work. The implication that art has a major place in scientific illustration is unfortunate; accuracy of representation is the chief criterion by which such illustrations should be judged. There have been some highly skilled and artistically talented illustrators, but art must be a secondary consideration.

The one essential rule in all taxonomic drawing is given by Ferris thus: *"Never cease studying the object until the drawing is finished."*

Ferris also gives some specific instructions for making drawings. Others will be found in Mayr, Linsley, Usinger, where there is also a short bibliography of books on this subject. Although in some specialties there is a strong feeling about the inadequacies of photographs as a part of descriptions, they have been effectively used in other instances. It is sometimes both possible and effective to give photographs to show the general appearance, even when details must be shown by drawings.

There are of course other uses of photographs where drawings will not serve. These are in showing the habitats in which the animals live and other non-taxonomic features. Use of photographs in publications may introduce difficulties or extra expense and must be planned in advance. In straight description of specimens, diagrams are inappropriate. In the representation of life histories or in the presentation of statistical data on populations, they are essential. They should be used whenever they will contribute to an understanding of the species.

TYPES IN DESCRIPTIVE TAXONOMY

The relation of type specimens and the ideas of typification are discussed in other chapter of this book, Species and Subspecies. In descriptive taxonomy, types are of considerable direct importance, and their employment is outlined here.

The use of types has grown with the development of taxonomy. By the end of the nineteenth century, they were being used by many taxonomists. Some of the early codes of nomenclature contained some reference to them, but, although some abuses arose, the *International Rules of Zoological Nomenclature* made no mention of the types of species.

The nomenclatural use of types is unequivocally required by the current Code, which regulates their employment. This does not, however, make it necessary to use types in any other way. Nevertheless, taxonomists do, with very few exceptions, select certain specimens as the basis for their descriptions, and these specimens are universally known as types.

When a describer has only a single specimen of a new species, or when he chooses to set aside a single specimen, it is the *holotype* (original single type). If he has other specimens which he considers identical, he may designate these *paratypes* (subsidiary original types). If one of the paratypes is of the opposite sex to the holotype, it may be called an *allotype* (first paratype of the other sex). If the original describer of a species does not set aside a holotype, his entire series is considered to be a type series; each specimen is *a syntype* (formerly called cotype). Later on, another taxonomist may select one of the syntypes to be a *lectotype* (single type selected subsequently). The remainder of the paratypes are then called *paralectotypes* (subsequent paratypes).

If a holotype is definitely lost or destroyed, another of the original syntypes is selected to take its place (it also becomes a lectotype). This could be chosen from what are called cotypes, syntypes, or paratypes. If the holotype and all other type specimens are lost or destroyed, some other specimen can be designated as ***a neotype*** (a new holotype) to take its place, under very rigid regulations.

The types are used as standards. There can be no question that a type (at least holotype, lectotype, or neotype) belongs to the species it typifies. By comparison with other specimens, the taxonomist determines if they too, in his opinion, belong to that species.

Although other specimens than the holotype may be used in the description, the type is always in complete agreement with all its details (except where some items were intentionally included to show variation). The description thus acts as a verbal picture of the type (and perhaps other specimens) for the use of persons who cannot examine the type itself.

The paratypes are thought to be unquestionably conspecific with the type (belonging to the same species), and they are often sent to other museums where they can act as stand-ins for the holotype. Thus, the descriptions and the paratypes serve to spread knowledge of the features of the type without risking the unique specimen by frequent shipment to every interested student.

If any question arises as to exactly what the species is, especially if it is found that the original series of specimens (holotype and paratypes) consists of more than one species, the holotype is the court of last appeal. It is always a 'representative of its species, even if all the paratypes prove to be something else that was originally confused with it.

A good description includes two distinct things. It cites the features of the holotype in detail, and it cites any variation in these features shown by the other specimens, as well as any features shown only by them. It should be made clear which is which. The first is a description of the holotype; the second should be a description of the entire species as nearly as it can be put into words at that time. Both aspects are important.

It has sometimes been assumed that taxonomists use the type specimen alone when describing a species, that the variation shown by other specimens is not considered, and that all "duplicates" or other specimens are disposed of or traded to other collections. These statements contain just enough truth to make it difficult to deny them, although they misrepresent the real situation.

There have been taxonomists who described only one specimen; there have been cases of exchange of most duplicates; there have been cases in which the variation of other specimens was not recorded. But none of these has ever been considered good practice. Work based on such procedures probably would not be entirely worthless, but it would be less valuable than it should be.

In order to select a type specimen to describe, even the persons who may have restricted their descriptions to a single type must have examined all the available specimens. The basis of the choice may have been sex, size, condition, source, ownership, or other, but there was a choice, based on some examination. If there was little or no diversity shown by the series of specimens (one or many, as the case may be), there is small need to dwell at length on this aspect.

If the series shows considerable diversity, the taxonomist will know that there is a chance that his "species" will eventually be found to consist of several. If he describes the "species" from all the specimens, including all the variation, it will be difficult to separate the description into two later on. He should therefore concentrate on one specimen, so that his entire description will always apply accurately to that one (the holotype).

Theoretically, the describer should describe the species. In practice, he can generally do so only in well-known groups where a new species is found as a segregate of a known but composite species. Otherwise, the "species" is not known but only a few specimens of it. (This is not usually even a statistical sample.)

There have been cases, especially in paleontology, in which the specimens other than the type (holotype) were arranged in sets to show the variation and these sets distributed to other collections. This is an excellent way to show the diversity in the original series. In some cases, these specimens have been labeled as paratypes.

These paratypes thus do not necessarily show the features of the holotype. This use of paratypes is condemned by most taxonomists, who believe that a specimen labeled as paratype should agree with the holotype in all pertinent features. These are the taxonomists who deny the claim of Simpson that types can serve only one purpose, that of an anchor for the name. These taxonomists know that types (and similar paratypes and other compared specimens) are constantly being used to show what the original species was like-as standards for comparison, and as a last resort in identification-as well as for the anchor for one or more names.

No taxonomist believes that the type will tell him what the species is, because the species consists of other sexes, other developmental stages, other seasonal forms, other phases, castes, positions, and so on. But he knows that the type will tell him one condition that indisputably does belong to that species, one point around which he can rally the diversity, the life forms, of the species.

There is every reason for treating the holotype as a specimen of unique value and use. Paratypes that agree closely with the type in every taxonomic feature are also valuable taxonomically and can spread the understanding of the original concept of the species to other collections and students. Any specimen that has been carefully compared with the holotype will have extra taxonomic importance because of that fact.

It should be carefully labeled to show all the relevant facts of the comparison (with what it was compared, by whom, when, and to what extent). There are scores of other terms that refer to specimens and include the root -type. Many of them have real value in taxonomy as specimens of particular sorts or histories.

The terms, however, are usually less informative than a descriptive phrase. They should be used with great care, if at all, because their meanings are not always inherent in the term and may not be widely understood. Among these are *hypotype* (a described or figured specimen), *topotype* (a specimen from the same locality as the type), *metatype* and *homoeotype* (a specimen compared with the type and believed to agree with its features), and *plastotype* (a cast of a type).

Type-locality. Because a species (or a subspecies) had a definite geographic range and its types were collected at some spot in that range, the place of collection can be of considerable importance in taxonomy. The place at which the holotype was taken is called the type-locality. In any description of a new species, this locality should 'be recorded as accurately as possible, using well-known points of reference and exact distances.

This appears to be a simple concept, easy to put into practice. There are confusing features, however. Some writers believe that the typelocality is the published locality rather than the actual place where the specimen was found. If the species was originally described from America septentrionalis, the type-locality would be North America. These writers then find it necessary to restrict the type-locality, to limit it to some reasonable part of the continent.

This concept of typelocality, which is in reality the published-locality, leads to endless difficulties. It has not been formally accepted in the rules of nomenclature, although there is mention of restriction of type-locality. There seems to be no good reason for not accepting the simple straightforward concept and definition that the type-locality is the place from which the type was collected.

It is seldom that a type-locality is published in the greatest possible detail. In addition to incompleteness, there have been cases of erroneous citation. Any later taxonomist can correct the statement of locality, make it more definite and explicit, or separate out the relevant part, just as he may correct and supplement the description of the species. When citing the locality of the type of a new species, it is important to record the relevant detail but not to obscure this with pointless data or ineffective minutiae.

DESCRIPTIVE PUBLICATIONS

Diagnosis

As suggested above, diagnosis is the statement of the features in which a species (or other taxon) is completely unique. These may not be the most important taxonomic characters, but they are the distinctive ones, the most immediately useful ones. Diagnosis is not really distinct from description, but it is always useful to have a separate statement of the distinguishing features.

Description must give both the features which make possible the grouping of taxa and those which serve to distinguish taxa. Diagnosis denotes merely the latter function. In nomenclature, diagnosis has an additional function. In order to publish a name for a new species, it is necessary to give some statement of the distinguishing features.

This statement is in principle a diagnosis. (Unfortunately, in many cases, the actual diagnosis is so sketchy that it serves little purpose except as an attempt to fulfil the requirement of the rule.)

Revisions and Monographs

Revisionary work in general is largely descriptive. Revisions and monographs usually include redescription of all previously known species as well as all new ones. The description may be on a more-detailed scale than the original, or it may be somewhat summary. Monographs tend to be more elaborate and complete than other revisions. They also generally cover a larger group of organisms.

There is nothing unique about revisions or monographs among descriptive publications. Besides the descriptions, they generally include most of the following: keys, complete synonymies, detailed distributions, records of locations and identity of types and other specimens, analysis of previous publications, and summaries of available knowledge of non-taxonomic sorts.

Keys, classifications, synonymies, and bibliographies are aspects of revisionary works which can be published alone. Their usefulness is great even when separated from the descriptive material. It is not always possible to do monographic work and, in lieu of this most complete work, any of its parts will be welcomed.

Keys

Taxonomic keys are devices for permitting the identification of taxa. The key may enable identification of species, genera, orders, or any other taxa. It may key out the species in a genus, or the genera in a family. It may key out several levels in succession. One recent key, to the phylum Pogonophora, keys out all the orders, families, and genera in the phylum. Separate keys to each genus then key out the species.

There have been a variety of styles of keys used, but those that have proven to be practical are all rather similar. Whatever real differences occur are usually the result of attempts to make the key serve other purposes than just identification. These other purposes may be classification (arrangement), sequence of primitive to specialized, phylogenetic speculation, and so on. Where these functions are appropriate for presentation, they should be separate from the key, both to prevent interfering with the function of identification and to make more effective presentation of the other data.

As long as the one purpose of the key is to aid in identification, there is little to choose between the minor forms of successful keys. The requirements of a good key are:

1. It must be workable, which means that
    (a) its arrangement must be self-explanatory,
    (h) it must be simple,
    (c) its couplets must he distinctive, and
    (d) its length must be reasonable.
2. It must be possible to work it in reverse.
3. It must use characters that are simple, clear, and direct.

4. It must be illustrated, if necessary for clarity.
5. It must be composed *only* of couplets that consist of mutually exclusive statements, with the first one positive, the second negative, or both positive if qualitative.
6. It must show clearly its limitations as to sex, developmental stage, age, and any other pertinent condition.
7. It must deal with all appropriate taxa, including any that cannot be keyed out.

There is really only one major type of key that is widely practical. An example is given here, with notes on possible modifications.

Key to the Suborders of Coleoptera

1. Hind coxae immovably fused to metasternuun, completely dividing first visible abdominal sternite Adephaga
   Hind coxae not fused to metasternum, not dividing first visible abdominal sternite 2

2 (1). Pronotum with notopleural sutures 3
   Pronotum without notopleural sutures Polyphaga

3 (2). Antennae filiform; wings with apex spirally rolled in repose Archostemata
   Antennae clavate to capitate; wings with apex folded in repose, never rolled Myxophaga

This key illustrates the capacity for reverse use, by means of the parenthetical numbers after the couplet numbers. The couplets consist of clear-cut characters, generally with positive condition first. Where necessary more than one character is used in a couplet. Appropriate characters are illustrated. The author has not been concerned with the order of the groups keyed out, as he deals with them later in the order Archostemata, Adephaga, Myxophaga, Polyphaga.

Some taxonomists have found the making of keys to be difficult or laborious. This would no doubt be true if one set out to construct a key to an unfamiliar group of animals. The making of keys should not be undertaken by anyone who is not thoroughly familiar with the taxonomy of the group.

An experienced person will know so much about the features of the group, its comparative zoology and its biology, that the making of the key should not be difficult at all at the genus or species level. There are exceptions, however, where certain groups prove difficult to key out. As one progresses up the hierarchic scale, the making of keys becomes more difficult because so much diversity is involved. There are Arthropoda without jointed legs, without an exoskeleton, without tracheae, and so on. Most arthropods will key out readily, but some will upset the simple key characters.

A key at this level is of little use if it works only for the obvious forms-those that could be placed without reference to the key. It is never sufficient to key out the common kinds alone and forget the exceptions. The user of the key will never know whether he has one of the exceptions or not. As pointed out in an earlier chapter, identification is a tricky business at best, and in many groups the keys are suitable only for use by specialists.

There have been times when it was claimed that keys, like classifications, should employ characters of great biological significance. This is entirely unnecessary. The important things are that the character be readily detectable and clear-cut in its alternative appearances and that these distinguish the groups already recognized by the taxonomist.

Classifications

Although keys are very common in taxonomy, formal classifications are rare, except as incidental adjuncts to other works. In some cases, arrangement is mistaken for classifying, but serial arrangement doesn't necessarily involve union into classes, which is the essence of classification.

The purpose of zoological classification is to present the classifier's views on the grouping and subgrouping of the animals involved. These views may involve belief in the phylogenetic origin of the groups, or intent that the grouping show new correlations of the features, or merely a summary of existing knowledge of the organisms.

Such classifications are useful as reference works, for teaching the diversity of animals, as evidence of relations that will help solve practical problems, and so on. Much of our classification has become so well known that it is taken for granted in ordinary daily life.

There have been few really new classifications published in the past half-century. The reason for this is that most of the real groupings have been recognized, and all that can be done now is to redefine them or make changes in detail. Several supposedly quite distinct schemes differ chiefly in the hierarchic level of groups or in the names selected.

Of course, shifts of position of individual taxa, splitting of taxa, union of taxa, and recognition of new levels are common in revisionary work. For example, three supposedly rather different classifications of Protozoa are shown in parallel columns in Figure elsewhere in this chapter.

At first glance there is little similarity between these three classifications, but if some of the unfamiliar names are replaced by synonyms and the nominal levels of the taxa are not indicated, these three schemes appear as follows:

Hyman 1940	**Copeland, 1956**	**Honigberg et al., 1964**
Protozoa	(pt. of king. Mychota)	Protozoa
Plasmodroma	Phaeophyta	Sarcomastigophora
Mastigophora	Mastigophora (pt.)	Mastigophora
Opalinida		
	Protoplasta	
Sarcodina	Sarcodina	Sarcodina
		(+ Sporozoa pt.)
Sporozoa	Sporozoa	Sporozoa (pt.)
		Sporozoa (pt.)
Ciliophora	Ciliophora	Ciliophora
Ciliata	Ciliata	Ciliata
(Opalinida)	(Opalinida)	(+ Suctoria)
Suctoria	Suctoria	

There are still differences between these three, but they are in reality only slight, consisting of difference of opinion as to whether two groups should be united or not at a higher level and whether an aberrant group belongs closest to one or another of the major groups.

Compared to the five-class scheme given in many textbooks (Mastigophora, Sarcodina, Sporozoa, Ciliata, and Suctoria), Hyman shows two major groups: 1 + 2 + 3, 4 + 5, Copeland shows four major groups: 1, 2, 3, 4 + 5. Honigberg et al. show four quite different major groups: 1 + 2, 3a, 3b, 4 + 5, with small parts of 3 and 4 transferred to 1+2.

Classifications are the means of presenting the groupings discovered in the diversity of animals. Here the hierarchic nature of grouping becomes evident, with groups, supergroups, and subgroups. Because the taxonomist believes that the correlations that give the groupings, and thus the groups themselves, are the result of evolutionary processes, he looks at classifications to see whether they contain any evidence of the phylogeny of the groups.

There usually is no direct evidence, but even indirect evidence can lead us to interesting speculation on the ancestry. It is thus from classification that most studies of phylogeny spring. There may also be feedback from the hypothetical phylogeny that will lead him to consider a change in the classification. At best, then, the classifications may be modified in detail because of phylogenetic speculation, but they are never based on phylogeny in the first place.

PHYLOGENETIC TREES

The diagrams used to record the supposed ancestry of a taxon are generally based on the prior classification of the group. This speculation is not a part of taxonomy as such, and the interested reader is referred to the extensive literature of Biosystematics, The New Systematics, and Evolution.

Synonymies

All revisionary and monographic studies must be based on the detailed study of past taxonomic work. The record of this study is ordinarily presented in the monograph in the form of a complete synonymy, which includes all such bibliographic data. A synonymy is a list of the synonyms (names) that have been applied to the taxon under consideration, including the name that is therein accepted as the correct name.

In a formal sense, the synonyms in zoological nomenclature include only such names as are acceptably published-what the 1961 Code calls "available." In actual practice, a synonymy generally includes more than just a list of the "acceptable" names and their bibliographic references. It will also include (1) any names that have been printed (but not acceptably) and may thus be mistaken for real zoological names, (2) expressions which are not names but have been attached to the taxon in question, (3) misidentifications, which are uses of wrong names for a species, and (4) bibliographic histories of all of these.

It is a commonplace error to speak of "the synonymy" and "the synonyms" of a name, meaning only its rejected synonyms. This does no harm so long as it does not obscure the fact that *all the names applied to a taxon are synonyms,* from which one is determined under the Code to be the currently acceptable one.

In arranging a list of synonyms, there are a variety of forms, arrangements, and special devices. If the list is very short, the arrangement will not be a matter of great concern, as the list can be rearranged mentally on the spot. If the list is long, it will have to be arranged for a specific purpose, to show (1) the chronological history of each name, (2) the chronology of all of them together, or (3) the bibliographic history of each name.

Many things are illustrated by this example, besides the abbreviated style. Some of these points are:

1. The species is now in the original genus even though it was on intermediate occasions transferred to other genera.
2. The widespread and variable species received several names in different parts of the world. These are now believed to be straight synonyms (subjective).
3. One synonym was published in synonymy and is therefore a stillborn synonym (objective).
4. Typographical errors or lapsus calamorum occur in the generic names and also in the specific epithet.
5. Homonymy occurs, which is somewhat unusual within one species. The 1961 Code holds that *S. fasciatus* Fuessly and *S. fasciatus* are not homonyms because they apply to the same species; the Laporte name is to be considered merely as a reference to the Fuessly name. This is a procedure that could lead only to synonymic confusion, because the names were, in fact, completely distinct and are, in fact, homonymous.
6. One unacceptable name appears. It has been ruled that tke word *tertius* in this case is a number, not a name. Because the word has been previously cited in synonymy, it is best to continue, as it may have acquired standing in some way in subsequent works. Listing it helps to avoid misunderstandings, if it is adequately annotated.
7. Forms named as varieties are now thought to be identical with the typical form. An aberration has been similarly suppressed, as well as a subspecies.
8. The minimum of bibliographic reference is given, including only the original work or the work in which the transfer to another genus is made.
9. The names were originally proposed in three different genera; that is, in three genera still believed to be distinct. The present placement in the original genus is the result of new evidence about the type species of that genus, so that the *Staphylinus* of 1952 is not the same zoological genus as that of 1758.
10. Some published references to names are not acceptable under the Code. To fail to cite them would hide the fact that they have been noted and found to be of unacceptable status. Frequently they later meet the requirements and become acceptable as of that later date. Listing the earlier reference,

with annotation, records the situation.

11. This synonymy is complete in these features: (a) it lists all the specific epithets that have been applied; (b) it lists all the generic combinations of all these epithets; (c) it lists all the original references, for the names and for the generic transfers (thus, for all the binomina); and (d) it lists all known misspellings of the epithets (but not all those of the generic names in other applications).

The purpose of the synonymy is to convey information about the names that have been applied, their status at the time of publication, any circumstances affecting their proposal, history, applicability, and so on. It is therefore highly desirable to annotate all synonymies fully.

Much bibliographic and taxonomic study can be wasted if the resulting synonymy fails to show all the information obtained and all the taxonomic conclusions reached.

Specifically, it will generally be assumed that any unannotated synonym is a subjective synonym in the opinion of the author of the synonymy, and that there are no special circumstances or technicalities involved.

Bibliographies

In taxonomic wdtks, a bibliography is usually a device to permit abbreviation and condensation of synonymies. It thus serves as a list of literature cited. In much taxonomic work, other than revisionary or descriptive, the listing of pertinent works may assume greater proportions and importance.

The extent of the taxonomic literature and the relevance of the works of all authors over a two-hundredyear period make the need for bibliographic aids very great. A variety of bibliographic works are cited in other chapter of this book. They may be consulted as samples of style, coverage, purpose, and so on.

The present book contains several types of bibliographies, from brief lists in the text to a substantial bibliography at the end of the text. Some books useful for the preparation of bibliographies will be found listed there.

Naming the Taxa

The description of individuals or groups is of little use unless each is identified with a name. The application of the names is a subject of such technicality that it is not directly covered by any chapter in this book except those on the conventions of zoological nomenclature. The naming of taxa, presumably new or previously unnamed ones, is so closely governed by the rules of nomenclature that a taxonomist cannot properly use a name at all without reference to the rules.

Professional taxonomists have come to look upon descriptions and names as responsibilities of the author. If he publishes them, he has a responsibility to all future workers to make them accurate, effective, and properly integrated into previous work. This responsibility includes being right in his opinion that the group is new, correctly placing it in the classification, making sure the relevant features are all recorded, and ensuring that all the information is made available to others, not buried in an unknown publication.

On the other hand, it is frequently impossible to be absolutely sure that a species is new or that it is certainly the same as some older species. In this circumstance, professionals frequently publish their data under a new name, knowing that it may eventually have to be "sunk" into synonymy. This is often preferable to running the risk of associating new data with an old name only to find out later that the supposed connection was nonexistent. It is easier to record a synonym than to erase data which have been erroneously associated with a name.

Just as there is no special honor attached to the publication of a new name, there is also no dishonor in having a name reduced to synonymy. Some worlIers in the past have been insulted by such an act by a colleague, but there is no justification for such a reaction. The science grows continually, by addition and correction, and no one can expect to know all that will be known to his successors.

9

PROFESSIONAL TAXONOMY

Of the twenty-five hundred taxonomists in the United States at the present time, roughly 50% are in academic situations, where taxonomy is their research interest and all but a few are teaching other subjects primarily. About 35% are in positions here described as professional, but only a handful of these are employed for full-time taxonomic research. The remaining 15% are not professionally or academically employed but work on taxonomy as a hobby or avocation.

TAXONOMISTS

From the earliest days of taxonomy, whether or not we take 1758 as the starting point, taxonomists have struggled to make known the kinds of animals that inhabit the earth. The number of people who have been involved in this work runs into the hundreds of thousands. Among them were carefully trained scientists, self-trained professionals, experienced amateurs, and dilettantes.

Among these were men of wide biological knowledge and understanding, very one-sided men of strong opinion, and men with no interest in theories or anything except the building of collections. The number of people in the world interested directly in the taxonomy of some group of animals must be at least ten thousand at the present time. Some spend all their time at taxonomic activities, some use it for relaxation only, and for some it is a research sideline.

Both professionals and amateurs have produced excellent taxonomic work, but it would probably be impossible to determine for the entire period of formal taxonomy (a little more than two hundred years) whether the professionals or the amateurs had done the best work. It is certain, however, that in number of workers the amateur group is far ahead, and there seems to be little doubt that the amateurs, who predominated during the first century and a half, have done the larger share.

Even if there has been little correlation between professional or amateur rating and the quality of the output, there does appear to be a direct relationship between the quality of work and the training and experience of the worker producing it.

More important than formal training are the ability to receive the ideas of others, a discriminating eye for the features of the animals, an interest in the previous literature, and a knowledge of the animals themselves. Nowadays, it is increasingly hard for a person to become proficient in taxonomy in his spare time; nevertheless, the fact that several respected present-day taxonomists have accomplished the feat shows that it is still possible.

What are the motives that bring zoologists to study the kinds of animals and their classification? The answer varies, but it always seems to involve an interest in the animals and in the systematization of knowledge, together with a satisfaction in assembling, possessing, and studying a diverse collection of specimens representing one sector of the diversity of nature.

Some taxonomists in the past may have been trying merely to increase their own importance as authors of new species or owners of large collections, and some may have been only interested in satisfying their employers; but the person who goes into taxonomy these days is almost sure to be interested in the animals themselves.

Of course there have been zoologists who felt forced to do some taxonomic work because they were unable to find a taxonomist willing or able to make the identifications for their ecological or evolutionary studies. These men have rarely become taxonomists in the full sense of the term, but many of them have made important contributions.

Training of Taxonomists

Taxonomy should, of course, enlist the services of biologists of the highest calibre and with the best possible training. The implication above that a large part of taxonomic work has been done by amateurs may seem to imply that this requirement has not been met. But increasingly in modern times taxonomic research, as distinct from the curating and identification aspects of taxonomy, has been performed by persons with either formal zoological and taxonomic training or extensive practical experience in taxonomy. The actual training necessary or desirable as a basis for taxonomic work is indicated by the outline of subsequent chapters in this book.

First, the knowledge of the animals themselves in all their aspects must be substantial. This should involve all the aspects of life suggested in the chapters on Diversity, and it may be gained from the living animals, from preserved specimens, and from the published records of what others have observed.

Second, a detailed familiarity with the taxonomic literature and the use of such stored data is essential in taxonomy, surpassing the need for this in other fields of biology.

Third, experience in the methods of collecting, handling, preserving, and studying specimens and kinds of organisms is indispensable. To this may be added the methods of reporting the observations-publication.

Fourth, a detailed knowledge of the rules of nomenclature and their application to species and other taxa, without which all other taxonomic work can be wasted.

Beyond all this a taxonomist is today expected to be well grounded in all the major fields of biology. He will be expected to deal to some extent with cytology, biochemistry, genetics, evolution, ecology, biogeography, parasitology, behavior, embryology, and perhaps paleontology.

To do all this requires the broadest possible background of zoology, in addition to a high degree of specialization in the taxonomic aspects. Almost any zoology department can provide the general training, but the special training in systematics can be obtained at only a handful of universities. But even where there are no formal courses, taxonomic training can sometimes be obtained by a sort of apprenticeship under the influence of an experienced taxonomist whose research is taxonomic even if his teaching is not directly so.

Academic Taxonomy

As an academic subject (or course of study), taxonomy is often entirely omitted from the biology curriculum. A random search of college catalogs might well turn up none at all under this name. It has sometimes been said that there are no courses in taxonomy but merely directed learning through experience.

This is certainly not so, because many schools offer courses specifically in taxonomic practice and theory; nevertheless, it is unquestionably true that taxonomy is missing from many curricula in which it could make a real contribution to the biological training of both undergraduate and graduate students.

In many schools taxonomic courses are offered in departments other than Zoology. Among those known to be offering such courses at the time this is written are the following:

University of Alberta (Entomology)
Amherst College (Entomology)
University of California, Berkeley (Entomology)
University of California, Los Angeles (Entomology)
Catholic University of America (Biology)
Cornell University (Entomology)
Duke University (Zoology)
University of Florida (Biology)
Fresno State College (Biology)
Harvard University (Biology)
University of Illinois (Zoology)
University of Indiana (Zoology)
University of Kansas (Natural History Museum, Entomology)
University of Maryland (Entomology)
University of Michigan (Museum of Zoology, Geology)
University of Mississippi (Biology)
University of Nebraska (Entomology)
Ohio State University (Zoology and Entomology)
Pacific Marine Station
Philadelphia Academy of Natural Sciences
University of Pittsburgh (Biological Science)
Purdue University (Biological Sciences, Entomology)
University of Rhode Island (Zoology) Rutgers University (Zoology)
Sam Houston State College (Biology)
San Jose State College (Natural Science)
University of Southern California, Hancock Foundation (Geology)
Southern Illinois University (Zoology)
Stanford University (Biology, Geology)
University of Tennessee (Entomology) Tulane University (Zoology)
Union University (Biology)
University of Utah (Zoology)
Walla Walla College (Entomology)

State College of Washington (Zoology)

University of Wisconsin (Entomology)

In many other schools taxonomy, although not offered in direct course form, is taught to some extent through the practical means of identifying specimens, seeing how they fit into the existing classifications, and preparing revisions for practice or publication.

This may be done under the guise of research, or it may be in a course on a group of animals. There is necessarily a good deal of taxonomy in courses in Mammalogy, Ornithology, Herpetology, Ichthyology, Entomology, Acarology, Protozoology, Parasitology, and Paleontology.

Where formal study of taxonomy is not included at an early stage in a zoological curriculum, it becomes necessary to teach some basic taxonomic ideas in other courses, because much of biology deals with kinds of organisms or with individuals that are referred to particular kinds.

It is not enough for comparative anatomy students to dissect "just any animal." It must be an animal of known position in the classification. Its structures are noted and interpreted in the light of its position in the classification, and by means of this position it is compared with other specimens known to occupy different places in the classification. The whole basis of classification thus becomes evident as do the similarities and differences between the successive specimens.

In some courses entitled Comparative Anatomy the comparative aspect is largely abandoned. The animals dissected are looked at primarily as stand-ins for man, and the work is considered to be merely a prelude to the study of medicine and human anatomy.

Other courses may also involve recognition or identification of species or more inclusive groups. Names are used, whether for species or for orders. But both classifications and names are taken for granted, and it is frequently assumed that the work of classifying animals is completed. How far this is from the truth should be evident to anyone who probes beneath the surface of the classification of animals as a whole.

Teachers

Taxonomic work is well-suited to research by college professors. It does not require expensive equipment; it can be conducted in short spaces of time between other responsibilities; and it can be published in small segments. Academic taxonomy can still make a large contribution to the taxonomy of animals, directly, in addition to the teaching of taxonomic ideas and methods to potential taxonomists. The people involved in academic taxonomy, the teachers, are usually not professional taxonomists, in the strict sense of being paid directly to do taxonomic research.

Those whose research is taxonomic and who teach only taxonomic courses are few. For the rest the research is something of a sideline, after their real job of teaching other subjects is done. This is no reflection on the individuals as taxonomists or teachers; it merely shows the lack of interest in taxonomy as a formal course subject in many schools.

PROFESSIONAL TAXONOMY

As a profession, taxonomy has never been attractive to any save the student with a real interest in the ordering or systematizing of knowledge, one willing to work in a glamorless field where rewards are primarily in personal satisfactions. Some taxonomists work professionally in museums and research institutes. The number of such positions is probably less than two hundred in the United States.

In some cases a large amount of time is spent in the more routine tasks of curating collections and identifying specimens. Often this is under the aegis of a public-supported organization, which must perform certain services for the public. Research time may be considerably reduced.

A few taxonomists work for large pest control organizations, usually public service authorities such as mosquito-abatement districts. Probably a thousand or more American taxonomists work for oil-producing companies and mineral-prospecting firms. These are paleontologists, who sometimes refuse to be called taxonomists. They study the fossils in order to predict where the oilor mineral-bearing rocks will be found.

A majority of these study the microfossils, Foraminifera, diatoms, and Ostracoda. They are often more highly paid than other taxonomists; but there are usually severe restrictions on their freedom of publication, because of the economic implications of their work. These are about all the professional jobs in taxonomy proper.

The number of such positions, especially outside economic paleontology, is low, and vacancies are not common. There are occasionally attractive temporary jobs on expeditions or in large projects, but these are usually filled by persons on leave of absence from their regular work.

It has become increasingly difficult in recent years for a biologically untrained person to work effectively in this field, although it is still possible for a person to train himself. But taxonomy covers such a wide range of groups, of activities, and of viewpoints that it is seldom hard to find a field of endeavor suited to the means, the time, and the training of any person interested in adding to the knowledge of the kinds of organisms.

THE ORGANIZATIONS OF TAXONOMY

In this age nearly all human endeavors have been organized in some way. Taxonomy is no exception. In general, the number of organizations is likely to reflect the number of people involved, and the distinctness of the organizations will be related to the isolation of the field from other branches of learning. Accordingly, the organizations of taxonomy are few, and most of them are not exclusively concerned with this one field.

Taxonomic Organizations

In the United States there is only a single organization which devotes itself entirely to taxonomy and attempts to cover all aspects of it in all groups of animals:

Society of Systematic Zoology; founded in 1948; publishes *Systematic Zoology, SSZ Newsletter, Directory of Zoological Taxonomists of the World,* and *Books on Zoology.*

In England, a comparable organization exists:

Systematics Association; publishes occasional symposia, including:

Bibliography o f Key Works for the Identification o f the British Fauna and Flora (1953).

The Species Concept in Palaeontology (1956).

Function and Taxonomic Importance (1959).

Taxonomy and Geography (1962).

Speciation in the Sea (1963).

Phenetic and Phylogenetic Classification (1964).

One supposedly international organization publishes a journal of direct taxonomic interest:

International Trust for Zoological Nomenclature (a private body formed to publish the decisions of the International Commission on Zoological Nomenclature) ; publishes *Bulletin of Zoological Nomenclature* and various Official Lists of names.

National societies concerned with one or two groups. Many societies have arisen to promote interest in particular groups of animals.

At first, most of these were active predominantly in taxonomy, but many later broadened their interests. Among the national societies of this type are:

American Society of Mammalogists; publishes *Journal of Mainmalogy.* American Ornithologists' Union (AOU); founded in *1883;* publishes *The Auk (1883-).*

Herpetologists' League.

American Society of Ichthyologists and Herpetologists; founded in *1916;* publishes *Copeia (1913-).*

Entomological Society of America; founded in *1953* by union of the former Entomological Society of America *(1906)* and the American Association of Economic Entomologists *(1889) ;* publishes *Annals of the Entomological Society of America (1908-), Miscellaneous Publications of the E. S. A., Bulletin of the E. S. A. (1955-), Journal of Economic Entomology (1908-),* and monographs under the name of the Thomas Say Foundation *(1916-).*

Entomological Society of Canada; founded in *1951;* co-publishes *The Canadian Entomologist (1868-).*

Lepidopterists' Society; founded in *1947;* publishes *Journal of the Lepidop*

terists' Society (previously *Lepidopterists' News) (1947-),* and

Memoirs of the Lepidopterists' Society (1964-) . American Malacological Union, founded in *1931.*

Society of Protozoologists; publishes *Journal of Protozoology.*

National societies for mixed groups. Several national organizations deal with a variety of groups brought together by some such aspect as their manner of living:

American Society of Parasitologists; founded in *1924;* publishes *The Journal of Parasitology.*

American Microscopical Society; publishes *Transactions of the American Microscopical Society.*

Society of Marine Borer Biologists and Chemists.

Paleontological societies. For those interested in fossils, including their taxonomy as well as other aspects, there are:

The Paleontological Society; founded in 1908; publishes *Journal of Paleontology* (1927-) (jointly with Soc. Econ. Paleo. and Miner., below) The Society of Economic Paleontologists and Mineralogists; founded in

1927; publishes *Journal o f Paleontology* (1927-). (See The Paleo. Soc., above)

Paleontological Research Institution; founded 1932; publishes *Bulletin of American Paleontology,* and *Palaeontographica Americana.*

Society of Vertebrate Paleontologists; founded in 1940; publishes *News Bulletin,* and *Bibliography of Vertebrate Paleontology and Related Subjects.*

Geological Society of America; founded in 1888; publishes *Bulletin of the Geological Society of America, Special Papers of the G. S. A., Memoirs of the G. S. A., Bibliography of Fossil Vertebrates, Treatise on Invertebrate Paleontology,* etc.

Regional societies on one group. There are regional societies, interested in certain groups of animals, often with national appeal and membership:

Wilson Ornithological Club; founded in 1888; publishes *The Wilson Bulletin.*

Cooper Ornithological Society; publishes *The Condor.* Ohio Herpetological Society.

New York Entomological Society; founded in 1892; publishes *Journal of the New York Entomological Society* (1893-).

Brooklyn Entomological Society; founded in 1872; publishes *Bulletin o f the Brooklyn Entomological Society* (1912-), and *Entomologia Americana* (1926-).

The American Entomological Society (Philadelphia); founded in 1859; publishes *Entomological News* (1890-), and *Transactions of the American Entomological Society* (1861-) .

Entomological Society of Washington; founded in 1884; publishes *Proceedings of the Entomological Society o f Washington* (1884-), and *Memoirs of the E. S. W.* (1939-).

Kansas Entomological Society; founded in 1925; publishes *Journal of the Kansas Entomological Society* (1928-).

Florida Entomological Society; founded in 1916; publishes *The Florida Entomologist* (1920-).

Pacific Coast Entomological Society; founded in 1901; publishes *Pan Pacific Entomologist* (1924-), *Memoirs o f the P.C.E.S.* (1951-). Hawaiian Entomological Society; founded in 1904; publishes *Proceedings of the Hawaiian Entomological Society* (1906-).

Cambridge Entomological Club; founded in 1874; publishes *Psyche* (1874-).

Entomological Society of Quebec; founded in 1951; publishes *Annals of the Entomological Society of Quebec* (1956-).

Entomological Society of Ontario; founded in 1863; publishes *Canadian Entomologist* (1868-), and *Annual Reports of the Entomological Society of Ontario* (1870-).

Entomological Society of Alberta; founded in 1952; publishes *Proceedings of the Entomological Society of Alberta* (1953-).

Entomological Society of British Columbia; founded in 1902; publishes *Proceedings of the Entomological Society of British Columbia* (1911), and *Occasional Papers of the E.S.B.C.* (1951-) . Connecticut Shell Club.

Hawaiian Malacological Society.

Helminthological Society of Washington; publishes *Proceedings of the Helminthological Society of Washington.*

Regional societies for many groups. There are also a few regional societies interested in a wide variety of groups:

Association of Southeastern Biologists. Cambridge Society of Natural History. Buffalo Society of Natural Sciences.

Society of Natural History of Delaware.

Biological Society of Washington [D.C.]; publishes *Proceedings of the Biological Society o f Washington.*

Elisha Mitchell Scientific Society; publishes *journal of the Elisha Mitchell Scientific Society.*

Southwestern Society of Naturalists.

Supporting Organizations

Many other organizations are occasionally concerned with taxonomy to the extent of supporting research or publishing its results. Among these are most general science associations, as well as academies of science:

American Association for the Advancement of Science; founded 1848; publishes *Science.*

American Institute of Biological Sciences; founded 1948; publishes *A.I.B.S. Bulletin* (now *Bio-Science), Quarterly Review of Biology, In Briefln Biology,* etc.

Society of the Sigma Xi; publishes *The American Scientist.*

Washington Academy of Sciences [D.C.]; publishes *journal of the Washington Academy o f Sciences.*

California Academy of Sciences; founded 1854; publishes *Academy Newsletter, Pacific Discovery, Occasional Papers of the California Academy of Sciences,* and *Proceedings of the C. A. S.*

New York Academy of Sciences; publishes *Annals o f the New York Academy of Sciences* (1877-).

Southern California Academy of Sciences; publishes *Bulletin of the Southern California Academy of Sciences.*

Kansas Academy of Science; founded 1872; publishes *Transactions of the Kansas Academy of Science* (1872-).

Virginia Academy of Science; publishes *Virginia Journal of Science* (1940-).

Museums. Museums are of all sizes and for many purposes. Some have been very active in the production and support of research and in the publication of taxonomic results. Among the more active nonuniversity museums are the following:

United States National Museum (U.S.N.M.); publishes *Proceedings of the United States National Museum, U.S. National Museum Bulletin,* etc. (The U.S.N.M. is part of the Smithsonian Institution which publishes *Smithsonian Miscellaneous Collections,* etc.).

American Museum of Natural History (A.M.N.H.); publishes *American Museum Novitates, Bulletin of the American Museum of Natural History.*

Chicago Museum of Natural History (formerly Field Museum of Natural History); publishes *Fieldiana.*

Los Angeles County Museum.

Royal Ontario Museum.

Several museums important in taxonomy are associated with major universities. At the risk of omitting some of equal standing, we may cite Museum of Comparative Zoology (M.C.Z.), at Harvard University; publishes *Johnsonia* (mollusks).

Museum of Natural History, at University of Kansas; publishes *University of Kansas Publication (Museum of Natural History).*

Museum of Vertebrate Zoology (M.V.Z.), at University of California, Berkeley.

Museum of Natural History, at Stanford University. Museum of Zoology, at University of Michigan.

A list of the museums of North America has been published, with the institutions listed by state, name, and field of interest:

American Association of Museums; published *Museums Directory of the United States and Canada* (1961).

Universities. Several universities sponsor publication of journals in the field of taxonomy:

Catholic University of America; publishes *Coleopterists' Bulletin.*

Pomona College; publishes *Journal of Entomology and Zoology.*

Stanford University; publishes *Microentomology.*

University of Kansas; publishes *University of Kansas Science Bulletin,* and University o f Kansas Paleontological Contributions.

University of Notre Dame; publishes *American Midland Naturalist.*

University of San Francisco; publishes *Wasmann Journal of Biology.*

Commercial supporters. One biological supply house publishes a small journal with articles of interest to taxonomists:

General Biological Supply House, Inc.; publishes *Turtox News.*

Plant societies. One international plant taxonomy organization deserves to be cited here:

International Association for Plant Taxonomy; publishes *Taxon,* and various directories.

10

Recording the Data

The results of research are of little use to anyone unless they are recorded. Even the observer or experimenter will find his data useless, unless he keeps a record of his results. For studies to have a lasting effect on science, for them to become part of human knowledge, the results, at least, must be published.

Publication is the virtually necessary prelude to use and criticism by other scientists, to repetition of the experiments, to analysis of implications in other fields, and to verification of consistency with other knowledge. The final judgment on a theory may not come for years, but in the end the faults and virtues of every work will be known.

The keeping of notes is not as pertinent to the study of classification as to some other fields, but it can be of very great value. It is beyond the scope of this book to describe the various methods of taking and storing notes, but the value of accurate and detailed records of data is pertinent to several aspects of taxonomy and may appropriately be emphasized here. References to this subject in the literature of systematics are not common.

A distinction will be made here between the notes taken in the field to accompany specimens intended for taxonomic study and notes taken in the course of research (taxonomic or other). The first are intended as permanent records to accompany the specimens from then on. The latter may be intended for permanent record in publication but are more likely to be of temporary nature to record the progress of the study.

FIELD NOTEBOOKS

It has already been noted that accurate records of the place, time, and circumstances of capture of the specimens are of great importance. In recent years, the employment of classifications in other branches of biology has become much more frequent, and the amount of data contributed by these fields to classification is becoming substantial.

It is therefore desirable for taxonomists to take maximum advantage of information available at the time of collection, even though this information is not the goal of the taxonomic study. When a taxonomic study is preceded by a period of planned collecting of specimens, thought is usually given to the problem of just what data also need be recorded to give the specimens maximum value.

The better this preliminary planning, the better the results in accuracy and usability of the data. However, it is often found that even carefully planned records turn out to be inadequate in some important but overlooked detail, especially when the study leads into unexpected avenues of investigation, as is often the case with good projects. Some examples may serve to highlight both the advance planning and its possible failures.

Data Sheets

In many fields of biology, whether experimental or observational, records are customarily kept on prearranged forms that facilitate the recording. Such forms are well-nigh indispensable in keeping the data uniform, complete, and capable of ready storage, but there can be serious disadvantages which must be recognized.

They provide spaces for all the types of desired data, and the notes are taken on the spot at the time of collecting. These forms help to ensure uniformity of data for all specimens, and encourage complete recording of data, because the blanks provided serve as reminders. In addition, the use of the forms encourages advance thought and planning and permanent storage of the uniform notes.

These forms have some disadvantages, which should not be overlooked. They tend to restrict the recording of any data not provided for, and they sometimes prove too elaborate for effective use.

Figure elsewhere in this chapter is a facsimile of one-half of a 4 × 7 inch sheet prepared by a student collector for use on a collecting trip to a new part of the world, where general collecting of insects was to be undertaken. He hoped to make the form so complete that the station number and a few circled words would be about all that was

Field No.__________
State______________
Locality___________
County_____________

POPULATION ECOLOGY

LOCALITY
Description:_________________________________

Elev. (m):______________________ Date:__________

ENVIRONMENT
Temperature:__________________ Time:__________

Weather:____________________________________

Soil:_______________________________________

Moisture:___________________________________

Vegetation:_________________________________

Condition of lupine:__________________________

Abundance:__________________ Food plant noted:________

Estimate No. Species Lupine________________

General:____________________________________

BEHAVOUR OF ADULTS
Nos:________________ Proximity of host plants:_________

Condition:__________________________

Activity:_____________________________________

Altitudinal range in vicinity:_____________________

Seasonal status:_______________________________

Field larvae observed:_________ Eggs observed:__________

% Parasitism:____________

Predominant Insects in Area:______________________

REMARKS

Figure 10.1: A collector's ecological data sheet.

necessary. The form turned out to be totally inadequate, and most records were kept by writing between the lines. (The peculiarities of the capitalization and printing were due merely to the fact that the student set the type by hand and printed the form himself!)

In general, it can be said that the usefulness of such forms in the long run depends on several factors: (1) the care used in their preparation, (2) the extent to which the possible future ramifications of the problem can be foretold, and, especially, (3) the temperament of the user in relation to keeping records and being conscientious in using the forms.

An example of two detailed forms prepared after years of preliminary experience and designed to give uniform data for a particular study is illustrated here. They were used by Dr. John C. Downey in a study of the population and variability of a species of butterfly living on lupine plants. The Population Ecology sheet was used in the field to record ecological and collecting data. It was designed to encourage the keeping of detailed environment records.

It proved to be effective in several ways: In addition to the advantages listed above, it made possible rapid comparison of some particular aspect on a series of the forms. For example, the temperature at the time of capture could be rapidly compared in various populations to show the effect of this feature on flight activity during the day. It often reminded the collector to note a factor that would otherwise have been overlooked.

A subsequent development highlights some factors in the keeping of such forms. A companion on one trip used a bound notebook to keep a journal, a combined diary-and-field-notes. At every stop, notes were made of all the usual features, as well as brief lists of other specimens taken incidentally and external factors affecting the trip, with mileages between collecting sites, names of intervening towns, and any unusual features or occurrences.

This journal proved to be so helpful that the forms were abandoned for the rest of the trip. However, the items of information listed on the data sheet were consciously entered into the journal, so that it served a dual purpose. In subsequent use on the trip the journal seemed entirely adequate. After return to the laboratory, when a specific feature was to be compared for each locality, it was found that the journal was more difficult to use than the forms, because the arrangement varied.

It was also found that the journal sometimes missed a pertinent fact that would have been recorded on the form because of the place reserved for it. This fault of the journal could be eliminated by any of a variety of means, such as use of a large rubber stamp at each new locality. The stamp would have the desired features of the form and would thus help to combine the good features of both types of notebooks.

If the journal were loose-leaf, one of the original forms could be inserted for each collecting station. One other advantage of a journal

SPECIMEN DATA RECORD

Sex: __________ Genitalia Dis. No. ________

Population
State: __________ County: __________ Locality: __________

Wings.
Length forewing __________ Length hindwing __________

Macules
all present.

missing macule no.: __________
additional macules: __________
fusions: __________
spot ratio, fore to hindwing: __________

Constellations
Forewing value: __________ hindwing value: __________
Placement: __________
Ground color: __________

Termen in male: __________
Blue of male: __________
Orange in female: __________
Blue of female: __________
Brown of female: __________

Body
length: __________
setae: __________

Genitalia: Male
F ______ H ______ U ______ E ______
Valve length ______ Valve width ______
D ______
Ratios: F/U ______ Forewing/Valve ______
Other: __________

Figure 10.2: A research data sheet.

is that it can be illustrated by means of pasted-in maps, photos, or other material. It would thus be possible to have the rubber-stamped form on gummed labels that could be pasted in where appropriate.

The advantage of this would be use of a bound rather than a loose-leaf notebook, the latter being subject to loss or disarrangement of pages. There is no end to the possibilities. Imagination and foresight are the ingredients necessary to devise an effective note-taking system.

Research Notes

The keeping of notes is necessary not only in the field to accompany the specimen collected but also in the laboratory, where the specimens are later studied. Here again, uniformity is an important benefit bestowed by pre-arranged forms. This results in direct comparability of the observations. These research notes are often the result of assembling the data for report or publication.

They are not only written but may be drawings, photographs, recordings, graphs, diagrams, etc., and merge into the permanently stored dissections, preparations, and specimens themselves. A good museum has not only the specimens but also the collecting notes, the research notes, and the resulting publications.

An example of a prepared form for research notes in the same project as described above (the butterfly taxonomy and ecology) is shown in Figure elsewhere in this chapter. Its principal advantages are permanence, completeness, and comparability.

THE CATALOGING OF DATA

The verb to catalog means rather different things to different taxonomists: (1) the cataloging of specimens, (2) the cataloging of species and groups, and (3) the cataloging of literature. They are discussed separately below.

Cataloging of Specimens

In some groups of animals, the specimens in the collections are recorded individually or in lots in what is called cataloging. This is sometimes in the nature of an accession record, showing how the animal was received, the data of its collection, its identification, and the place of storage in the collection.

In the higher vertebrates, this generally takes the form of assignment of an individual number to every specimen and the recording of the relevant information on a card to be filed in a card catalog either numerically, systematically, geographically, or all of these.

In collections stored in fluid preservatives, such as those of many aquatic invertebrates, the individuals may not be cataloged but merely the lots. Each collection will receive a number, or each species in each collection.

In insect collections such cataloging is extremely rare, because the large numbers of both species and specimens make it entirely impractical. It is sometimes possible to include on the pin labels a reference to a lot number or catalog number, but this has generally proven to be of temporary value at best.

As a means of keeping extra data associated with specimens, such procedures as cataloging of specimens are highly desirable. In practice, however, the time and cost have proven so high that cataloging has often been deemed unjustified. As detailed data becomes more necessary to fill the demands on taxonomy, methods must be found to keep track of data in an economical manner.

One class of specimens is, however, almost universally cataloged. These are the type specimens on which the species are based. In major museums these type catalogs are usually bound books in which the types are serially recorded by number. The number on the specimen refers back to the notes on how, when, and by whom the specimen was made a type.

Cataloging of Species

Checklists and catalogs are often physically somewhat different, as explained in a later section, but they are similar in being basically lists of species. Such lists of the species, either of one group or of one region, are sometimes made on cards primarily for personal use, but they are often prepared with publication as the goal.

They may list the species of a given region, the species of a given group for the world, or the species or specimens in a particular museum or collection. When such a catalog is made on cards for personal use, it is not clearly distinct from the next type. A card catalog of the species in any group from any region may simply consist of a card for each species, with the original author, date, and reference, the formal synonyms (other names for that species), and notes on any other information desired by the collector.

The cards serve as a list of the known species. For publication, the cards are carefully arranged and transcribed into a list for the printer. The published catalog may contain only the names themselves, or it may contain a great deal of additional information about each one.

Cataloging of Literature

In general, taxonomic cataloging of literature is the assembly of an annotated bibliography of the previous work on a group of organisms. It is usually more than a mere list of the published books and papers, as its purpose is to arrange taxonomic and nomenclatural information, not library information. Because flexibility in arranging the data is essential, cataloging is nearly always done on cards or sheets that can be arranged as desired or handled with the aid of mechanical devices.

The catalogs of *species* are frequently not prepared for publication. Complete catalogs of the *literature* are also first of all for personal use of the taxonomist, but they are sometimes published. They are extremely valuable, if well prepared, but they are so expensive to publish that at best they are usually combined with the catalog of species.

The catalog is made from the original books and papers. If these works are then sent back to a library, the value of the catalog will be greatly reduced. The catalog may contain an abstract of the information in each publication, but it serves primarily as an index to those publications. The works will have to be consulted again on many occasions, if the catalog is in active use.

It is impossible to foresee all the problems that will necessitate reference back to the original. Therefore, a taxonomic catalog should be assembled in conjunction with a set of the pertinent papers and books, so far as possible. Cataloging of the literature is essential for serious taxonomic work.

On many groups of animals, the literature is so diverse, so voluminous, so scattered, that the taxonomist can assemble it only through years of effort. His catalog must be highly accurate and complete, unless it is to be misleading, because many taxonomic decisions are based on the data in the catalog. The extent to which the quality of detailed taxonomic work depends on the knowledge of previous work is sometimes not fully realized.

The failure to uncover one pertinent paper published at any time since 1758 might quite possibly render an entire analysis useless and produce a whole series of conclusions that would be logical but erroneous. This has happened many times. It can be prevented only by the most thorough bibliographic work and properly designed cataloging of the historical data.

It is said that there are almost as many methods of filing reprints as there are scientists filing them. Something of the same sort could be said about the methods of cataloging. This is not entirely bad, because cataloging should be carefully planned to fill the needs of the situation at hand and therefore should vary with the circumstances. The first step in any sort of literature cataloging is to determine the exact nature of the data desired and the manner in which it is to be filed.

This will determine the course of the rest of the work. The exact limits of coverage must also be decided at this time. Inadequate planning at the beginning can result in the necessity to repeat the early work when a change in coverage or data becomes necessary. It is always best to plan a more detailed and complete catalog than the minimum which at first seems to be all that would be required. For example, when the author of this book started to catalog the family Staphylinidae, he spent several years covering the eighteenth-century books and then worked on publications of the early nineteenth century. From the beginning, he included several groups that had sometimes been placed in the family and sometimes not, such as the Micropeplidae.

Had these been omitted and later found to belong in the family, much of the search would have had to be done over. After a large part of the cataloging was complete, it was discovered that the genus *Inopeplus,* always placed in a distant part of the Coleoptera, probably belonged in the Staphylinidae. Only by reexamining much of the early literature on beetles could this group be brought into synonymic harmony with the rest of the Staphylinidae.

This job is too large to repeat, and the genus will probably remain for a long time imperfectly cataloged. The second part of the cataloging work is bibliographic-to determine all the publications that have any bearing on the problem at hand. In a synonymic study this means every publication in which any of the members of the group have appeared. It is not enough in synonymic work to study only the major works.

In many cases every use of each name must be examined and evaluated. This job continues as long as taxonomic work is being done. Unknown older papers are forever turning up, and new publications are appearing daily in many groups. There is no cut-off point between 1758 and today. The difficulties encountered in the bibliography depend on the previous cataloging, the existence of published bibliographies, the extent and completeness of recent monographic works, the size of the group, the volume of the accumulated literature, the geographic spread of the literature, the number of languages involved, and other factors.

A good catalog cannot be produced without excellent bibliographic foundation, and good taxonomic work cannot be done on a monographic scale without adequate cataloging. The third step is to obtain each of the appropriate publications and extract from it all the data pertinent to the catalog. In a small catalog, the entire pertinent section may be copied onto the card. Or a reprint or photostat may be cut up and pasted on the cards. In an extensive catalog, the best that can usually be done is to make the card serve as an index to where the data is to be found, with annotations as extensive as possible of the data itself.

When the group being cataloged is a large one, the catalog will have to be little more than an index to the literature-an index to all the names and to every reference to each. Two cards from such a file are reproduced as Figure elsewhere in this chapter. They are both from one work, showing an important reference (to a new species description) and a minor reference (a species merely compared to a new species). The first card shows that this species was described as new in the cited publication, was placed in a particular subgenus, and came from a certain locality. This is about all one could expect to find about this species in this publication.

The second card represents a reference to the species *P. planus* that some catalogers would consider too trivial to record. However, in comparing this species with the new one, some previously undescribed features may have been mentioned. Furthermore, this may be the first time that the species has been placed in this particular subgenus.

This emphasizes that no citation can be considered too trivial in cataloging. Generic names, particularly, are governed by such strict rules, that every time they are printed, and every spelling variation, may prove to be of the highest importance in nomenclature.

Some catalogers try to catalog the relevant works in chronological order. If one knows in advance all the relevant works, it will hardly he necessary to catalog them at all. Furthermore, it is in practice simply impossible to do this, and the cataloger will save much time and effort by taking books as they come, searching in all possible places for additional references to his species, and keeping a meticulous record of what he has already cataloged.

A bibliography of the publications cataloged is an important part of the catalog. It should be in standard form, complete, accurate, and annotated to show the extent of the data therein, the library where the book is obtainable, and the date on which it was cataloged. In large catalogs, it has been found extremely useful to keep a duplicate bibliography in chronological order.

Not only taxonomic data and nomenclature can be organized but geographical and bibliographical data also. Taxonomy involves all of these, and simultaneous use of all data is essential to sound results.

Since animals can only be referred to by names, nomenclature is a key factor in cataloging data about animals. Although we say that the "correct" name of a certain species is *Ocypus olens,* this name is correct only at the present time.

We must recognize that the species was originally called *Staphylinus olens,* that it was later called *Goerius olens,* then *Dinothenarus olens,* then *Ocypus (Goerius) olens,* as well as *Ocypus major, Ocypus maxillosus,* and *Ocypus unicolor*. It must be cataloged under each of these and several others, although it would be possible to file them all at one place. (This latter is not practicable or desirable in a large catalog.)

```
Phloeonomus pinicola  n.sp.                    1920

Champion ---- Ent.Mo.Mag.,56,p.241,242.

Subg. Phloeostiba
Desc., notes
Kumaon
```

```
Phloeonomus planus Payk.                       1920

Champion ---- Ent.Mo.Mag.,56,p.242.

Subg. Phloeostiba

D.f. P.pinicola n.sp.
```

Figure 10.3: Examples of literature catalog cards.

The following synonymy gives the principal names under which the data on this species would be filed.

Staphylinus olens Muller *(1764)* (1)
Goerius olens (Muller) Westwood *(1827)* (2)
Ocypus olens (Muller) Curtis *(1829)* (3)
Emus olens (Muller) Dejean *(1833)* (4)
Physetops olens (Muller) Motschulsky *(1858)* (5)
Anodus olens (Muller) Motschulsky *(1858)* (6)

Ocypus (Goerius) olens (Muller) Mulsant and Rey *(1876)* (7)
Dinothenarus olens (Muller) Heyden *(1887)* (8)
Staphylinus (Goerius) olens Muller (Ganglbauer, *1895)* (9)
Staphylinus (Ocypus) olens Muller (Fauvel, *1897)* (10)
Staphylinus major Degeer *(1774)* (11)
Staphylinus maior Degeer *(1781)* (emendation *of major)* (12)
Goerius major (Degeer) Stephens *(1829)* (13)
Ocypus major (Degeer) Bertolini *(1872)* (14)
Staphylinus maxillosus (Schrank, *1781)* (not Linnaeus, *1758)* (15)
Ocypus maxillosus (Schrank) Gemminger and Harold *(1868)* (16)
Goerius maxillosus (Schrank) Reitter *(1909)* (17)
Staphylinus unicolor Herbst *(1784)* (18)
Ocypus unicolor (Herbst) Gemminger and Harold *(1868)* (19)
Goerius unicolor (Herbst) Reitter *(1909)* (20)
Emus morosus Dejean *(1833)* (21)

Cross-referencing is essential. Attention to spelling is necessary not only to avoid new errors but also to prevent omission of data published under a misspelling. For example *Goerius* has also been misspelled *Georius* and *Coarus*.

In the latter case, the data would be lost in a distant section of the file if it was not recognized and crossindexed. The mechanics of filing the data require careful attention also. Ordinary cards and guides are usually not adequate. Guide cards can be obtained with three tabs across the top, and ones with five tabs may then be used as subguides. Other subguides can be made by having cards cut from stock in a size %-inch higher than the catalog cards, so that a typed line at the top serves as a guide.

Cards of various colors can be used, and there are clip signals that can be attached to show special features. These must be worked out to serve the needs of each catalog, but the mechanical devices should aid the user, not merely add to the work. Catalogs are the basis of most taxonomic work, and without published catalogs the bibliographic workload of many taxonomists would be greatly increased.

PUBLICATION

No research has much impact on science until it is made available to other scientists. This can be done orally-in conversation or by presentation of reports at meetings of scientists-or it can be done by correspondence or the circulation of printed reports. Only the latter means is customarily implied by the word publication, and it is also the only effective means of disseminating taxonomic information. In using taxonomic knowledge, it is often the most recent monograph which is consulted first, because it will be the most complete.

Nevertheless, the opinion of the monographer must be in conformity with the earliest work, the original publications, or it will be set aside. In the final analysis, all taxonomy and all nomenclature must be consistent with original sources, and intervening work, even of monographic nature, will be of secondary importance.

If the monographic work is well done, it may supplant the earlier work to a large extent, but this happens only in the better-known groups, where a high degree of taxonomic stability has been achieved. Taxonomic papers retain their value or interest for the specialist for decades or even centuries. In many cases a publication will remain the only source of data on the subject for fifty years or more.

This makes publication of data, analysis, and conclusions of prime importance in this field. In taxonomy, publications may take the physical form of books, pamphlets, journal articles, symposium chapters, etc.; they may be primarily factual, theoretical, methodological, essayistic, or critical; they may be analytical or synthetic; and they may range in size from a one-paragraph note on a new observation to a multivolume monograph.

The major types of taxonomic publications are listed below, with notation of some of the features and purposes of each. Publications presenting new zoological data. The largest number of taxonomic publications present the results of studies (observations) on the comparative attributes of animals. These publications include all the ordinary descriptive papers, whether the subjects are new species, life-history stages, distribution, or biochemistry.

Comparative Studies

The basis for all taxonomy and classification is comparative data. Therefore the first type of study required for systematic work is the study of the diversity of the group and the variation of the included species. The more that can be learned about these two things, the better the taxonomic work can be.

Comparative anatomical studies have been made in several parts of the animal kingdom, but the lack of them in many groups is a serious deterrent to sound classification. In the vertebrates, where comparative anatomy seems to be far advanced, there are many conspicuous gaps in the knowledge, so that sound classification has been delayed. In some phyla and classes of the invertebrates, nearly all the available anatomical data stands by itself, not effectively compared with data on the other groups. Even in such a largely comparative study as Hyman's compilation on *The Invertebrates,* there is little attempt to tabulate or compare item-for-item the numerous data presented.

To be effective these studies must be analytical, determining the nature and extent of variation. Frequently, they must explore new aspects, as new techniques become available. Their purpose is to discover and record all the ways in which species or individuals are similar or unlike, and the extent to which the data can be reasonably used in segregating and combining groups.

These comparative studies may be taxonomic contributions. Among them are life history studies, embryological studies, zoogeographies, stratigraphies, ecological studies, and behavioral studies, as well as comparative anatomy, comparative physiology, and comparative biochemistry.

Descriptions of New Taxa

The simplest type of direct taxonomic paper is the description of one or more new species or other taxa. Although some writers hint that such single contributions are to be frowned upon as inadequate, they sometimes include all the requirements for making a contribution to science.

Descriptive Revisions

Also called synopses and reviews, these papers summarize some aspects of the taxonomy of a group of species and incorporate the writer's views on the classification. They also enable others to identify the species. In extent of coverage, they range all the way from the previous type up to monographs. They may deal with species, or they may be limited to a study of the genera.

Monographs

These are the most complete systematic works, dealing with all the known facts about the species covered, usually not restricted so much as revisions in coverage. They have been described as "complete systematic publications (involving) full systematic treatment of all species, subspecies, and other taxonomic units and a thorough knowledge . . . of the comparative anatomy of the group, the biology of the species and subspecies included, the immature stages in groups exhibiting metamorphosis, and detailed distributional data."

This is an ideal. It is sufficient for a good monograph to bring together all that is known and add the writer's analysis and systematic conclusions. However, a monograph is necessarily exhaustive in its bibliographic background, because this is essential to assembly of all the existing information.

Faunal Studies

Merging with revisions and monographs are detailed studies of the fauna of a single region. Monographs are restricted to a single group of animals and can be prepared only by an experienced specialist on that group. Faunal studies cover all animals of an area or at least all those in a major group. The author generally is not a specialist but has studied the local fauna, made keys to the species, or tabulated their occurrence.

Atlases

These are comparative studies in picture form. They present anatomical data by means of illustrations.

Classifications

The studies which deal only with the grouping of animals and the arrangement of the groups into categories of the hierarchy are not very numerous, although much of this type of work at lower levels is included in monographs and even revisions. These papers may cover all the genera in a class (Simpson's *Classification of Mammals),* all the families in a class (Wetmore's A *Classification for the Birds of the World),* all the phyla in the Animal Kingdom (Hyman's *The Invertebrates, vol. 1,* chap. 2), or the subgroups within a group at any level.

Publications presenting new studies of names. Nearly all taxonomic revisions and monographs deal with names extensively, but a few papers deal only with the solution of the problems involved in using the correct name for each taxon.

Nomenclature Studies

These are studies of the names themselves, their derivation, orthography, validity, typification, synonymy, homonymy, and so on. They are not to be confused either with nomenclators (which list names) or with studies of rules of nomenclature. Examples are the following extensive generic name studies.

Knight, J. Brooks, *1941.* Paleozoic Gastropod Genotypes. *Geol. Soc. America, Spec. Pap. 32, 510 pp. 96 pl., 32* figs.

Blackwelder, R. E. *1952.* The Generic Names of the Beetle Family Staphylinidae with an Essay on Genotypy. *United States Nat. Mus. Bull. 200,* 483 pp.

Publications presenting methods of study. The working out of new methods to learn more about animals is a very important activity, one of those tending to keep the field up-to-date in techniques and outlooks. The study of rules of nomenclature amounts to study of methods of perfecting the system of naming.

Methods

Reports on the methods found useful in any aspect of taxonomy are valuable aids to other taxonomists. They may be methods of collection, preservation, storage, observation, examination, preparation, cataloging, filing, classification, measuring, comparing, recording, or any other aspect faced by taxonomists.

Rules of Nomenclature

These are studies of the nomenclature rules, especially those analytical papers that offer solutions to problems of nomenclature. These papers are generally short and cannot be listed here. They will be found listed in the subject indexes of the *Zoological Record* and in *Biological Abstracts*.

Reference Publications

Works of reference are usually major works, requiring years of work and resulting in lightening the work load of all other workers in the field. Some works listed above could also be included here, such as classifications, because they are much used for reference by non-specialists.

Catalogs and Checklists

Both of these words have been used for rather different things. A checklist is literally a list of names prepared for the purpose of checking off certain ones. In the groups that have been popular with collectors-birds, butterflies, and beetles-these have been used to record the species in the collection.

If the species were numbered consecutively, the numbers could be used as a shorthand notation when referring to the listed species. Through extension of meaning, the word checklist has come to refer, in work with vertebrates especially, to any tabulation of species, even if it includes most of the features usually found in catalogs.

A catalog is a tabulation of species which also cites some of the following information about each: (1) the original description reference, (2) later references, (3) synonyms with references, (4) range, (5) type locality, (6) genotypes of generic names, (7) annotations of various sorts, and (8) other pertinent data. Few catalogs are able to present all of these data. The circumstances dictate what will be shown in -each case. The extreme use of the term catalog is the descriptive catalog, in which the species are actually described.

Keys

Most revisionary or monographic works include keys for the identification of the genera and species. In some cases such keys may be published separately, either singly or collected into a volume that covers a major group. An example is:

Bradley, J. *C. 1930. A manual of the Genera of Beetles of America North of Mexico. Keys for the Determination of the Families, Subfamilies, Tribes, and Genera* . . . , Ithaca, N.Y.; Dow, Illston and Company.

Handbooks

Books designed to enable the layman or non-specialist to identify the more common local species may be a product of taxonomic endeavor, but they usually do not form a part of the real taxonomic literature. They may be in the form of field guides or in the form of student manuals. Occasionally they are scholarly volumes of relatively complete taxonomic treatment.

Bibliographies

Inasmuch as nearly all taxonomic work is largely dependent on previous literature, guides to this literature are of universal importance to taxonomists. Most taxonomists must do a great deal of bibliographical work in their own research, and some of the results are published for the use of all. There is no end to the variety, extending from large summaries through annual lists to studies of some one work or serial.

Nomenclators

Lists of names, usually generic, intended for reference to ·show what names have been used and where, are called nomenclators. They differ from checklists in being alphabetically rather than systematically arranged.

Critiques

Less strictly taxonomic are certain papers that discuss the attitudes or work of taxonomists. These are very important in directing attention to goals, pitfalls, and inadequacies. They are not very numerous but may be cited under two headings.

Book Reviews

Reviews of new books in taxonomy are not different from reviews of any other sort of book. It is not common to review monographic works, but brief notices are sometimes published to announce such works. The few general books that are published on taxonomy are reviewed in appropriate journals.

Essays

Many of the types of works cited above are primarily concerned with the presentation of taxonomic data. It is sometimes believed that such works should not contain discussions of methods, concepts, theories, the relation of taxonomy to other fields, or critical analysis of other work. Consequently this discussion material is frequently published in the form of essays.

11

Publication of Data

Information accumulated by an individual is not really part of science until it is communicated to other scientists-made part of the general knowledge of the subject. For this purpose, communication is possible only by words, or symbols representing words, and by pictures. Words combine into statements by means of which concepts are described. The statements may be vocal or written.

Vocal statements are seldom heard by more than a few of the directly interested persons in the world, even at large meetings, but many types of scientific contributions have been initially presented in this manner. Similarly, written communications (letters, information sheets, and drafts of possible publications) seldom reach more than a few people and have little effect on science, particularly taxonomy.

This leaves as the only effective means of communication the direct publication of the knowledge. The word publication could involve, besides printing, such practices as distribution of recordings or microfilm, but in science it seldom does.

In taxonomy, all forms of reproduction other than printing are specifically outlawed or recommended against if there are any nomenclatural considerations. Nearly all dissemination of taxonomic knowledge is through formal publication by printing, in books, technical periodicals, or separate pamphlets.

GENERAL PROBLEMS OF PUBLICATION

Rather diverse problems face the taxonomist preparing to publish taxonomic data and conclusions. In order to undertake a taxonomic publication a zoologist needs rather extensive taxonomic experience. Just how extensive depends on the type of publication.

Recording new localities or new facts about a well-known species would require only a minimum of background. Describing as new a species formerly mixed with another species, or transferring a species to a new genus, would require very substantial knowledge of the technical aspects of both taxonomy and nomenclature.

What to Publish

There have been many published comments on the abuses of publication, suggesting that there are limits to what should be published. There is no possibility of setting standards, however, and the individual must follow his own conscience. He should be careful with his facts, reasonable in his interpretations, considerate of his colleagues, and critical of his own efforts; he should publish everything that contributes usefully to the knowledge of animals; and he should try to publish in the most useful form possible.

Single large publications are often more useful than a series of small ones, yet frequently it is difficult to obtain the publication of a large work, no matter how good. Some projects that result in diverse data are best published in separate papers in different journals. It is thus often possible to justify either a single large paper or a series of small ones. Many factors may be relevant to the decision.

Some employers judge a taxonomist's qualifications or activities by the number of his papers. Few scientists believe this to be a good criterion, but, if the situation exists, the individual cannot afford to ignore it. No real monograph should ever be broken up into short papers, but any peripheral aspects may profitably be reported separately, whereupon they actually become more available than in a large work.

There are no limits to the things that may be worth publishing in taxonomy. A single taxonomist might publish examples of all the following, over a period of fifty years or so:

New records of species from new localities
Revision of a genus or larger group
Description of an unusual structure
Monographic study of a group
Checklist or catalog
Notes on synonymy and records
Description of a new species or genus

Study of genera in a larger group
Classification of phyla, classes, orders, or families
Essay on taxonomic trends or ideas
Essay on theory of taxonomy
Description of a previously unknown larval form
Notes on a new method of study, collecting, or storage
Itinerary of an expedition for collecting
Study of the nomenclature of a group
Comparative study of a group
Biography or bibliography of a taxonomist
Preliminary notes for a new classification
Regional or faunal studies
Essay on relation of taxonomy to some other field
Critique of new proposal
Studies on nomenclature rules and problems
Summaries or tables for reference
Index to literature
Studies on dates of taxonomic books
Systems for citing or filing literature
Book reviews

These by no means exhaust the possibilities. Taxonomists are interested in pertinent aspects of most other zoological sciences and appreciate summaries of these for their special benefit by other taxonomists. They are interested in learning where to find collections, who is working on a particular group, in what museums there are noteworthy collections, the history of taxonomy, how taxonomy directly benefits other fields, how animals can be identified by non-taxonomists, how to teach taxonomy, and many other subjects.

Diversity in the publications of a taxonomist adds spice to his efforts, broadens his outlook, makes more of his ideas available to others, and increases his understanding of taxonomic problems.

Where to Publish

It seems useful to comment briefly on taxonomic works published in inappropriate journals. Recently a zoological student discovered a population of animals that seemed to represent a new species. He was without any direct training or experience, and his advisors were not taxonomists. He wrote a paper describing the species as new and submitted it to an appropriate taxonomic journal, which turned it down because it failed to meet taxonomic standards. It was thereupon submitted to a game management journal, which published it because it had some practical aspects. The paper, as published, showed the inexperience of its author in taxonomic matters.

It is now in a journal that carries little such material and is not well known to workers on this group of animals. Several conclusions can be drawn from this: (1) Taxonomic experience is necessary for the publication of new species and other technical taxonomic material; (2) a taxonomic paper should be published only in a journal devoted largely to such material; and (3) a rejected manuscript should be rewritten until it is acceptable to the most appropriate journal; anything else shows willingness to publish under lower standards.

It is a sad addition to the above story that the description therein fails to conform to several of the requirements of the rules of nomenclature and will probably be held unacceptable. In this condition, it not only fails to fulfil the desired end of describing, naming, and making known a newly discovered species, but it places the author on record in the literature of this species for all time as an inadequate taxonomist, because the reason for rejection of the oldest name will always have to be cited.

It must be admitted that journals sometimes reject manuscripts because of lack of space or other reasons besides inadequacy of the manuscript. However, there is no part of the animal kingdom so isolated that there is only one journal appropriate for taxonomic papers dealing with it. Numerous alternatives are available, before resorting to a non-taxonomic journal. There are cogent reasons for publishing taxonomic papers only in taxonomic journals.

First, most taxonomists subscribe to the chief journals in their field and thus obtain the paper immediately. Second, the taxonomic journals are the ones most likely to be indexed in the *Zoological Record*, often by special arrangement between the editors. Third, the taxonomic journals are more likely to be available in the centers where taxonomic work is being done and thus available to those who must come there to see collections, literature, and specialists.

Fourth, more respect is engendered by a good paper in an appropriate journal than by the same paper in an equally professional and prestigious journal whose subject of specialization is not taxonomic. Fifth, the *1961 Code of Nomenclature* has instructions to editors of taxonomic papers, which are very unlikely to be known to the editors of nontaxonomic journals.

Authorship of Taxonomic Papers

Occasionally, in the general monthly *Science*, there have been series of letters discussing the problems raised by multiple authorship of articles. In some fields, short articles are not infrequently signed by five or more authors. It may be that the aspect of obtaining "credit" for a share of the work is important.

It may even be sufficient justification. But such a practice lays a real burden on librarians, bibliographers, and all who need to cite these papers. The most common solution is to cite such a paper as "Mothy et al." (Mothy and others.) This effectively reduces the credits of most of the authors back to zero! In taxonomy, the problems are not merely those of the bibliographer.

The name (or names) of the new species will be cited whenever that species is referred to, very likely for centuries to come. A name such as *Pseudopentarthrum subcylindricum* Champion is clumsy enough as is, but to have as authors, for example, Boisduval and Lacordaire would extend the name over fifty letters; while to extend it to three or more authors imposes a burden on the user too great to be accepted, so that drastic abbreviation or curtailment will be practiced.

Although there are a great many monographic papers signed by two authors, and double authorities for names are thus common throughout the animal kingdom, it can be doubted that two men actually collaborated in the preparation of each description. If they did not, the species should be credited to the one who prepared the description.

It looks clumsy to find a species cited as *X-us albus* Bonhomme, in Malheuse and Bonhomme, 1892, but in citing the species only Bonhomme need be given. The longer form is a reference to the publication. Probably the best solution when two people collaborate, and especially if there are more than two, is for one to publish the new species separately and then to collaborate on the rest of the study, if appropriate.

There are many sorts of taxonomic papers which do not involve description of new species or groups. Co-authorship is often advantageous for these, but even here it is well to avoid multi-authorship whenever possible.

Ethics in Publication

In many of the professions, there are codes of ethics that have the support of organizations and individuals in the field. Taxonomy has gradually built up such standards for certain practices, and it has also adopted a very elaborate code of behavior in one particular subject-zoological nomenclature. Beyond this technical aspect, discussed later, there are some things of which people need to be reminded that involve the giving of credit for prior study or data, the accumulation of a collection, the borrowing of specimens, the exchange of specimens, the suppression of hard-toexplain data, the use of unfounded criticism, deliberate pre-empting of a field of study, use of research funds improperly, and all aspects involved in contacts with other taxonomists.

Not all of these are directly involved in publication, but most of them may be reflected in the published results. Specifically, professional ethics in taxonomic publication involves: (1) integrity, (2) the giving of credit for the help of others, (3) courtesy and forebearance in language, and (4) humility.

Integrity

Integrity requires scrupulous adherence to fact, presentation of all sides of a situation, leaving room for difference of opinion, and doing all the things that one would normally be expected to have done to establish facts. It does not require conformance to fads or popular schemes; in fact, it requires the taxonomist to follow his own conscience even when it challenges the ideas accepted by others.

The giving of credit for the help of others

No scientist or scholar produces his contribution to knowledge without help both from the past and from contemporary colleagues. In taxonomy most "new" work is a reworking of previous data, often with only a relatively small addition of fresh data and no really new ideas. Every person publishing in taxonomy should have a proper respect for the previous work, even though he is now in a position to improve on it. In a short time his work, also, will be improved on by his successors.

It is customary for this respect to take the form of direct acknowledgment. In taxonomic material itself, the references to previous work and the name of the author of each species fulfill this requirement. In the general aspects of books and papers there are a few more direct acknowledgments that may be appropriate. For example:

1. Cite the name of the collector of specimens used.
2. Acknowledge the specimens lent or donated.
3. Identify all unpublished data provided by others.
4. Acknowledge permission to use previously published material.
5. Give credit to persons preparing photos, drawings, tabulations, and so on if their contribution was more than clerical.
6. Acknowledge assistance of advisors, manuscript critics,

financial aid, facilities made available by institutions, and so on.

7. Acknowledge permission to quote from unpublished letters or manuscripts.

All of these admonitions must be treated with sense. It is possible to carry acknowledgment to ridiculous lengths. When material is brought together from many sources, the only reasonable acknowledgment may be in the bibliographic citations.

People whose business it is to help in the publication, but who have no other connection with taxonomy, need not be cited except in special cases. The overloading of a paper with references to every person who ever wrote on the subject may serve only to hide the contribution of the writer.

Courtesy and forebearance in language

There are admonitions to be found against the use of emotional phraseology, indulging in controversy, and personal attacks on other scientists. All of these admonitions will bear repetition, but they also cry out for a more understanding statement. Although personal attacks are never justified in taxonomic papers, emotion is not necessarily bad and may be worth communicating.

Controversy, furthermore, is the source of much clarification of ideas; the admonition should be rather not to take offense at argument or criticism, but to study it for its possible contribution.

Humility

Humility is not always highly regarded these days. What is intended here is the avoidance of making claims for the importance of conclusions. The facts will speak for themselves, regardless of whether the author claims "a transcendent hypothesis" or only the discovery of a "new" fact. The "new" fact is new to him and to the literature he happened to see.

It may not be new to the reader. The claim of newness does not increase the importance of the discovery, if it is one, and it doesn't soften the criticism if it turns out not to be. Much use of the first person in writing shows lack of humility. In formal writing, the first person is usually restricted to the Preface of books and to some essays. Whenever necessary, exceptions to this rule are allowable.

Never refer to the value of your own work. You are not a disinterested judge and no qualified colleague will pay any attention to your rating of yourself. Do not be misled into thinking you can shift the blame to the editor or the advertising department or someone else who speaks well of you.

A problem related to ethics is the attitude of a taxonomist to the new species which he describes. There have been persons who sought professional status or other recognition because of the number of new species they had named. Whatever the motives of individuals may have been in the past, professional taxonomists do not now rate another taxonomist by the number of species he has named.

Rather, they ask about the effectiveness of his revisions, classifications, and monographs. They look upon the publication of a new species not as an honor but as a responsibility-a responsibility to other taxonomists to have made this species recognizable, to have determined correctly that it is previously undescribed, and to make all information about it available to all other workers.

If there ever was a cult of new-species worshipers, it is fast dying out, even though there are still thousands of new species in museums waiting to be described.

TECHNICAL PROBLEMS OF PUBLICATION

There are many aspects of taxonomic publication that have special requirements. Some of these are discussed briefly below.

Descriptions

Many of the problems of publishing descriptions of animals or taxa are cited in Chapter 15, Descriptive Taxonomy. Only one further point requires emphasis here: in taxonomy description serves two purposes. First, it records and conveys to the reader the data about the thing described.

Second, it establishes part of the legal basis for a new name. For the latter, the describer must know and take into account the implications of the rules of nomenclature and the procedures which have come to be accepted as standard in that part of taxonomy.

Works that are relevant to this subject or have direct suggestions on preparation of descriptions include:

Ferris, G. *F. 1928. The Principles of Systematic Entomology.* Stanford, California; Stanford University Press.

Keen, A. M., and Muller, *S. W. 1956. Procedure in Taxonomy.* Stanford, California; Stanford University Press.

Mayr, Linsley, and Usinger. *1953. Methods and Principles of Systematic Zoology.* New York; McGraw-Hill Book Co.

Rensch, B. *1934. Kurze Anweizung fiir zoologisch-systematische Studien.* Leipzig; Akademische Verlagsgesellschaft M.B.H.

International Code of Zoological Nomenclature. . . . London; International Trust for Zoological Nomenclature. *1961.*

Keys

Publication problems with keys involve principally the style of key most useful to the person identifying specimens. Keys do not need to use characters of great biological significance. They are often most effective with simple characters that happen to have clear-cut distinctions that can be readily used.

Keys are not classifications; there should not be any attempt to combine the two, as this generally does violence to both functions. Some forms of keys waste a great deal of space on the page by indenting each couplet farther than the one above it.

In a very short key this will not be serious, but in long keys it will probably be unreasonably expensive. In general, a key of several hundred couplets will be less useful than the same couplets arranged as a series of keys. For example, to key out the 124 families in Arnett's beetle book cited on p. 298 would have taken 123 couplets.

A mistake anywhere along the line, when using the key, might appear only at the end, when the identification proved to be wrong. Going clear back to the beginning to check all couplets could be unnecessarily time-consuming. Instead Dr. Arnett arranged the key to the order as separate keys to the four suborders and to ten groups within one of these.

The user can thus verify the suborder before proceeding to key out the group, and he can then verify the group before keying out the family. One of the keys is 47 couplets long, one has 27 couplets, and the rest have fewer than this.

Classifications

The technical problems of publishing classifications are those of obtaining a style which permits communication of a maximum amount of information. The major problem is the tendency of authors to try to incorporate into a classification what they believe to be the phylogeny of the groups. This would be appropriate if the phylogeny were an independent source of data. It is not, because all ideas of phylogeny are based on comparative studies of the taxonomic features of the animals.

The classification should use this comparative data directly; it should be little influenced by speculation on phylogeny based on these same data. There will, of course, always be some feed-back from phylogenetic studies to the taxonomic data on which it was based.

The conclusion here is that if phylogeny has been studied, it should be presented separately from the classification. The latter is a listing of groups, in which the sequence is a minor consideration and the history of no direct interest. (It is not intended here to imply that there is no connection between classification and phylogeny.

There is an inescapable connection in that they are both based on comparative data. Furthermore, every classification after the first one may be influenced by the phylogenies derived in large part from the earlier classification. It is principally the fact that a classification lends itself mechanically to phylogenetic conclusions that makes it seem that the two are connected, whereas the real connection is indirect, through the comparative data.

The taxa are probably of evolutionary origin, so we tend to think of them as evolutionary facts, whereas they are comparative facts which very likely justify evolutionary conclusions.)

Synonymies

The tracing of the various names applied to each genus or species and the forms of all these names is tedious and timeconsuming, but it is absolutely necessary to effective taxonomic work. The publication problems are chiefly the reactions of editors, who find the cost of the tabular material high and the reader appeal low. As a result synonymies are seldom published except in monographic works, where subsidized publication may be stretched to include them.

Bibliographies

On a small scale, bibliographies accompany many types of publications. They are more likely to be selective than exhaustive. Large bibliographies are difficult and expensive to publish, but they are of unending benefit to specialist, librarian, and general zoologist alike.

Nomenclatural Aspects

First of all, the publication of new zoological names is deeply affected by certain provisions of the rules of nomenclature. The 1961 Code specifies that any material affecting nomenclature must be published in conformance with the following stipulations

(1) It "must be reproduced in ink on paper by some method that assures numerous identical copies." This means that microfilms, microcards, and other photographic reproductions are not acceptable. It also means that mimeographing and hectographing (Ditto or spirit

duplicating) are not to be used.

(2) It "must be issued for the purpose of scientific, public, permanent record." This means that it cannot be intended only for those at a particular meeting, nor for a limited group of colleagues or students. It also means that distribution of a few copies of proof sheets is neither acceptable nor sufficient.

(3) It "must be obtainable by purchase or free distribution." This is to ensure the availability of copies to the zoological world at large.

(4) The document must not be anonymous, although before 1953 such anonymous publications were usually held to be acceptable.

(5) "Mere deposit of a document in a library" does not satisfy the distribution requirements, whether or not it is suitably printed. This rules out dissertations or theses which are made in too few copies for general distribution.

If nomenclature is affected by the proposed publication, the author should conform to these requirements exactly. They are not unreasonable. While they do not really ensure satisfactory methods of printing and distribution, they are helpful in eliminating unsatisfactory methods.

Languages

The description of new taxa, to be acceptable under the rules of nomenclature, should be written in English, French, German, Italian, or Latin. This is an attempt to make all new publication available to all workers, who cannot possibly deal with all the many languages of the earth.

In the past only local works have been published in other languages, but important works have been published in more recent years in Japanese and Russian. So far as the zoologists represented in the International Congresses of Zoology are concerned, these five languages are the acceptable ones for all papers of nomenclatural interest. Most taxonomic papers by Dutch, Danish, and Swedish writers, for example, are published in English.

Many papers in the past have had descriptive matter in Latin, regardless of the language of the text, and, of course, in botany a Latin diagnosis is always required. Historical documentation. Because nomenclatural aspects are usually prominent in taxonomic studies, it is necessary to know the entire history of every taxon discussed, especially the name-history.

It is therefore frequently necessary to include chronological summaries, often in the form of synonymies. A high degree of accuracy must be maintained in these items in every publication.

Spelling of names. In nomenclature, all erroneous spellings become a matter of record and are studied, as they *may* produce real problems later on. Spelling variations should be avoided, even at the cost of extra proofreading, final checks back to original sources, and letter-for-letter rechecking at every opportunity.

PREPARATION OF PAPERS

The remainder of this section will be devoted principally to listing some of the books that will aid a taxonomist in planning, writing, and obtaining publication of technical papers.

Manuals of Style

Most serial publications, in which nearly all taxonomic papers are published, require certain special forms of presentation. These may affect title, abstracts, tables, illustrations and their legends, and bibliographies. The manuscript must be prepared with these style requirements in mind, or it will have to be done over.

Preparation of Illustrations

What to illustrate and how to prepare the illustrations for publication are discussed in numerous books and papers.

Common Errors

There are some common errors that may be pointed out individually because of their special applicability to taxonomic papers.

Names in Apposition in Titles

When a species is referred to by both common name and Latin name in a title, the names are separated by a comma. The names are in apposition-they refer to exactly the same thing.

"Notes on the housefly, *Musca domestica.*" (1)

Here, "the housefly" is not merely a loose expression for some indoor insect but a definite name for the species *Musca domestica.* Since "the housefly" and *"Musca domestica"* refer to exactly the same thing, they are said to be in apposition.

"Notes on the fly *Musca domestica.*" (2)

Here, "the fly" is not equivalent to the species named and is therefore not separated by a comma. The latter expression (2) is equivalent to saying "the particular kind of fly which is called *Musca domestica.*" The former expression (1) is equivalent to saying "the housefly (also known as *Musca domestics).*"

These two forms can be distinguished only with knowledge of what "housefly" and "fly" denote. The word "the" is restrictive, but it is not equal to the task of restricting "fly" to any one species, as it can with "housefly."

"Notes on a fly, *Musca domestica.*" (3)

Here, the comma is used even though "fly" is indefinite, because "a fly" is in apposition to the Latin name. The Latin name could be omitted without making the title entirely meaningless. In the second form above, omission of the Latin name would leave only "Notes on the fly." This is taxonomically meaningless, because there is no such thing as "the fly."

The article "a" in this situation always denotes a particular thing, although ordinarily it is permissive; therefore in such cases it involves apposition and a comma.

The rule must be that if the two expressions are fully synonymous (if they refer to exactly the same thing), either expression could be omitted without making the entire statement meaningless; they are in apposition and must be separated by a comma. If not, the comma must be omitted.

Actual examples of an erroneous and of a correct use of the comma are the following:

"The locust, *Zonocerus variegates L.*" (4)

(The comma should have been omitted, because that species is not "the locust" but only "a locust.")

"The morphology . . . of the green peach aphid, *Myxus persicae* (Sulzer)." (5)

(The comma is correct because the two expressions are fully synonymous, in apposition; either one could be omitted.)

Use of Abbreviations

There is a great temptation to abbreviate words or names in certain circumstances. Although it is sometimes permissible to do so, it is best to avoid this wherever possible.

Where the Latin name of a species is repeated several times in a page or section, it is permissible and sometimes actually helpful to abbreviate the generic name after the first use of it.

Musca domestica . . . M. domestica . . . M. domestica (6)

It must be noted, however, that if more than one such genus is abbreviated in a paper, there may be two with the same initial.

In descriptions or technical material, abbreviations may be troublesome to the reader. Even so-called standard abbreviations may not be familiar to students in other parts of the world. Much taxonomic work is eventually worldwide in interest. It is therefore best to write out words and terms wherever possible, even in charts and tables.

In bibliographies most journals and publishers will permit or insist upon abbreviation of the scientific periodicals cited. The author must conform to these requirements, but it is always better to err on the side of writing out too much rather than too little. Most systems would abbreviate *Revue d'Entomologie* as *Rev. Ent.* However, there are also journals entitled *Revue Entomologique* and *Revista de Entomologia.*

Both of these would also be abbreviated as *Rev. Ent.* To be explicit, these must all be written out. It is a mistake to assume that there is no duplication of an abbreviation, unless one has at least checked the *Union List of Serials.*

An excellent but little-known system of abbreviating names of journals has been in use for many years by the Smithsonian Institution and the U.S. National Museum. In essence, this system recommends: (1) write out all titles consisting of a single word; (2) use all the principal words of the full title; (3) never insert words not in the title, except in parenthesis; (4) write out in full all words of one syllable and all proper nouns; (5) abbreviate other words by stopping before the second vowel; (6) if any confusion is anticipated, write out the word or add syllables; and (7) use the exact wording of the full title and retain its order. Exceptions are noted for compound germanic words and for all cases where confusion between titles may occur.

Use of generic name alone. It is common in non-taxonomic papers to find references to the structure or behavior or some feature of a genus. For example:

It is obvious that no genus has a proboscis and that it is impossible to draw a picture of a genus. It must be assumed in such cases that the author means "in some unspecified species of *Gyrocotyle.*" This would be clearer if it were written ". . . of *Gyrocotyle sp.,*" meaning "of one species of *Gyrocotyle,*" or, if all the species share this feature, as ". . . of *Gyrocotyle* spp.," meaning "of the species of *Gyrocotyle.*"

Where various animals are being discussed, and there is only one species per genus, it does no great harm to refer to them by the generic name alone. The generic name assumes something of the nature of a common name, and some writers do not italicize it in such a situation. For example:

Necator americana is the original American hookworm. . . . Necator (8) is a worm of historic sociological significance.

It would seem to be a pomposity to repeat the scientific name in such instances. It is only necessary to be careful that there is no possibility of confusion.

The First Subspecies

When in a previously known species a population is found that is recognized to be a subspecies, there is a tendency to record the facts in such a manner as this:

X-us albus David (1866). Black, length 7-9 inches. Range: New England to Virginia.

X-us albus carolinensis n. subsp. Tinged with gray, length 6-8 inches. Range: Coast of South Carolina.

The new population has a few features that fall partly outside the range of the previously known specimens, and it comes from a peripheral locality.

Assuming that zoologically the new population *does* represent a new subspecies, the above descriptions are misleading. The *species* occurs from New England to South Carolina (or from New England to Virginia, and in South Carolina). Its specimens are black or grayish black, 6-9 inches in length. Only the nominotypical (or nominate) subspecies *X-us albus albus* fits the first description above.

The rule should be that every species consists of at least one subspecies; if there is only one recognized, it is not mentioned; if there are two or more, the nominate one must be distinguished, and any description given under the specific name *must* cover *all* the subspecies.

Quotation of Foreign Languages

In quoting from works in foreign languages, and especially in citing foreign titles in bibliographies, it not infrequently happens that alterations are made in the orthography (spelling). The names of authors, titles of papers, and names of journals should be quoted in the exact form of the original, so far as physically possible, and any deviation should be shown as such.

In German, all nouns are capitalized; in French, accent marks are universally used; in many languages, capitalizing of particles in personal names is a matter of individual preference and cannot be changed by others. For example:

W. C. van Heurn
V. S. Van der Goot
J. De La Paz
J. R. de la Torre Bueno
M. A. V. D'Andretta
J. d'Aguilar
J. C. Von Bloeker
H. von Boetticher
A. M. da Costa Lima
E. A. Da Rosa
J. de Beaumont
L. A. P. DeConinck

Errors in the quotation of names and titles may be the fault of the author, the editor, or the printer. In any case, it is the responsibility of the author to see that the final form is correct.

Over-use of Technical Terms

All science uses technical terminology and finds that accuracy in communication depends upon accuracy of definition and use. It is, however, possible to over-do the use of such terms. The following example was quoted by J. R. de la Torre Bueno in an editorial entitled "Heavy, Heavy Science." It was originally published in the *New York Sun.*

"It would appear from what evidence is available that the act of oviposition is immediately stimulated by the crepuscular diminution in the intensity of illumination and the rise in relative humidity as the diurnal temperature decreases."

Translation:

"Egg-laying seems to be stimulated by twilight and the dampness of evening."

In addition to unnecessary use of technical terms in ordinary writing, there is a tendency for taxonomists to coin terms for use in their descriptive work. Sometimes these are necessary and reasonably employed. At other times they are synonyms of equally acceptable terms or not even needed at all.

New terms should be proposed only after thorough search has shown that no suitable word is available, and then only with assurance that it is correctly formed. Dictionaries are full of useful but forgotten words that can be effectively used. A useful book is:

R. W. Brown. *1954. Composition of Scientific Words.* Published by the author. (Obtainable from Smithsonian Institution, Washington, D.C.)

Inadequate Titles

In addition to misusing commas, many faults can be found in the titles of papers and books. They may be too short or too long, indefinite or unnecessarily detailed, ambiguous or so specific as to be intelligible only to a specialist. It would be difficult to illustrate all of these.

Titles that are too short and too indefinite include:

Nouveautes diverses.

Remarques en passant.

Geanderte Namen.

New neotropical myrmecophiles.

Miscellaneous notes and new species.

Titles that are too long and include unnecessary matter are:

Esploracion cientifica praeticada par orden del Supremo Gobierno i segun las instrucciones del doctor don R. A. Philippi, par don Carlos Juliet, ayudante de la Comision esploradora del mar i cost as de Chiloe i Llanquihue, a bordo del "Covadonga."

Illustrations o f exotic entomology, containing upwards o f six hundred and fifty figures and descriptions of foreign insects, interspersed with remarks and reflections on their nature and properties. [With subtitle] A new edition brought down to the present state o f the science, with the systematic characters o f each species, synonyms, indexes, and other additional matter.

A title that is specific but ambiguous as to the locality of the specimens is:

Eine neue Odacantha (Ins., Col.: Carabidae) des Senckenberg-Museums. Titles intelligible only to a specialist on the (unnamed) group are:

Stilpnastus nov. gen.

Addenda au genre *Petalium.*

La larve du genre *Scirtes.*

On the genus *Opoleon, Gorh.*

Synopsis of the species of the tribe Lebiini.

A title should always be carefully selected with at least the following considerations in mind:

1. Reasonable brevity is desirable.
2. The necessary information must be communicated.
3. Unnecessary information should be omitted.
4. Both general and specific information should be given. 5. The title should aid in indexing the article by subject.
6. It should not include punctuation, abbreviations, or local words not intel ligible everywhere in the world.

THE DISTRIBUTION OF PUBLICATIONS

Taxonomic publications are normally distributed by two rather different means. In the first place, papers published in serials (magazines, journals, reports, occasional papers, or other named series) are automatically distributed to the mailing list of that serial, whether by subscription, exchange, or gift.

If published in or as a separate book, the sale of the book will automatically provide this primary distribution. An author has little to do with this aspect, except to consider the extent and selection of distribution in deciding where to publish his paper. In the case of commercially published books, this primary distribution will probably be the only type of distribution.

In the second place, some serials provide the author with extra copies of his paper removed from the volume. These copies are called reprints, author's extras, or separates. These terms are often used loosely, but they do have definite meanings that can be readily distinguished.

Author's extras are pages removed unchanged from extra copies of the publication. They frequently contain parts of other papers and may not show the place and date of publication. This fact causes them to be sometimes regarded as a nuisance, but they are the most accurate type of separate copy so far as exact duplication of the serial paper is concerned. (The bibliographic reference can and should be added later.)

Separates (or separata) are copies printed from the same type as the original but with all extraneous matter eliminated. If the article begins in the center of a page in the serial, it will begin in the same place in the separate. It may have a line of type added to show the bibliographic reference of the original, but it is otherwise identical to the original (in completeness, arrangement, and pagination).

Reprints are, strictly speaking, copies rearranged to fit most satisfactorily on a page and thus not printed at the same time as the original but from substantially the same type. Pages may be renumbered, the text arranged differently on the page, new type set for the title, etc. These copies give the least assurance of duplication of the original and are definitely disadvantageous in taxonomic papers. The word reprint is often used loosely to include all three types of copies.

In working from separated copies of articles, especially older ones, it is very necessary to recognize those which differ in any material way from the original. It is often desirable to compare a copy with the serial, and then to note upon it that it has been so compared and found to be (or not to be) in agreement with it in all pertinent ways.

The purpose of these extra copies is direct distribution by the author to interested colleagues. Whether the copies are supplied free (still a common practice in taxonomic journals) or are purchased by the author (usually at cost), they are mailed out to specialists on the particular group to serve as convenient personal copies in place of the inconvenient library set of the periodical.

The mailing of "reprints" is a kind of professional courtesy. It frequently results in an informal exchange of papers, to the benefit of both parties. The mailing may be as soon as possible after publication, or it may be periodic, containing several papers at a time.

The purchase and distribution of separates is a good practice for several reasons.

1. It makes papers available in the most convenient form to those in the field most likely to profit from them.
2. It serves as a notice that the writer is still active and is interested in other people's papers on this subject.
3. It makes the paper available to persons who do not have ready access to the complete serial.
4. It serves as a record for the writer's employer that he is producing research, and aids in the maintenance of files of his work.
5. It enables a teacher to use copies of his papers (and those of others also) in his teaching, as sources of data, as examples of methods, and so on.

DEALERS IN SECONDHAND BOOKS

In a few branches of taxonomy there are dealers specializing in books of technical nature. Some of these sell also papers of smaller size and even reprints. Because the normal mark-up on such secondhand items is high, often 100% or more, some taxonomists have looked upon these dealers as unprincipled profiteers.

It is doubtful if any of them ever made more than a moderate living. A more realistic view is that they are really indispensable and should be encouraged to continue their service to the science. Such dealers provide places where reprints and monographs can be obtained by those who need them.

They are an unexcelled means of distributing these papers. A person who is willing to buy a paper is probably one who will use it. What better way is there to ensure that copies will get to the persons who really need them? Some taxonomists make a practice of giving or selling a few reprints of their papers to secondhand-book dealers. The practice has much to commend it.

12

ORIGIN

One of the greatest mysteries of biology, one that may never be fully solved, is that of the origin of life on Earth. Fossil evidence suggests that microscopic life was abundant at least 3.5 billion years ago, and the first living things may have appeared less than half a billion years after Earth's crust solidified.

A plausible mechanism for the origin of life is suggested by the results of experiments in which presumed ancient environmental conditions were mimicked. This chapter deals with spontaneous generation, comparative metabolism, stromatolites and other fossils, the geologic time table, meteorites, the primitive atmosphere, and chemical evolution. Else where in this chapter, we shall be dealing with the diversity of life-the different kinds of organisms that now surround us, as well as those that once lived but are now extinct.

Then, in the other part of this chapter, our attention will turn to evolution, the process that led to such diversity on our planet. Now, however, let us consider the beginnings of life itself. How did the first living inhabitants of Earth get here? Did they arise in a single, instantaneous event; did they come from outer space; or did they result from the continued operation of chance events and simple chemical reactions over hundreds of millions of years?

SPONTANEOUS GENERATION: OLD IDEAS

It was only in the last century or two that serious doubts arose about the origin of life. The practical person "knew" that new life appeared all the time: flies and maggots from rotting meat, and barnyard manure, lice from sweat, glowworms from rotting logs, eels and fish

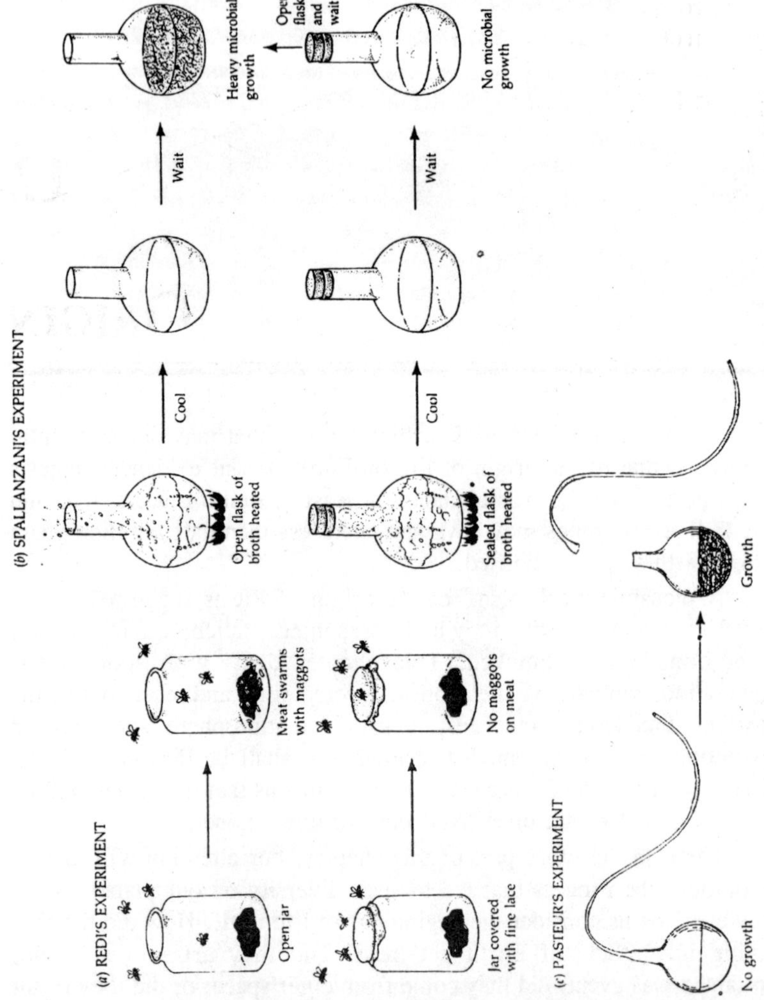

Figure 12.1: Tests of spontaneous Generaeration.

from sea mud, and frogs and mice from moist earth. No less an authority than Aristotle had vouched for such commonsense observations.

For over two thousand years, *spontaneous generation*—the formation of living things from nonliving matter—was accepted as a fact of nature. A few people questioned whether spontaneous generation ever really occurred.

Did maggots really arise spontaneously from decaying meat, for example? Francesco Redi, an Italian physician, demonstrated in 1668 that maggots in meat were only the larvae of flies and that if the meat were protected so that adult flies could not lay their eggs no maggots appeared. However, when the Dutch lens grinder and microscope maker Anton van Leeuwenhoek discovered microorganisms in 1676, spontaneous generation received new support.

Although many people were ready to concede that worms and maggots did not appear spontaneously from nonliving matter, they were less confident about the subvisible creatures that Leeuwenhoek could find everywhere. The Italian biologist Lazzaro Spallanzani showed that, if broths were placed in sealed containers and adequately sterilized, they remained devoid of life.

However, he failed to convince his contemporaries, partly because others were performing the same experiments with less care and obtaining different results. Also, some people objected that Spallanzani's techniques not only killed the microorganisms already present but also rendered the air unfit for the generation and growth of new ones.

Experimental methods were not good enough to rule out spontaneous generation for those who wanted to believe in it. The great French chemist and microbiologist Louis Pasteur finally laid spontaneous generation to rest in 1862, in response to a competition for a prize set up by the French Academy of Sciences.

Pasteur won the prize for a series of meticulous and conclusive experiments that showed that microorganisms came only from other microorganisms and that a genuinely sterile broth or solution would remain sterile indefinitely unless contaminated by living creatures. His most elegant experiment involved swannecked flasks, which were open to the air (ruling out the "spoiled air" objection raised against Spallanzani).

The flasks were heated strongly to kill any microorganisms present and then cooled slowly; the shape of the necks kept new microorganisms from falling into the nutrient medium in the flasks-and no new growth ever appeared. The old aphorism, *omne vivum e vivo* ("all life from life") became dogma. Pasteur delivered his famous lecture to the French Academy in April, 1864.

On the fourteenth of May that year, a meteorite shower fell near Orgueil, France. A century later, scientists would find these meteorite fragments helpful in studying the evolution of life, as we shall see presently. They also uncovered a century-old fraud that misfired.

Spontaneous Generation Revisited

Pasteur answered an old question, but his results posed a new and more fundamental question: If all life comes from preexisting life, where did the first life come from? In spite of its inherent interest, this question did not attract serious scientific attention for over half a century.

In 1924 the Russian biologist Alexander I. Oparin published a short monograph in Moscow entitled *The Origin of Life*. Although it was never translated from Russian and had no impact on scientific thought at the time, it laid out a sequence of events and conditions that would now be accepted by most biologists as similar to those that actually did lead to the beginnings of life on Earth.

Five years later, the eminent British biologist J. B. S. Haldane independently arrived at similar ideas and published them in *The Rationalist Annual,* again to little effect. Not until after Oparin expanded his ideas into a book-Origin *of Life,* which was published in 1936 and translated into other languages-did the problem of the appearance of life on Earth receive serious attention.

Experimental work finally got underway in the 1950s, when suitable techniques and equipment became available; and it continues today. Any reasonable theory for the origin of life on Earth must rest on three kinds of evidence: evidence for a common genetic and metabolic heritage in modern organisms (the province of comparative biochemistry), fossil traces of ancient life (studied by paleobiologists), and laboratory experiments simulating plausible early Earth conditions.

To these we should like to be able to add a fourth kind of evidence: comparisons of independent appearances of life on more than one planet-the province of "exobiology." In fact, no extraterrestrial life forms have yet been discovered; but exobiological studies have contributed importantly to our ideas about chemical evolution on early Earth. (These studies have dealt with topics such as the atmospheres of Jupiter and Saturn, molecules in interstellar space, and the chemistry of meteoritic stones.)

Evidence from comparative biochemistry, paleobiology, and laboratory simulations has converged to suggest a general picture of the origin of life. We shall examine these types of evidence, one at a time, and then suggest a series of events that may have occurred long ago on this planet. At the present stage of knowledge, such a scenario is undoubtedly incomplete, but it is unlikely to be in serious error in its main points.

A COMMON METABOLIC HERITAGE

The central metabolic processes of modern eukaryotes are essentially the same. As discussed in other chapter of this book, organisms extract energy from foods by glycolysis, followed by either fermentation or

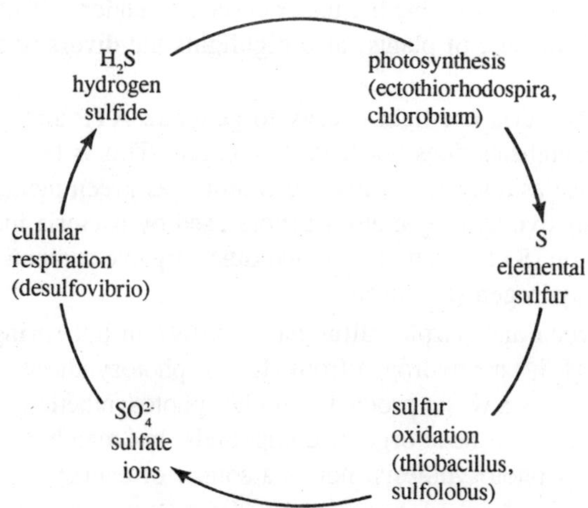

Figure 12.2: Sulfur in Prokaryotic Energy Metabolism.

aerobic respiration. Plants, as well as some protists, have the added ability to synthesize foods for later use by the process of photosynthesis. These patterns are evident throughout the eukaryotic kingdoms.

Many other metabolic reactions are identical or closely similar in all eukaryotes; and, where they differ, they are often merely variations on the same basic theme. In terms of metabolism, the real diversity of life is much more evident in prokaryotes.

The prokaryotes display a staggering variety of mechanisms for energy storage and food synthesis that have no parallel in the eukaryotes. For example, oxygen gas is not the only possible oxidizing agent for cellular respiration. Many bacteria use oxygen just as do plants and animals.

Others, such as *Desulfovibrio desulfuricans,* can use sulfuric acid for respiration, a process that yields hydrogen sulfide (H_2S) instead of water (H_2O). Still others can conduct reactions in which carbon dioxide is thé oxidizing agent; these organisms liberate methane gas (as in the methanogens) or acetic acid in place of water.

The denitrifying bacteria oxidize their foods with nitrate ions (NO_3) and give off nitrous oxide (N_2O), nitrogen gas (N_2), or ammonia (NH_3). Of all the possible energy-yielding chemical reactions involving oxidation, the eukaryotes use the one that reduces oxygen gas to water. Even the idea that respiration itself is a universal metabolic heritage is disproved by bacteria. Many bacteria manage quite well with only the energy they receive from fermentation and do not respire at all.

Moreover, a number of plants and fungi, as well as a few protists, have the option of anaerobic life under certain conditions. Photosynthesis, a universal attribute of plants, also highlights the diversity of bacterial metabolism.

Many bacteria use light energy to generate ATP and NADH, but their photosynthesis does not liberate oxygen. This is because they do not use water as a source of hydrogen atoms as green plants do. Some of the alternative hydrogen atom donors used by bacteria include H2S, thiosulfate ion ($S_2O_3^-$), fatty acids, and other organic compounds-or even molecular hydrogen (H_2) itself.

The green and purple sulfur bacteria live in hot springs or other sources of H_2S, take hydrogen from H_2S for photosynthesis, and release sulfate (SO_4^{2-}) as a waste product. Another photosynthetic group, purple nonsulfur bacteria, need organic compounds, but mainly as a source of hydrogen for photosynthesis, not as a source of energy.

Other bacteria are not photosynthetic at all but obtain energy from chemical reactions. A few species of *Pseudomonas* use the energy of the reaction between hydrogen and oxygen to synthesize carbohydrates from CO_2 and H_2. Some sulfur bacteria (thiobacilli) are not photosynthetic but obtain their energy by oxidizing H_2S to sulfur, or sulfur or thiosulfate to sulfate ions. Other *Thiobacillus* species oxidize ferrous ions (Fe^{2+}) to insoluble ferric hydroxide. Some nitrifying bacteria oxidize ammonia to nitrite (NO_2^-), and others oxidize nitrite to nitrate (NO_3^-).

The important point to recognize in bacterial metabolism is that the eukaryotes use just one particularly efficient set of reactions from among the many possible pathways. (The reasons for such specialization by the eukaryotes relate to characteristics of the environment in which they arose and, possibly, to their suspected endosymbiotic origin)

The genuine diversity of life is obscured if one looks only at the eukaryotes. The bacteria help one to see what *is not* common to all organisms.

What the Common Heritage Tells Us

What remains after all the variation is stripped away is the process of *glycolysis*. There is no type of living cell-bacterial, protist, plant, animal, or fungal-that does not extract energy from organic molecules; and all except certain bacteria use glucose as a standard fuel.

Because comparative biochemistry implies evolutionary ancestry as clearly as does comparative anatomy, one may conclude that the original ancestor of all organisms, prokaryotes and eukaryotes alike, absorbed its food from its surroundings and extracted energy from it without the use of molecular oxygen.

In short, it was almost certainly an anaerobic heterotroph. The presence of glycolysis in all cellular organisms provides a valuable clue to the conditions under which life began. Life probably emerged when and at a site where organic compounds were abundant, not only as sources of energy, but as sources of the materials from which life could evolve in the first place.

There was probably little or no oxygen gas, for aerobic respiration is so much more efficient than fermentation alone that it is difficult to imagine that oxygen-using organisms would not have evolved at the beginning, had O_2 been readily available. Another argument against the presence of free oxygen is the very existence of large supplies of organic matter. Had O_2 been prevalent, it would have spontaneously oxidized the supply of organic matter much faster than it could have been produced by nonbiological means.

One sometimes overlooks the fact that the vast amount of organic matter on the surface of the planet today and the gaseous O_2 around it are both results (in part) of the activities of living organisms. If all life were to end today, in a few thousand years all of the organic matter would have been oxidized to CO_2 and water, and the remaining atmospheric oxygen would have been locked up in Earth's crust in the form of mineral oxides. In short, the atmosphere of early Earth lacked more than transient traces of free oxygen.

THE FOSSIL RECORD

The fossil record of living organisms is relatively plentiful for most of the last 600 million years. Any recognizable trace of an organic structure preserved from prehistoric times is a fossil (Figure 3a). Some of the most dramatic examples are the mammoths that were frozen intact in the icy soil of Siberia.

The mineral cast of a bone of a vertebrate and the calcified shell of a mollusk are also fossils. In such specimens, the original calcium carbonate or other hard material was gradually dissolved and replaced with mineral substances by the infiltration of ground water. A fossil may consist of nothing more than the cast of the impression of the hard surface of a bone or shell in the originally soft sediment.

Occasionally the only trace of an organism is its footprint or the remains of a burrow that it dug. One of the best ways for a particular organism to become a fossil is to die in some favorable spot, such as in quicksand, where it will be quickly covered by sediment destined to become part of a long-lasting geologic formation. As millennia pass, mud turns to shale, sand to sandstone, and peat to coal. The traces of the organism locked in such sediments may remain essentially unchanged for hundreds of millions of years.

When the rocks are later split open by the geologist's hammer (or, in the case of more ancient rocks, studied by other means), the fossils are exposed to inspection. Fossils can usually be dated according to the age of the rock strata in which they lie. As a general rule, the deepest strata are the oldest, provided that the formation has not been drastically folded or deformed.

The age of the rock can be determined by techniques using trace quantities of radioactive isotopes of uranium, thorium, rubidium, or potassium, and the stable end products of their decay. Uranium-238, for example, spontaneously decays into lead at a slow but precisely known rate. By comparing the amount of ^{238}U still present in a rock or mineral with the amount of lead derived from its decay, geochemists can estimate the age of a sample within an error seldom in excess of 5 percent. Different kinds of fossils are used to correlate rock strata in different locations and to delineate eras in the history of life.

Geologists divide Earth's history into four *eons*: the Hadean Eon (beginning with the origin of the planet 4.5 billion years ago and extending for approximately 700 million years), the Archean Eon, the Proterozoic ("primitive life") Eon, and the Phanerozoic ("visible life") Eon.

The Proterozoic and Phanerozoic Eons are subdivided into *eras*, and the eras of the Phanerozoic Eon are further subdivided into *periods*. The oldest probable fossils discovered so far are 3.5 billion years old, which means that life was already abundant when Earth was only 1 billion years old, in the middle of the Archean Eon. Geologists believe that the solid crust of Earth may not have formed until approximately 4 billion years ago, which would indicate that life appeared only a few hundred million years after the crust itself.

Numbers in the billions are so large that they have little meaning for most readers. To convey a real sense of the relative age of fossil organisms, it is useful to scale down the history of Earth to a hypothetical 30-day month. Each "day" on that geologic calendar represents approximately 150 million years.

On that calendar, the Hadean, Archean, and Proterozoic Eons stretch across the first 26 days. The Cambrian Period, which opened the Paleozoic Era 600 million years ago, marks a great divide in the fossil record.

By the dawn of the Cambrian, on the twenty-seventh day, the

Table 12.1: Earth's Geologic History.

EON	*ERAERA*	*PERIOD*	*BEGAN*
Hadean			4.5 bya
Archean			3.8 bya
Proterozoic			2.5 bya
Phanerozoic			600 mya
	Paleozoic	Cambrian	600
	mya	Ordovician	500
	mya	Silurian	440
	mya	Devonian	400
	mya	Carboniferous	345
	mya	Permian	290 mya
	Mesozoic	Triassic	245
	mya	Jurassic	195
	mya	Cretaceous	138 mya
	Cenozoic	Tertiary	66 mya
		Quaternary	2 mya

ancient seas teemed with life. Representatives of every modern group had appeared, except for vertebrates, mosses, and vascular plants.

Precambrian Rocks

Below the earliest Cambrian strata there is a striking dearth of fossils. Various explanations have been offered for the apparently dramatic explosion of life in the Cambrian Period: changes in the radiation level of the sun, climatic changes, an increase in the oxygen content of the atmosphere past a critical point for respiration, or, simplest of all, the replacement of soft-bodied creatures with organisms having shells, armor, and skeletons that would leave more substantial fossil remains.

Moreover, in later eras, many of the Precambrian rocks have been heated or deformed by geologic processes in ways that would tend to obliterate faint traces in the fossil record. Some years ago, it was thought that the record of Precambrian life was meager and unimpressive. However, the situation has changed because paleontologists now know how and where to look for the microscopic remains of one-celled organisms.

If we can rid ourselves of the bias that equates plants and animals with life and regards all microorganisms as pretty much alike, then we see that the record of Precambrian life is surprisingly rich. Over most of the surface of Earth, Precambrian rocks are covered by later deposits. The "shields," where large areas of Precambrian rock are exposed or at least accessible-are shown in Figure elsewhere in this chapter. Some of the most convincing examples of Precambrian life are listed in Table II, and the locations of these finds are marked on the map.

ANCIENT PROKARYOTES

Modern cyanobacteria and other photosynthetic bacteria that inhabit shallow salt and fresh waters as well as thermal pools lay down successive calcareous (calcium-containing) and siliceous (silicon-containing) layers that form composite, flat to domed structures called *stromatolites*.

An example of a modern stromatolite is shown in Figure elsewhere in this chapter. The stromatolite grows layer by layer, with the apex

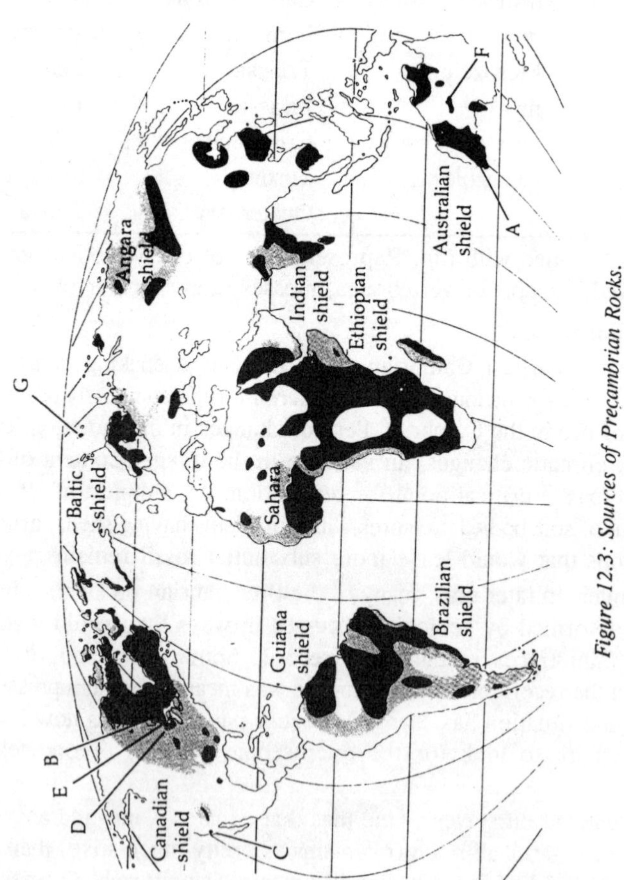

Figure 12.3: Sources of Precambrian Rocks.

of the dome upward, like a stack of nested thimbles. The oldest well-dated fossils of likely biological origin are 3.5-billion-year-old sedimentary structures from a site in the torrid desert of Western Australia, ironically called North Pole.

Three lines of evidence indicate the presence of traces of life in the ancient rocks of North Pole. The first line is based on stromatolitelike structures found in at least two separate samples of rocks, approximately 2 kilometers apart. These structures suggest the occurrence of cyanobacteria or other photosynthetic bacteria in the waters that covered parts of North Pole 3.5 billion years ago.

The second line of evidence is the discovery of hollow, spherical, carbon-containing structures ranging in diameter from 1 to 12 micrometers-approximately the size of modern prokaryotic cells-in rock samples from the site. Several groups of investigators have discovered what appear to be carboncontaining structures corresponding to fossils of filamentous bacteria; this is the third line of evidence.

Each of these pieces of evidence is subject to criticism, but it is highly unlikely that all are simultaneously invalid. These North Pole (Australia) fossils are the oldest convincing signs of life that have been found so far on this planet. It is likely that the methanogens (bacteria that produce methane from carbon dioxide) arose before the other kinds of bacteria that we know today.

If this is true, it could indicate that a substantial amount of evolution had already occurred well over 3.5 billion years ago, in-asmuch as the North Pole fossils seem to be from cells that came after methanogens. Some investigators believe that photosynthetic organisms such as cyanobacteria, which apparently occur in North Pole fossils, could not have been the first living things to appear, and that it is likely that they were preceded by nonphotosynthetic forms for some considerable time.

One of the most dramatic and varied collections of Precambrian organisms occurs in a geologic formation called the Gunflint chert, an outcropping of 2-billion-year-old rock in the Canadian Shield, exposed near the Minnesota-Ontario border.

Thousands of canoelsts have followed the Gunflint Trail in an effort to get back to nature and turn back the clock a few years, never realizing that they could turn the clock back 2 billion years simply by examining the rocks at their feet. Unmistakable microorganisms, including cyanobacteria, have been found here, as well as organisms that lack close modern parallels. A variety of hydrocarbons are present in the Gunflint rocks, along with stromatolites.

Eukaryotic and Multicellular Organisms

The life forms discussed so far appear to have been prokaryotes-bacteria. The first true plants-green algae-may be represented in the Beck Springs dolomite from California. In these specimens, 1.4 to 1.2 billion years old, can be seen what have been claimed to be eukaryotic cells on the basis of their large diameters and of the branching patterns of the filamentous forms.

What appear to be cysts of eukaryotes have been found in shales approximately 1.4 billion years old from the Belt Supergroup, in Montana. If the interpretations of the Beck Supergroup fossils are correct (some paleobiologists have challenged them), then life arrived at the eukaryotic stage at least 600 to 800 million years before the Cambrian Period.

Both prokaryotic cyanobacteria and, according to some researchers, eukaryotic green algae (showing true nuclei) can be seen in the Bitter Springs chert from Australia, in surprisingly undistorted form. These rocks have been dated as between 900 and 700 million years old.

Thick-walled unicellular fossils, bearing thick, tubular spines, are beautifully preserved in 800-million-year-old rocks from Spitsbergen, Norway. These cells, approximately 500 μm in diameter, were clearly eukaryotic.

The first signs of multicellular life date to 670 million years ago, less than 100 million years before the Cambrian Period. The most ancient traces of multicellular organisms include worm tracks, body fossils, and impressions in sandstone of soft-bodied worms, jellyfish, and other creatures with no modern descendants.

Then the Precambrian fossil record blends into the Cambrian. The enormous increase in the number of fossils at the beginning of the Cambrian has yet to be explained satisfactorily. In brief, the interval from approximately 3.5 billion to 800 million years ago-from the seventh to the twenty-fourth day of the calendar in Figure elsewhere in this chpater can be described as the age of the prokaryotes.

At the beginning of this period, there flourished simple organisms morphologically similar to bacteria, some of which may have been photosynthetic. At that time, Earth probably had an atmosphere composed of nitrogen, carbon dioxide, water vapor, some carbon monoxide (CO), and perhaps a trace of hydrogen gas, but no free oxygen gas.

During the course of the following 2.5 billion years, these organisms diversified and developed both photosynthesis and cellular respiration, a development that led ultimately to eukaryotes and then to multicellular creatures that we would recognize as fungi, plants, and animals.

The main conclusion to emerge from recent studies of Precambrian microfossils is that well-preserved cellular remains of life are much more common on Earth and have been here much longer than anyone previously suspected. Many workers now estimate that the first living systems appeared some time during the first few hundred million years of the planet's existence-the first three days or so on our calendar.

METEORITES AND EXTRATERRESTRIAL LIFE

Even the most primitive Precambrian bacteria were probably complicated structures compared with nonliving matter. Their discovery sheds no light on the central question of chemical evolution: How did nonliving matter organize itself into a living system? One possibility is that life did not originate on Earth at all but was "seeded" here by an extraterrestrial object such as a meteor.

Earth is steadily bombarded with showers of meteors, presumably the debris of shattered asteroids; and some of this material contains organic molecules also found in living systems. Most meteorites are stony or metallic; but a relatively small number are soft and crumbly, with a high carbon content. These soft meteorites are called *carbonaceous chondrites*, and the meteorites that fell in a shower around Orgueil belong to this category.

They have been studied in recent years by several research groups using techniques similar to those used for detecting microscopic Precambrian fossils. The results have been inconclusive and have generated much heated debate. A variety of hydrocarbons have been found; and some of the organic compounds are optical isomers, which are usually associated with syntheses carried out by living organisms.

It should be noted that some amino acids found in meteorites are ones not found in organisms on this planet and, hence, cannot be contaminants introduced after the meteorites fell. Spheroids and other organized bodies of some complexity have been reported, but contamination of the meteorite samples by airborne spores and pollen has confused the issue.

In at least one instance, the organized bodies turned out to be ragweed pollen. Most of the complex organized bodies have proved to be terrestrial contaminants, and those that are definitely meteoric in origin are sufficiently simple that they may be natural mineral formations rather than artifacts of life. Perhaps one should be encouraged by the negative (or at least ambiguous) results of meteorite analysis. These trials serve as a control for the Precambrian fossil analyses.

Had the meteorite evidence looked fully as good as the Precambrian rock evidence, it would have been necessary to question our apparent ability to find "life" and "organisms" every-where we looked for them. The fact that such welldeveloped organisms are not found in meteorites is reassuring in regard to what has been found in terrestrial deposits.

The presence of hydrocarbons and other "biochemical" compounds in the meteorites indicates that at least the first step in molecular evolution-the formation of complex organic compounds-can occur spontaneously even in space. If these meteorites are not evidence for life on some shattered planet, they may be evidence for the universality of the organicchemical-rich environment in which life could develop.

PRIMITIVE EARTH: ATMOSPHERE AND ENERGY SOURCES

The air we now breathe consists of approximately four parts of nitrogen gas (N_2) to one part of oxygen (O_2), with traces of other gases such as carbon dioxide (CO_2), argon, and water vapor. From the earliest times, N_2 has probably been the most abundant gas in the atmosphere; but O_2 has been a latecomer, not appearing in significant quantity until at most 2.3 billion years ago.

Hydrogen gas, initially present in abundance, was lost, because it could not be held by Earth's gravitational field; but other, heavier gases such as carbon dioxide, water vapor, carbon monoxide, and perhaps ammonia and methane were apparently present in the primitive atmosphere.

Debate continues as to the exact composition of the atmosphere at the time life had its beginnings, but the key difference from today is the lack of significant amounts of oxygen gas. Another important aspect of the primitive environment was the array of energy sources at hand-sources of energy that could be used to drive endergonic chemical reactions.

Possible energy sources for syntheses would have been ultraviolet radiation from the sun, lightning, and, to lesser extents, radioactive decay in Earth's crust and heat from volcanoes and hot springs. By far the most plentiful energy source would have been visible light. However, visible light is relatively poor in energy per quantum; and it did not become significant in biochemistry until the evolution of photosynthesis.

Ultraviolet light, which has more energy per quantum, can break the covalent bonds in organic molecules and thus could have promoted a variety of chemical reactions leading to new products. This bond-breaking and synthetic activity is why ultraviolet radiation is lethal to microorganisms and is used to sterilize space-probe components.

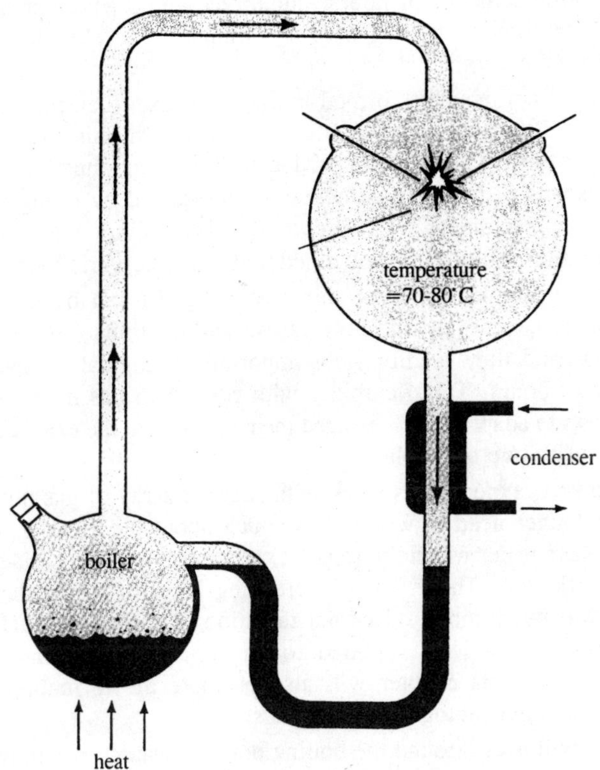

Figure 12.4: Miller's Apparatus.

Laboratory Simulation

By 1952 scientists, among them Harold Urey of the University of Chicago, were proposing that life evolved on Earth in a primitive reducing atmosphere of hydrogen (H_2), water, methane (CH_4), and ammonia (NH_3), from organic compounds that had been synthesized by nonbiological means. (Note that our picture of the composition of the primitive atmosphere has changed somewhat since then.)

In 1953, Stanley L. Miller, one of Urey's graduate students, made the first careful experiments to show that organic compounds, including amino acids, could be synthesized under plausible primitive-Earth conditions. Miller set up a recirculating system of hydrogen, ammonia, and methane gases and water vapor, and passed these gases over a spark discharge to simulate lightning.

After a week of circulation, he opened the flask and analyzed the contents; he found a great variety of organic acids and amino acids. In fact, within a matter of hours, numerous amino acids, simpler acids, and other compounds began to accumulate. The electrical discharge produced the compounds shown in Figure elsewhere in this chapter.

Those compounds, formed in the gas phase, then reacted in water to yield all the substances in Figure elsewhere in this chapter. Optical isomers of the products were produced in equal amounts-in this respect, the products differ from compounds synthesized by living organisms. Further experiments by Miller and many others have shown that comparable results can be obtained under a wide variety of conditions.

For example, different mixtures of gases can be used-different proportions, or even different gases, within limits (free O_2 must be absent)—and they readily yield important biological compounds in a matter of hours. This flexibility with respect to gas mixtures allowed biologists to adapt as they changed their views as to the exact composition of the primitive atmosphere.

In fact, experiments work with such an array of gas mixtures that we no longer need to worry very much about the *exact* nature of the atmosphere under which life began. Other energy sources besides lightning will work, too. There was no screening layer of ozone then, so that there was much more ultraviolet radiation falling on the surface of the planet-and ultraviolet supplied to an apparatus like that of Figure elsewhere in this chapter will also promote the formation of amino acids and other biological compounds.

So will heat (around the boiling point of water), which may mimic the environment around the volcanoes of the early Earth. In sum, experiments of the type pioneered by Miller work regardless of the exact chemical and physical conditions-as long as oxygen gas *is excluded-leading us to the assurance that reactions of this type happened regularly during the eons before life appeared.

Thus, over millions of years, the oceans of Earth became enriched with the products of these simple reactions. Laboratory simulations have shown that these products include amino acids, lipids, organic acids, simple sugars, the monomers of nucleic acids, and even compounds that are related to chlorophyll.

The easiest nucleic acid base to obtain in primitive Earth experiments, incidentally, is adenine. Cytosine, guanine, thymine, and uracil must be obtained by more complex reactions, but adenine is simply a pentamer of hydrogen cyanide. Irradiation of solutions of adenine, ribose, and phosphate compounds with ultraviolet light of wavelengths 240290 nm leads to the synthesis of ADP and ATP. It is likely that these high-

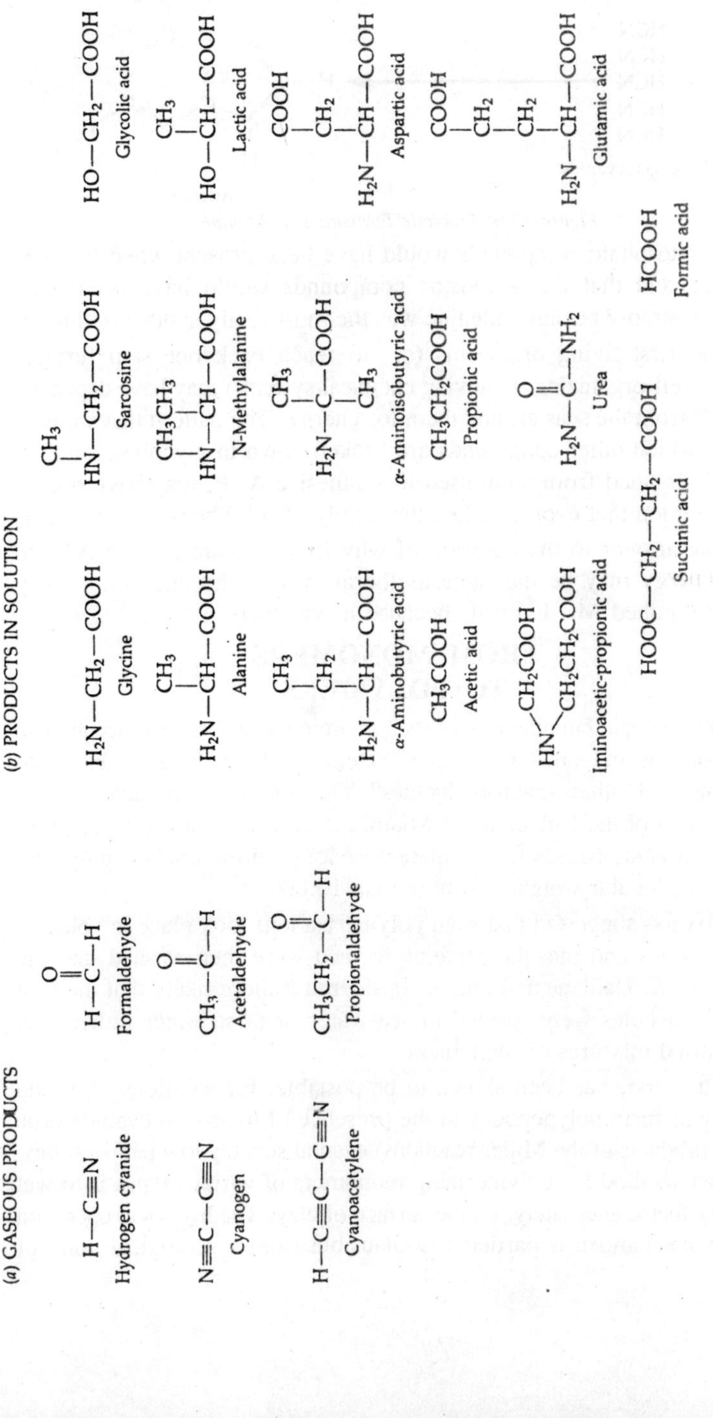

(*a*) GASEOUS PRODUCTS

$H{-}C{\equiv}N$
Hydrogen cyanide

$H{-}C({=}O){-}H$
Formaldehyde

$N{\equiv}C{-}C{\equiv}N$
Cyanogen

$CH_3{-}C({=}O){-}H$
Acetaldehyde

$H{-}C{\equiv}C{-}C{\equiv}N$
Cyanoacetylene

$CH_3CH_2{-}C({=}O){-}H$
Propionaldehyde

(*b*) PRODUCTS IN SOLUTION

$H_2N{-}CH_2{-}COOH$
Glycine

$HN(CH_3){-}CH_2{-}COOH$
Sarcosine

$HO{-}CH_2{-}COOH$
Glycolic acid

$H_2N{-}CH(CH_3){-}COOH$
Alanine

$HN(CH_3){-}CH(CH_3){-}COOH$
N-Methylalanine

$HO{-}CH(CH_3){-}COOH$
Lactic acid

$H_2N{-}CH(CH_2CH_3){-}COOH$
α-Aminobutyric acid

$H_2N{-}C(CH_3)_2{-}COOH$
α-Aminoisobutyric acid

$H_2N{-}CH(CH_2COOH){-}COOH$
Aspartic acid

CH_3COOH
Acetic acid

CH_3CH_2COOH
Propionic acid

$HN(CH_2COOH)(CH_2CH_2COOH)$
Iminoacetic-propionic acid

$H_2N{-}C({=}O){-}NH_2$
Urea

$H_2N{-}CH(CH_2CH_2COOH){-}COOH$
Glutamic acid

$HOOC{-}CH_2{-}CH_2{-}COOH$
Succinic acid

$HCOOH$
Formic acid

Figure 12.5: Miller's data.

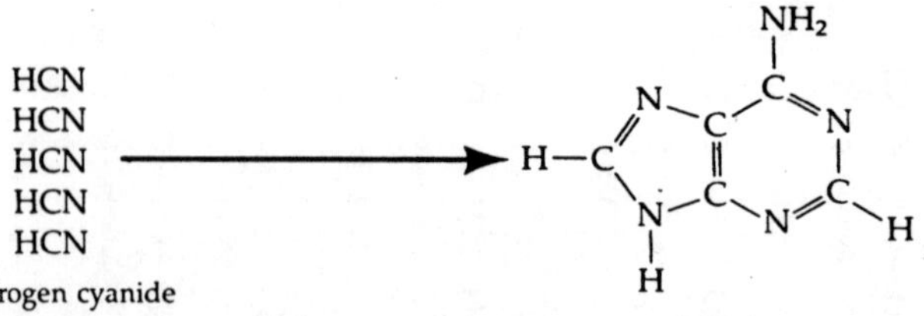

HCN
HCN
HCN ⟶ Adenine
HCN
HCN
Hydrogen cyanide

Figure 12.6: Prebiotic Formation of Adenine.

energy phosphate compounds would have been present when life was evolving and that the adenosine compounds would have been most common simply because adenine was the most easily synthesized base.

The first living organisms (or, to reach back one step further, perhaps self-organizing, nonliving chemical systems) may have depended on ATP from the seas around them for energy. The pattern that we now see, in which other compounds are broken down in glycolysis and the energy obtained from them used to synthesize ATP, may have been a later addition that evolved when the supply of ATP began to run short.

The answer to the question of why living organisms use ATP to store energy may be the same as the answer to the question of why people climbed Mt. Everest: because it was there.

FROM MONOMERS TO POLYMERS

Once simple building blocks such as amino acids began to accumulate in the oceans and smaller bodies of water, could they be assembled into proteins and other macromolecules? The answer is a clear "yes." Sidney Fox of the University of Miami found that heating a dry mixture of amino acids causes the formation of long "proteinoids," polymers having molecular weights of more than 10,000.

Fox has suggested that such polymerizations took place in volcanic cinder cones and that the proteins formed were then washed into the sea. J. B. S. Haldane and others considered it more likely that the first macromolecules were formed in sea water or pond water rather than from dried mixtures of monomers.

This, too, has been shown to be possible, for solutions of amino acids will form polypeptides in the presence of hydrogen cyanide (one of the products of the Miller reactions) even at suitably low temperatures. Another method for polymerizing monomers of various types is to wet and dry them, alternately, on the surface of clay. The historical operation of this mechanism is particularly plausible from a geological point of view. As in the experiments of the Miller type, in which simple molecules were formed, many different conditions have been shown to be compatible with the formation of proteins and other polymers.

Again, it is not necessary to know the exact details of the early physical environment in order to be sure that proteins and nucleic acids were formed during the era of chemical evolution. On the other hand, it is unlikely that we shall ever know which mechanism of polymerization was most important in leading to the appearance of life.

MICROSPHERES

The remaining steps in the origin of life on Earth are the ones about which we know the least, and it is possible that they will remain shrouded in mystery. Clearly, though, they must have involved the accumulation of biological polymers and other compounds into isolated droplets of increasing complexity. There are, in fact, several ways in which such accumulation can be accomplished in the laboratory.

For example, Fox found that his "proteinoids" have a remarkable tendency to form *microspheres* approximately 2 μm in diameter when hot, concentrated solutions of the proteinoids are slowly cooled. These microspheres show a double-layered boundary resembling a membrane (although lacking lipids), and they swell or shrink as the salt concentration in the solution is changed.

If allowed to stand for several weeks, the microspheres absorb more proteinoid material from the solution, produce buds, and sometimes divide to produce "second generation" microspheres. Cleavage or division can also be induced by changing pH or adding magnesium chloride. These microspheres should not be taken to be the ancestors of life. Rather, they show some of the remarkable self-organizing properties of relatively simple chemical systems.

They illustrate how many of the phenomena normally associated with living organisms can be duplicated by much simpler assemblages. One method for the accumulation of chemical substances into partially organized structures was proposed by the Irish physicist J. D. Bernal.

This method involves small clay particles-such particles have electrical charges that attract and bind substances such as proteins. Methane, ammonia, and water vapor can be subjected to electrical discharge; and among the products are spheres, one-quarter of a micrometer in diameter, consisting of mixtures of biological molecules bound to claylike particles eroded from the glass of the reaction chamber.

Coacervates

Another accumulation method was proposed and studied by Oparin.

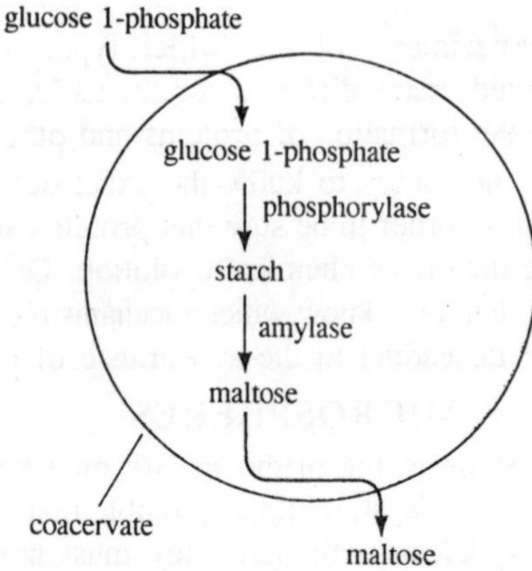

Figure 12.7: Models of Life's Precursors.

He spent most of his career studying *coacervate drops*. If you shake a mixture of a little olive oil in water, the oil will temporarily break up into a mass of tiny droplets.

If, instead, you use a large protein such as gelatin and a polysaccharide such as gum arabic, the result is the formation of coacervate drops, which are much more stable. As with the oil-water system, the coacervate preparation is divided into two separate phases: the interior of the drops (primarily protein and polysaccharide, with some water) and the aqueous solution around them (mostly water, but containing some protein and polysaccharide).

Coacervate drops will form in solutions of many different kinds of polymers: proteins, nucleic acids, polysaccharides, and various synthetic polymers. Coacervation is simply a matter of physical chemistry, not of life, yet coacervate drops show several properties relevant to the origin of life.

Many substances, when added to a coacervate preparation, are preferentially concentrated within the droplets. Lipids can coat the boundaries of droplets with "membranes" and strengthen the droplets against destruction. Some droplets made from complex solutions contain separate internal phases, one inside the other, like a nucleus within a cytoplasmic phase.

If coacervates are prepared so as to contain enzyme molecules, they can absorb substrates, catalyze a reaction, and let the products diffuse back out into the solution. Coacervates containing phosphorylase, for example, will absorb glucose 1-phosphate from the surrounding medium and polymerize it into starch.

If a second enzyme, amylase, is also present in the coacervate, it will break up the starch into maltose, which escapes into the solution. The coacervates containing phosphorylase and amylase are, then, small factories for converting the monosaccharide glucose 1-phosphate into the disaccharide maltose. The energy for the overall process comes from the high-energy phosphate in glucose 1-phosphate.

Oparin even succeeded in making coacervates containing chlorophyll, that would absorb an oxidized dye from the solution, use light energy to reduce it, and return the reduced dye to the surroundings.

LATE STAGES OF CHEMICAL EVOLUTION

It is possible that the immediate precursors of living organisms were capsules of chemical reactants similar to coacervate droplets. Some coacervates would enclose reactions that led to the early breakup of the droplets; others would enclose reactions that made them more stable.

The more stable coacervates would survive longer and could possibly grow at the expense of their surroundings by absorbing chemical substances derived from the remains of less stable droplets. If wave action or other mechanical forces broke a large coacervate into many small droplets, each of these might be able to absorb material and grow on its own. This stage of evolution would be purely a matter of chemical competition.

Any nonbiological catalysts that accelerated the rates of favorable reactions in a given type of coacervate would give it a great advantage over more slowly reacting droplets. Chemical selection, therefore, would favor catalyzed reactions. It is not hard to imagine how more and more efficient (and elaborate) catalysts would be developed and retained by chemical selection, until finally the evolving system stumbled onto the ultimate improvement of proteinlike catalystsenzymes.

Oparin postulated the existence of organized, metabolizing, but nonreproducing systems that he called *protobionts*. According to this reasoning, the breakthrough that led to truly living organisms was the development of *reproduction*: the ability of a successful chemical system to ensure its survival by duplicating itself.

The molecules in which the instructions for duplication are stored in modern living creatures are DNA or RNA. Yet the *living* unit of life is not just the nucleic acid, but the entire cell or virus. The organism is as helpless without its nucleic acid as a computer without a program, but the DNA or RNA alone can no more live than a program without a computer can do calculations. The coupling of a protobiont with genetic instructions may have occurred many times; at some time, one or more of the new, living things were successful in establishing themselves.

Will a totally new form of life on Earth be assembled from nonliving matter, along lines such as these, in the future? Almost certainly not. For one thing, any simple biological molecules released into today's environment are quickly consumed by already living things.

For another, such molecules are no longer accumulating through the mechanisms described above-Earth's atmosphere has changed. Oxygen, too, can oxidize biological molecules. In addition, it gives rise to the ozone that filters ultraviolet from the sunlight falling on the planet.

In so doing, it blocks one of the sources of energy once available for promoting chemical reactions. In sum, spontaneous generation is a thing of the past.

13

TAXONOMY AND PHYLOGENY

This chapter deals with the goals of classification; cladistic, phenetic, and evolutionary systematics; taxonomic hierarchies; taxonomic characters; homology; analogy; taxonomic keys; and the phylogeny of life.

We use terms such as mosses, ferns, conifers, insects, fish, birds, and mammals when we talk about organisms. Each of these words summarizes many features of those groups of organisms, and it would be impossible to discuss organisms collectively without using those or equivalent terms.

These words are all based on a classification scheme by which we compare and assemble organisms into groups, thus making possible more sophisticated forms of scrutiny. The science of the classification of organisms is called *taxonomy*. *Systematics* is the study of the relationships among all organisms.

It deals both with taxonomy and the inferences drawn from taxonomic systems about the evolution of life. Modern biology uses classification systems to indicate both similarities and differences among organisms and also evolutionary relationships. Both of these goals cannot be fully realized in any single classification system devised so far, and compromises between the goals must be made.

The study of the pathways organisms followed as they evolved is called phylogeny. Interpretations of phylogenies are often expressed as *phylogenetic trees*, which graphically represent lines of descent among organisms. In this chapter we consider the goals and methods of taxonomy and show how biologists use classification systems to express evolutionary relationships among living and fossil organisms.

THE GOALS OF CLASSIFICATION

Dealing with a complex world requires an ability to recognize similarities and differences among objects. All animals are probably taxonomists of some sort, but humans have developed taxonomic skills to a much greater extent than have other species. The basic role of classifying is simplification of description.

A useful classification system divides the objects under consideration into categories according to criteria that are useful in guiding our behavior toward them. The objects within any one class necessarily differ in detail, but they must share certain essential features that determine their placement in the same group.

Classification systems are based on features whose utility depends on what we hope to accomplish with the system. For instance, if we were interested in a system that helped us decide what plants and animals were desirable as food, we might erect a classification based on palatability, ease of capture, and quantity of edible parts each type possessed.

Early Hindu classifications of plants were made in this way. One such classification divided plants into four categories: (1) trees bearing fruits without flowers, (2) trees bearing flowers as well as fruits, (3) herbs that wither after fruiting, and (4) other herbs with spreading stems. The interests of ancient Hindus centered on horses and elephants, the two most important domesticated species.

Hindus were skilled in setting fractures and dislocations in these animals, and their hospitals for animals date back to at least the third century B.C. Special studies were made of snakes and their poisons. Classifications of animals were made from several points of view, such as type of reproduction, habitat and mode of life, usefulness to people, and number of senses.

One ancient system divided animals into (1) those with placentas, (2) those formed from eggs, (3) those that generated spontaneously (worms, mosquitoes), and (4) those born of vegetable organisms. Another system divided animals into (1) those born of moisture and heat, (2) viviparous or placental species (mammals), (3) egglaying species, and (4) those that burst forth from the ground (frogs).

We would not use such systems today, but they served the needs of the ancient Hindus. It is inappropriate to ask whether those classifications, or any others, including contemporary ones, are right or wrong. Classification systems can be judged only in terms of their utility and internal consistency. To evaluate any classification system we must first ask, "What is it trying to accomplish?"

Cladistic, Phenetic, and Evolutionary Systematics

Because no one system of classification can satisfy all of the needs of modern biology, several systems are currently in use, each with its strong supporters. They differ in the emphasis they place on different criteria for classification.

Phenetic systematics is based strictly on phenotypic similarities among living organisms. As many traits as possible are measured, and all are assumed to be of equal importance. Known or presumed evolutionary relationships are not used in erecting the classifications. Phenetic similarities are presented graphically as *phenograms*. Figure elsewhere in this chapter presents a phenogram for five hypothetical *taxa* (singular: taxon, a taxonomic category).

In this diagram the horizontal lines do not indicate common ancestry but show only the level of phenetic similarity between the two taxa they connect. Taxa C and D are phenetically the closest. Cladistic systematics is based entirely on how long ago two species shared a common ancestor. A *Glade* is a series of organisms descended from a common ancestor. A cladistic classification uses only information on the length of time since the species separated.

How much they have changed since separation is not considered. Cladistic relationships are presented graphically as *cladograms*. A cladogram of the hypothetical taxa from Figure elsewhere in this chapter shows the sequences of their origins from one another. The distance between any two parallel lines simply indicates the amount of time since their separation. In this cladogram, D and E might be placed in one taxonomic group; C, D, and E grouped together into a higher category; whereas A and B are placed in still another.

Evolutionary systematics uses information from both phenetic and cladistic studies. Its classifications are based both on the length of time of separation of the taxa and the nature of evolutionary changes that occurred after separation. Not all traits are given equal value.

The relationships of evolutionary systematics are presented as *phylogenetic trees*. A phylogenetic tree for our imaginary taxa shows both when they split from one another and how much they diverged or

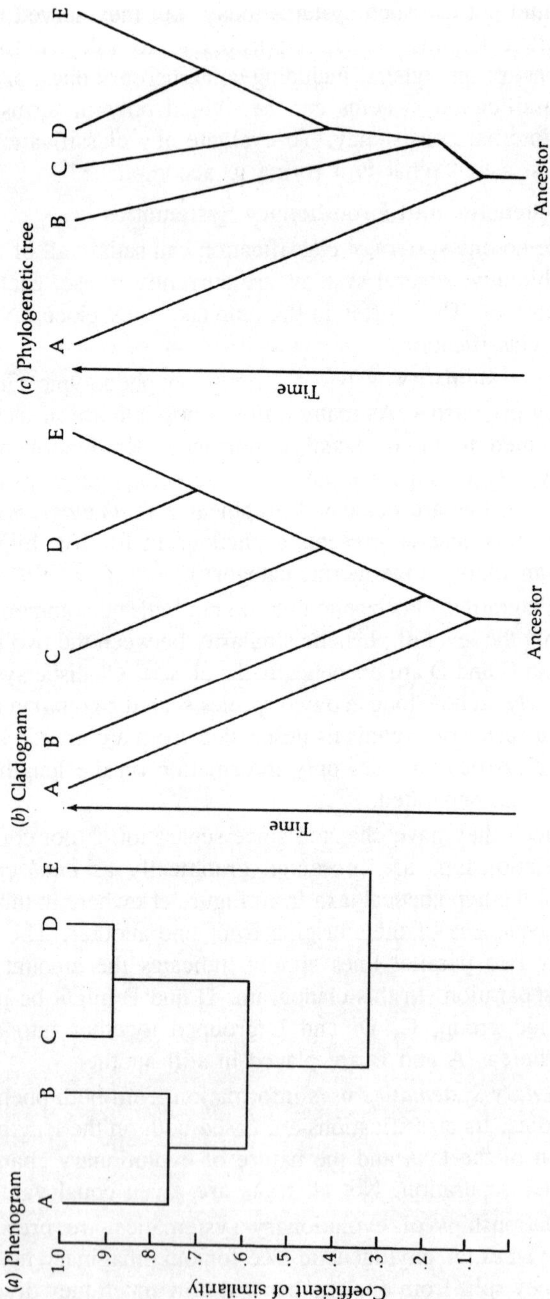

Figure 13.1: Types of Classifications.

converged after separating (Figure lc). The phenetic similarity of C and D is due to their lack of divergence after separation.

Each system has advantages and disadvantages. Phenetic and cladistic systems are more objective than evolutionary systems, and they are simpler because they don't attempt to express two types of information in one system. On the other hand, in a purely phenetic system, morphologically similar but unrelated organisms may be placed in the same group, whereas closely related but morphologically divergent ones are placed in different groups.

This is less likely to happen if many traits are used. Cladistic systems provide no information about degree of similarities among organisms. Currently used classifications of organisms are of all three types, although evolutionary systems predominate. As an example, crocodiles are generally grouped with reptiles because of their morphological similarities (a phenetic classification) even though they share a more recent common ancestor with birds than with other reptiles and would be grouped with birds in a purely cladistic classification.

No serious confusion need result from the use of more than one system, provided the criteria being employed are clearly indicated.

Taxonomic Hierarchies

Most classification systems group smaller units into successively larger ones. The number of features shared by members of the larger groups are fewer than the number shared by members of smaller units. For instance, ostriches, owls, hummingbirds, and sparrows are quite different animals, but they share more features with one another than they do with whales, cats, mice, and deer.

By calling them birds and the second group mammals, we direct attention to certain significant features that serve to unite members of the group and distinguish them from members of other groups. In other chapter of this booki the full biological meaning of the species concept will be examined in detail.

For the present purposes, we can define a *species* (singular and plural are the same) as a population or series of populations of organisms within which a significant amount of genetic exchange occurs under natural conditions but which is relatively isolated genetically from other populations.

The first step in erecting a classification system is to decide what basic units (species) are represented. Among sexual species, the best criterion is whether or not populations of organisms interbreed when they are in contact with one another. If they do not come into contact, the amount of difference between them is compared with the amount of difference between populations that do live together without interbreeding. If the difference is as great or greater than that between populations that live together without interbreeding, they are treated as different species. Among asexual organisms, only phenetic information can be used to decide on basic units.

In the system used today, based on the work of the great Swedish biologist Carolus Linnaeus, each species is assigned two names: one identifying the species itself and the other the *genus* to which the species belongs.

A genus is a group of species that resemble one another (the plural of genus is genera and its adjectival form is generic). In many cases the name of the taxonomist who first proposed the species name is added at the end. Thus, *Homo sapiens* Linnaeus is the name of the modern human species. *Homo is* the genus to which the species belongs, *sapiens* identifies the species, and Linnaeus was the first person to have used the species name *sapiens*.

You can think of the generic name *Homo* as being equivalent to your surname and the specific name *sapiens* as being equivalent to your first name. This two-name system, referred to as *binomial nomenclature*, is universally employed throughout biology. The generic name is always capitalized, but the species name is not. As we have done in this paragraph, both the generic and specific names are always italicized, whereas common names are not.

The next step is to group the species into higher taxonomic categories. The first task is to decide on the number and limits of the genera. As is shown in Figure 3, this choice is somewhat arbitrary. It is equally valid to group the ten imaginary species into one genus or to split them into three or more.

However, extreme splitting or lumping of species is less useful than intermediate types of groupings. If every species were put into its own genus or, conversely, if all were lumped into one genus, the genus would not carry any information not already present in the designation of species. There is taxonomic taste, but it is always tempered by the overall purpose of the classification system.

Once the limits of the genera have been decided upon, the taxonomist groups them into *families*. Figure elsewhere in this chapter shows how similarities among species making up different genera could form the basis for grouping different genera into a single family or setting them apart in several families. A family can contain a single genus or many

(*a*) Lumping 10 species into a genus

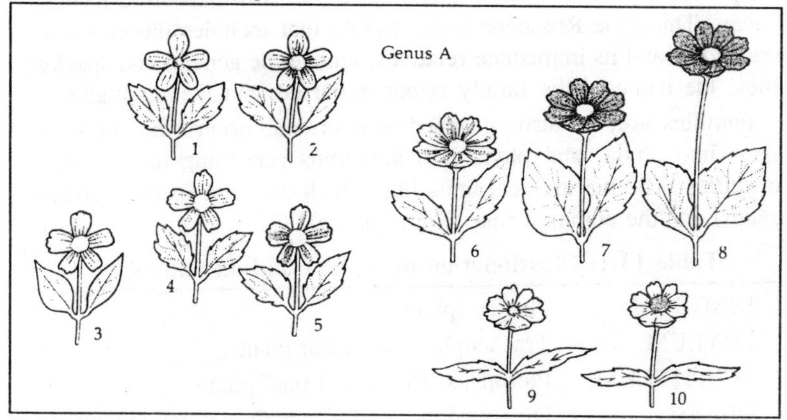

(*b*) Splitting 10 species into 3 genera

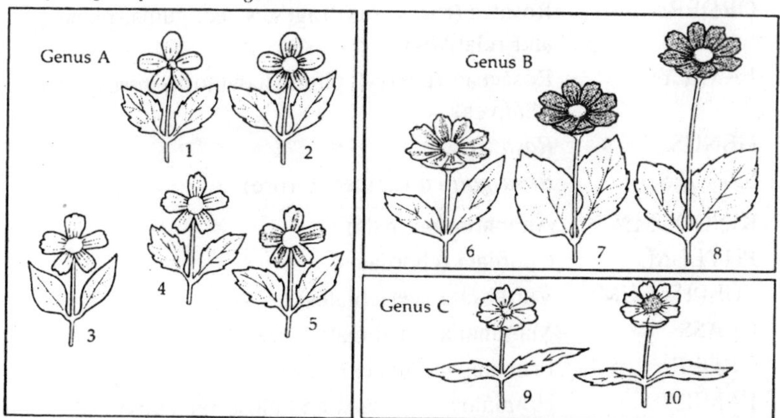

Figure 13.2: Clustering of imaginary species into genera.

of them. A family can even contain but a single species if that species is judged to be sufficiently unique from all other species. But again, families must contain, on the average, a number of genera if they are to be useful in describing a different level of similarity among organisms than that expressed with genera.

In animal classification, the names of families are identified by -idae endings. Thus, Formicidae is the family that contains all ant species, whereas Hominidae contains humans and a few of our fossil relatives. Family names are derived from the name of a member genus. Formicidae is derived from *Formica* (just remove the *-a* and add -idae), and Hominidae is derived from *Homo*. Plant classification follows the same procedures except that the ending -aceae is usually used instead of -idae. Thus, the Rosaceae is the family that includes the genus of roses *(Rosa)* and its immediate relatives. Unlike the generic and species names, the name of the family is not italicized, but it is capitalized.

Families are, in turn, grouped into orders, orders into classes, classes into phyla, and phyla into kingdoms according to the same procedures. The hierarchical units into which our own species *(Homo Sapiens)* and the common rose *(Rosa gallica)*.

Table 13.1: Classifciation of a plant and an animal.

KINGDOM:	Plantae (plants)
PHYLUM:	Tracheophyta (vascular plants)
SUBPHYLUM:	Pteropsida (ferns and seed plants)
CLASS:	Dicotyledoneae (plants with two cotyledons)
ORDER:	Rosales (roses, saxifrages, sweet gums, planes, and relatives)
FAMILY:	Rosaceae (cherry, plum, hawthorn, roses, and relatives)
GENUS:	*Rosa* (roses)
SPECIES:	*Rosa gallica* (domestic rose)
KINGDOM:	Animalia (animals)
PHYLUM:	Chordata (chordates)
SUBPHYLUM:	Vertebrata (vertebiates)
CLASS:	Mammalia (mammals)
ORDER:	Primates (primates)
FAMILY:	Hominidae (humans and close relatives)
GENUS:	*Homo* (modern humans and extinct relatives)
SPECIES:	*Homo sapiens* (modern humans)

TAXONOMIC CHARACTERS

The more information available, the better classification systems can be. New knowledge from all areas of biological inquiry is rapidly incorporated into modern taxonomies, sometimes causing important revisions in those systems. Many types of characters are used in classifying organisms.

Living organisms have been measured for many decades, and most species descriptions are based on *gross morphology*, that is, sizes and shapes of body parts. In addition, this is the type of information most readily available from fossils. Therefore, most inferences about phylogenies have traditionally been based primarily on morphological data. The early *developmental stages* of many organisms reveal similarities with other organisms that are lost by the time adulthood is reached.

For instance, larval, but not adult, sea squirts (tunicates) have a dorsal supporting rod-the notochord-which reveals their evolutionary relationship to other chordates. Examination of the adults would not suggest this relationship. Fossils tell us little about the behavior of organisms of the past, but living organisms often reveal their close affinities by similarities in their behavior.

This information is most useful for detecting relationships within rather than between lower units, such as families and genera. The German ethologist Konrad Lorenz showed that close similarities in behavior patterns supported other evidence suggesting that species of ducks with quite different plumages were nonetheless very closely related.

If organisms can cross and produce fertile hybrid offspring, we can be certain that they are closely related. Successful *hybridization* sometimes reveals that organisms that look very different may be very similar genetically. The *sequences of amino acids in proteins* provide information about genetic similarities and differences that is relatively free of environmentally induced changes.

Amino acid sequences can now be determined relatively quickly by a process that sequentially removes amino acids from the amino terminus of polypeptides. The cleaved amino acids are then identified by gas-liquid or thin-layer chromatography or by mass spectrometry.

A direct measure of genetic distance is given by the number of amino acid replacements that have occurred since the taxa from which the proteins are obtained shared a common ancestor. A phylogenetic tree of some hooved mammals based on amino acid comparisons of their fibrinopeptides-the molecules responsible for blood clotting-is shown in Figure elsewhere in this chapter. It is very similar to the one developed earlier by taxonomists, using gross morphological traits.

If foreign proteins are introduced into an animal, they cause an *immunological reaction*, that is, the production of specific antibodies. If antibodies produced in response to a foreign protein are mixed with the original protein, there is a reaction that results in the formation of large antigen-antibody aggregates that precipitate from solution.

The more similar the proteins, the stronger the reaction. Albumin has been used extensively in taxonomic studies because it evolves rapidly and consists of a single polypeptide of approximately 580 amino acids. Phylogenetic relationships among some frogs, as estimated by albumin

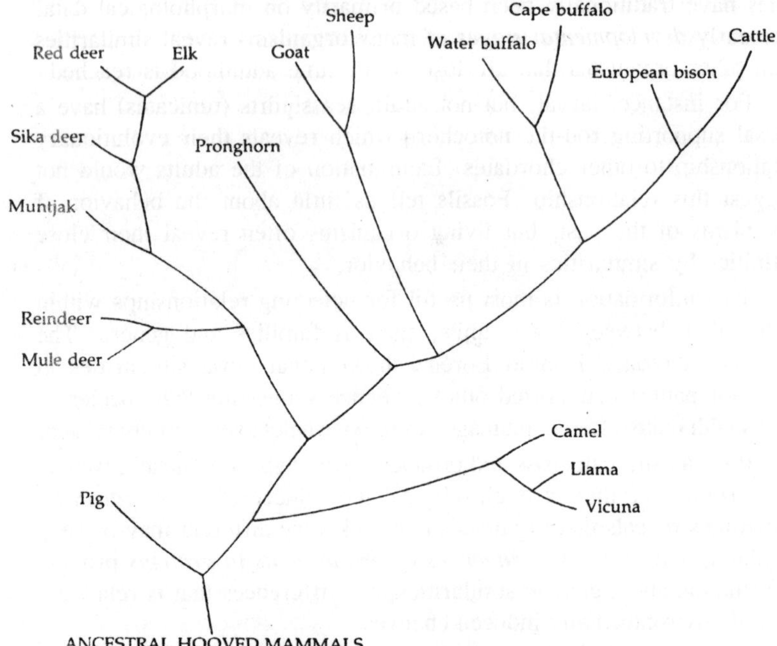

Figure 13.3: Phylogentic tree of some Hooved Mammals.

antigen-antibody techniques, are shown in Figure elsewhere in this chapter. The methods suggest that the frog *Anotheca spinosa,* originally thought to be related to marsupial tree frogs (Amphignathodontinae), is really very closely related to several North American tree frog *(Hyla)* species.

All proteins have an electric charge that is determined by their amino acid composition. Therefore, when in solution, they move in an electric field. Proteins with similar charges move at similar rates, and an estimate of the amount of difference between proteins can be made from the amount of difference in their mobility.

Some proteins, such as collagens of bone and skin, keratins, and seed proteins, are often well-preserved over geological time, allowing the method to be applied to fossil materials. Several different *electrophoretic techniques* exist, and, used in combination, they can detect most of the amino acid differences among proteins. However, current techniques can be used only on structural proteins, which constitute only approximately 1 percent of the total proteins of eukaryotes.

The best taxonomic character is the structure of the genes themselves- the *nucleotide sequences*. These are being determined in several ways,

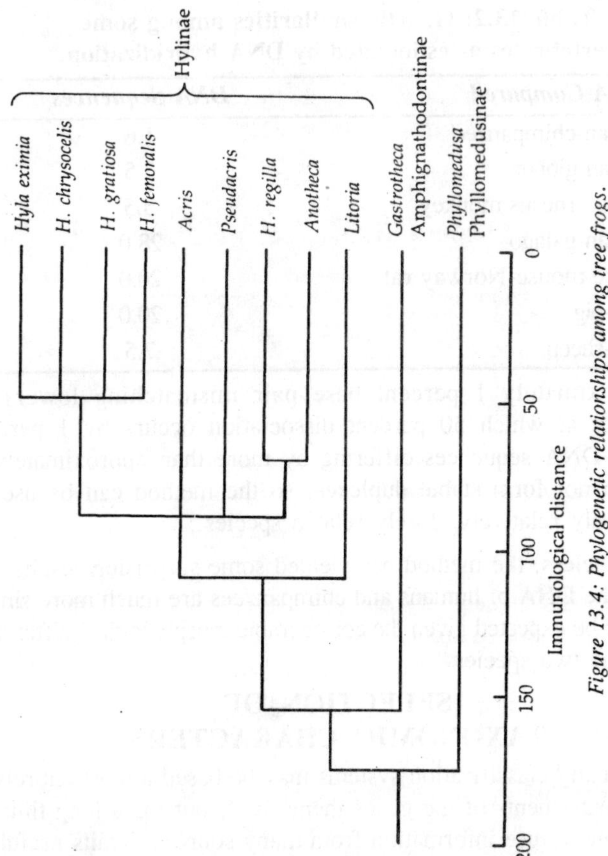

Figure 13.4: Phylogenetic relationships among tree frogs.

the most important of which is cleavage of DNA and RNA into short sections by the use of enzymes that recognize specific nucleotide sequences. These sections are then separated electrophoretically.

The two strands of the DNA double helix can be separated by heating, but they re-form again when cooled. If DNA from two species is mixed and heated, the separated strands will form interspecific double helices when cooled.

However, because of differences in the base sequences of the two DNAs, the strands do not match up well, and these hybrid helices can be separated at lower temperatures than double helices formed by heating and cooling the DNA of a single species. The relationship between degree of mismatching of the DNA and thermal stability is very regular.

Table 13.2: Genetic similarities among some vertebrates as estiomated by DNA hybridization.

TAXA Compared	*DNA Sequences*
Human-chimpanzee	1.6
Human-gibbon	3.5
Human-rhesus monkey	5.5
Human-galago	28.0
House mouse-Norway rat	20.0
Cow-pig	20.0
Cow-sheep	7.5

Approximately 1 percent base pair mismatching lowers the temperature at which 50 percent dissociation occurs by 1 percent. However, DNA sequences differing by more than approximately 20 percent do not form stable duplexes, so the method can be used to compare only relatively closely related species.

Nonetheless, the method has yielded some surprising results. For instance, the DNA of humans and chimpanzees are much more similar than would be expected given the considerable morphological differences between the two species.

SELECTION OF TAXONOMIC CHARACTERS

Eventually classification systems may be based almost entirely on direct measurements of the genes themselves, but for a long time we will continue to use information from many sources. Traits useful for determining evolutionary relationships among organisms must be measurable, describable, and relatively invariable, regardless of the environment in which the organism grows.

For a plant whose leaves have different shapes, depending upon whether they grow in the water or in the air, the shape of its leaves would not be a good taxonomic character. It is also desirable to make some assessment of the rate at which the character changes during evolutionary time.

A trait that changes rapidly is useful for studying relationships among closely related species, but it is not useful for determining relationships among higher taxonomic categories. The converse is true for slowly changing traits. The existence of fertile hybrids between birds with very different plumages shows that plumage patterns in birds can evolve rapidly and with little genetic change.

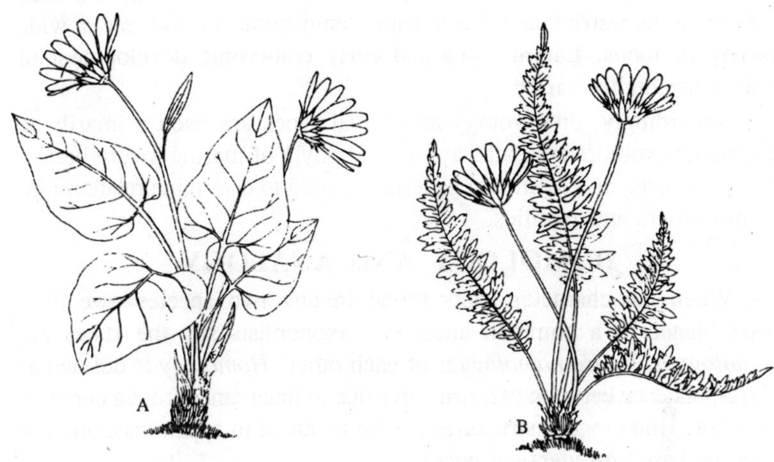

Figure 13.5: Taxonomic grouping based on plant structures.

Also, males and females of the same species often have strikingly different plumages. Consequently, taxonomists do not use plumage patterns in establishing higher categories among birds. Similarly, two interfertile plants may have strikingly different leaves but almost identical flowers. Because flower structure generally changes slowly, plant classifications are heavily based on reproductive structures.

For groups with good fossil records, direct measures can be made of the rates at which different features have evolved. Nucleic acid analyses and amino acid sequences in proteins, especially when combined with fossil evidence of the splitting of groups, provide very accurate estimates of the average rates of change in genes and their direct products.

Although the same procedures are used with all organisms, for several reasons the characters upon which classifications are based differ. Not all organisms possess similar measurable features. Flowering plants offer branching patterns, leaf shapes, specialized cells, reproductive structures, and so on. Bacteria have none of those features. Certain traits are developmentally flexible in some groups but quite independent of environmental conditions in others.

Also, traits that evolve rapidly in one group may evolve slowly in another. Many marine organisms shed their eggs into sea water. The larval stage feeds upon small algae in the water for a period before settling to the bottom and changing into an adult. Because conditions for survival of such larvae have been similar for long periods of evolutionary time, larval types of many marine invertebrates have evolved very slowly. The opposite is true among insects whose larvae exploit a wide variety of terrestrial and fresh water environments and eat a wide variety of foods. Larval types and early embryonic development of insects are highly varied.

Accordingly, embryology and larval types are used primarily to determine evolutionary pathways among phyla of marine invertebrates. Among insects, developmental patterns are used to determine relationships within orders and families.

HOMOLOGY AND ANALOGY

When the character traits found in any two species owe their resemblance to a common ancestry, taxonomists say the states are *homologous*, or are *homologues* of each other. *Homology* is defined as correspondence between two structures due to inheritance from a common ancestor. Homologous structures can be identical in appearance and can even be based on identical genes.

However, such structures can diverge until they become very different in both appearance and function. Nevertheless, homologous structures usually retain certain basic features that betray a common ancestry. Consider the forelimbs of vertebrates.

It is easy to make a detailed, bone-by-bone, muscle-by-muscle comparison of the forearm of a person and a monkey and to conclude that the forearms, as well as the various parts of the forearm, are homologous. The forelimb of a dog, however, shows marked differences from those of primates in both structure and function.

The forelimb is used for locomotion by dogs but for grasping and manipulation by people and monkeys. Even so, all of the bones can still be matched. The wing of a bird and the flipper of a seal are even more different from each other or from the human forearm, yet they too are constructed around bones that can be matched on a nearly perfect one-to-one basis.

The wing of a fly shares the same function as a bird's wing, and the two organs even resemble each other to a slight degree in external form. Yet close examination shows that the two organs are completely different in their basic structure. The entire wing of the fly is a membranous outgrowth of the external skeletal covering of the body. Its main supports are not bones but rather columns of hardened protein combined with a complex polysaccharide called chitin.

The bird and fly wings are said to be *analogues* of each other. *Analogy* is defined as a resemblance in function that is based on *convergent evolution*, that is, structures becoming more similar to one

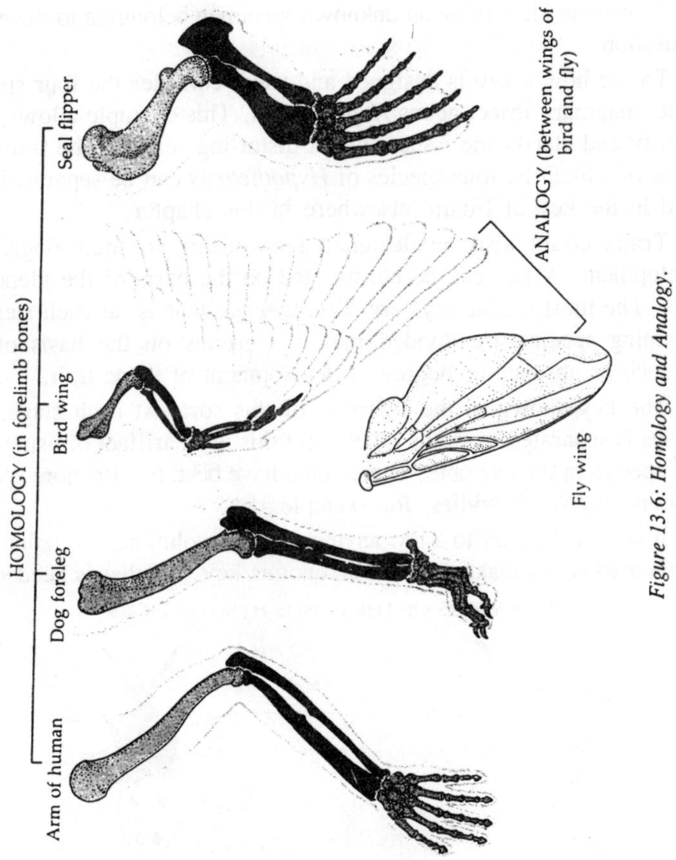

Figure 13.6: Homology and Analogy.

another than they were in earlier ancestors of the organisms being compared.

Evolutionary taxonomists must decide whether characteristics shared by the groups to be classified are homologous or analogous because evolutionary classifications use homologies extensively but ignore analogies. A phenetic classification uses both but assumes that careful measurements will detect the real, closer similarities of homologous, as compared to analogous, structures.

TAXONOMIC KEYS

Taxonomic systems are used not only to indicate relationships among organisms; they can also be used to help identify unknown organisms. A taxonomist normally publishes written descriptions of the new organisms being characterized for the first time. In addition, a revision of a group is usually accompanied by a *taxonomic* key designed to aid someone identifying an unknown specimen belonging to the group in question.

To see how a key is designed and used, consider the four species of the imaginary insect genus *Hypotheticus*. This example allows us to simplify and clarify the issue without distorting reality. The traits, by means of which the four species of *Hypotheticus* can be separated, are listed in the key of Figure elsewhere in this chapter.

Traits could also be designated according to their degree of development. A key can be constructed on the basis of the identified traits. The most useful keys are *dichotomous*, that is, at each step the remaining species are divided into two groups on the basis of the presence or absence or degree of development of some trait.

The key shown in the figure is of this sort. At each stage, one species is separated from the others, but this is an artifact of using only four species in the example. There could have been two or more species with entirely white bodies, for example.

It is not necessary to know anything about evolutionary relationships within a group to make a useful taxonomic key. All that is needed are

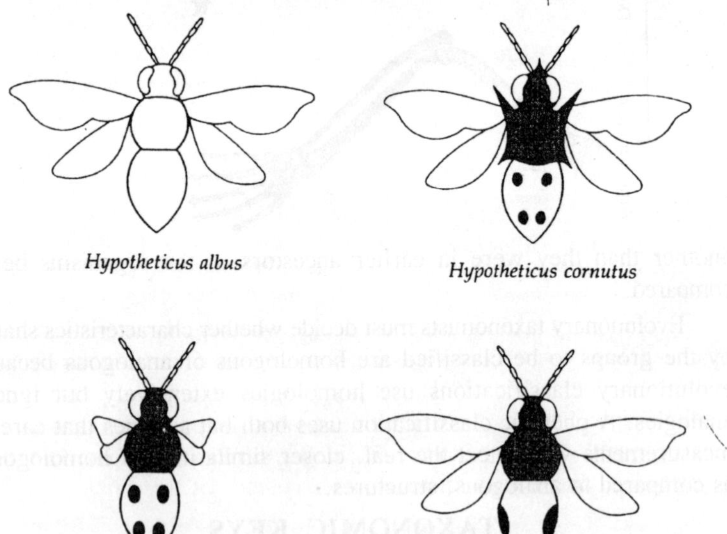

Figure 13.7: A key to species of Hypotheticus.

traits that clearly separate the species. If information is available about evolutionary relationships within the group, that knowledge can be used to construct a key that reflects those relationships.

Such keys are often called *natural keys* for the same reason that taxonomies based on evolutionary relationships are considered natural. Other keys are usually called artificial keys, and because they are often much easier to use than natural keys, they are in common use. For example, it is convenient to be able to identify plants that are not in flower. To do so requires the use of keys based on leaf and stem features. The keys found in many guide books are based on these traits.

Phylogenetic Trees of Life

In the early nineteenth century, paleontologists began the arduous task of reconstructing the history of life on Earth by the study of fossils. This task, which is still ongoing, is providing a wealth of information about the organisms that lived in the past, the rates at which organisms changed, and which species were derived from one another.

By indirect methods, such as estimating the time required to lay down deposits of rocks, geologists judged that Earth must be at least hundreds of millions of years old. There were some objections from physicists, such as Lord Kelvin, who estimated on the basis of the rate of cooling of Earth, that it could be only approximately 20 to 40 million years old-not enough time to permit the amount of evolution that biologists and geologists were convinced had taken place.

As it turned out, because Lord Kelvin had neglected to include the heat released by radioactive decay in his calculations, he seriously underestimated the age of Earth. Much uncertainty still surrounds the early evolution of life and relationships among the very simple prokaryotes. New discoveries are being made regularly in this area, principally through the applications of molecular biology techniques.

Therefore, any phylogenetic tree of life is likely to be replaced rather quickly by modified versions. The tree used in this book, based on the best information available today, is shown in Figure elsewhere in this chapter. It does not provide details about lower taxonomic categories and is intended to provide only a frame of reference for the more detailed treatments found in other chapter of this book.

14

MONERA AND PROTISTS

This chapter deals with diversity among the viruses and the kingdoms Monera and Protista. The subject of this and the next two chapters is the diversity of living things, approached kingdom by kingdom. Our aim is to provide an overview of the major groups of monera, protists, fungi, plants, and animals, with emphasis on how they differ from one another.

There is no better place to begin than with the various microorganisms. In terms of sheer numbers of individuals, the microscopic organisms-monera, protists, and viruses-are the most successful of all creatures on Earth. It has been pointed out that the number of bacteria in one's mouth outnumbers the humans who have ever lived. In spite of their minute sizes, the microorganisms outdo all other groups in such terms as metabolic diversity and ability to occupy extreme and diverse habitats.

VIRUSES

Unlike the organisms making up the five taxonomic kingdoms of the living world, the viruses are *acellular*; that is, they do not consist of cells. Unlike the cellular creatures, they do not conduct energy metabolism-they do not produce ATP, and they are incapable of fermentation, cellular respiration, or photosynthesis. The question of whether viruses should be viewed as "alive" was discussed in other chapter of this book, but leading virologists have firmly claimed the property of "life" for their subjects in recent years.

Table 14.1: Common sizes of microorganisms.

Microorganism	*Type*	*Typical Size Range (Cubic Micrometers)*
Protists	Eukaryote	5,000-50,000
Photosynthetic	Prokaryote	5-50 bacteria
Spirochetes	Prokaryote	0.1-2
Mycoplasmas	Prokaryote	0.01-0.1
Pox viruses	Virus	0.01
Influenza virus	Virus	0.0005
Polio virus	Virus	0.00001

Whole viruses never arise directly from preexisting viruses. They are obligate parasites, that is, they depend upon specific hosts for their reproduction and development. Animals, plants, and bacteria can serve as hosts to viruses.

Outside host cells, viruses exist as individual particles called *virions*. The virion, the basic unit of a virus, consists of a central core of either DNA or RNA (but not both) surrounded by a capsid, or coat, composed of one or at most a few kinds of proteins. These proteins are so assembled as to give the virion a characteristic shape.

Many animal viruses also acquire a membrane consisting of lipids and proteins as they bud through host cell membranes, and many bacterial viruses have specialized "tails" made of protein.

Reproduction of Viruses

Animal viruses attach to the plasma membrane of the host cell and are then taken up by endocytosis, a process that leaves them trapped within a membranous vesicle inside the cell. After the membrane breaks down, the viral protein capsid must be digested by the host cell, whereupon the viral nucleic acid can take over the host's metabolism.

The host cell replicates the viral nucleic acid; in addition, the viral nucleic acid serves to direct the synthesis of new capsid protein by the protein-synthesizing system of the host. New capsids and new viral nucleic acid combine spontaneously; and, in due course, the new virions are released by the host cell.

The release of animal viruses is usually by budding through virus-modified areas of the plasma membrane (or sometimes the nuclear envelope), so that the completed virions are surrounded by a membrane somewhat similar to that of the host cell.

Plant viruses and bacteriophages must get through a cell wall as well as the host plasma membrane. Infection of a plant usually results from attack by a virion-laden insect vector (intermediate carriers of disease from one organism to another are called vectors). The insect uses its proboscis to penetrate the cell wall, and the virions then escape from the insect into the plant.

Bacterial viruses are often equipped with tail assemblies that inject the nucleic acid into the host bacterium. Escape from plant or bacterial cells is by lysis of the host cell, rather than by budding as in animal hosts. Some *bacteriophages* have lytic life cycles (cycles that result in rapid lysis of host cells); but others have *lysogenic* life cycles, in which the viral and host nucleic acids replicate at the same time and the virus may be present as a "*silent*" provirus for many bacterial cell generations.

How does a virion recognize a suitable host-or how does the host recognize the virion? There is a specific interaction between proteins of the bacteriophage tail and of the host cell wall, in the case of some bacterial viruses. The recognition of membranesurrounded animal viruses is probably accomplished by means of the host plasma membrane.

The viral membrane is obtained, at least in part, from the previous host; and it can readily fuse with the plasma membrane of a new host cell. It is not known how the nucleic acid of other viruses gets into the host cell. Free viral nucleic acid, without a capsid, can sometimes infect host cells; but this mode of infection (only known in the laboratory) is less than one-thousandth as effective as infection by intact virions.

Plant viruses, such as tobacco mosaic virus, can be artificially introduced without the assistance of insect carriers if a leaf or other part is bruised mechanically before a suspension of virions is applied.

Classification of Viruses

A common way to classify viruses separates them, first, on the nature of the nucleic acid component (DNA or RNA) and then on whether the nucleic acid in the virion is single- or double-stranded. Further levels of classification depend upon such factors as the overall shape of the virus and the symmetry of the capsid.

As illustrated in Figure elsewhere in this chapter, most capsids may be categorized as *helical* (coiled like a spring, as in tobacco mosaic virus), *icosahedral* (a regular solid with 20 faces), or *binal* [with a polyhedral (many-faced) head and a helical tail]. Another level of categorization is based on the presence or absence of a membranous envelope around the virion; still further subdivision relies on capsid size and other criteria. In Table elsewhere in this chapter we show only the major levels of description and some examples; technical names of the taxonomic groups are omitted.

The distribution of viruses in terms of host organisms is puzzling. Viral diseases of flowering plants (angiosperms) are very common, but they are rare in the cone-bearing seed plants (gymnosperms), ferns, algae, and fungi.

Almost all vertebrates are susceptible to viral infection, but among invertebrates such infections are common only in arthropods. A group of viruses called *arboviruses* (short for arthropodborne viruses) causes serious diseases such as encephalitis in humans and other mammals.

Though carried within the arthropod vector's cells and transmitted to the other host through a bite (certain arboviruses are carried by mosquitoes, for example), they apparently do not affect the insect host severely-just the bitten and infected mammal.

THE KINGDOM MONERA (PROKARYOTES)

The kingdom Monera, which includes all organisms with prokaryotic cells, has the most ancient origins of any group still present today. Its earliest fossil representatives date back at least 3.5 billion years; and, as noted in other chapter of this book, these ancient traces indicate the occurrence of considerable diversity among the prokaryotes even during the Archean Eon.

The prokaryotes reigned supreme on an otherwise sterile Earth for over two billion years, adapting to new niches and to changes in existing ones. The monera have spread to every conceivable habitat on the planet, including the insides of other organisms. By any standard, they must be judged enormously successful and highly adapted creatures.

Contrary to the assertions of simple structure and function that one often reads, the monera of today are astoundingly diverse, and it is likely that they represent the current products of many independent evolutionary lines that have been separate for hundreds of millions of years. That is, in spite of their common prokaryotic heritage, they have been following their separate evolutionary paths for most of the history of life on the planet.

In addition, each of these evolutionary lines has spread over the surface of Earth and adapted to many or most of the possible environmental challenges, so that diversity is great within each of the lines. The result is a taxonomist's nightmare. Attempts to classify the monera on the basis of evolutionary affinity have met only limited success, while others based on morphological similarities are patently artificial.

There are at least three possible motivations for setting up schemes of classification. One, favored by many biologists, is to group organisms by evolutionary affinity, providing where possible a natural classification. A second one, followed by the great classic, Bergey's Manual of Determinative Bacteriology, is to group the species in such a way as to facilitate the identification of unknown organisms.

Yet another, appropriate to an introductory book, is to set up groupings that display the diversity of the living world, without in the long run being excessively concerned about incorporating all the newest evidence. In this book, we follow *Bergey's Manual* in dividing the kingdom Monera into two phyla or *divisions*. (Note that both botanists and bacteriologists prefer the term "division" to "phylum."

However, to maintain uniformity in these chapters, we shall use the term "phylum" for plants and monera, just as we do for the other kingdoms.) The *Manual* subdivides the larger phylum into 19 "parts." We are acting here on the assumption that a more compact treatment is appropriate for an introductory biology course, so we shall consider only some of the groups recognized by the *Manual*.

PROKARYOTES *VERSUS* EUKARYOTES

The architectures of prokaryotic and eukaryotic cells were compared in other chapter of this book, and you may wish to review Figures elsewhere in this chapter. The basic unit of the monera is the prokaryotic cell, which contains a full complement of genetic and protein-synthesizing systems, including DNA, RNA, and all the enzymes needed to transcribe and translate the genetic information into protein.

The cell also contains at least one system for generating the ATP it needs. As discussed in other chapter of this book, the prokaryotic cell differs from the eukaryotic cell in three important ways. First, the genetic material of the prokaryotic cell is not organized within a membrane-bounded nucleus, and the DNA is not part of a DNA-protein complex (chromatin).

The elaborate mechanism of mitosis is missing; prokaryotic cells divide by their own elaborate method, fission, after replicating their DNA. Second, prokaryotes have none of the familiar membrane-bounded cytoplasmic organelles-mitochondria, chloroplasts, Golgi apparatus, endoplasmic reticulum that occur in the cells of eukaryotes; but the cytoplasm of a prokaryotic cell may contain a variety of mesosomes and photosynthetic membranes not found in eukaryotes.

Table 14.2: Selected groups within the kingdom Monera.

Group	*Representative Genera*
Phylum Bacteria	
Phototrophic bacteria	*Chlorobium, Ectothiorhodo spira, Rhodospirillum*
Sheathed and appendaged bacteria	*Sphaeropilus, Caulobacter*
Gliding bacteria	*Beggiatoa, Thiothrix*
Spirochetes	*Borrelia, Treponema*
Curved and spiral bacteria	*Bdellovibrio, Spirillum*
Gram-negative rods	*Bacteroides, Escherichia, Pseudomonas, Rhizobium, Salmonella, Vibrio*
Gram-positive rods	*Bacillus, Clostridium*
Gram-negative cocci	*Neisseria, Nitrosococcus*
Gram-positive cocci	*Staphylococcus, Streptococcus*
Methanogens	*Methanobacteria*
Actinomycetes	*Actinomyces, Corynebacterium, Mycobacterium, Nocardia, Streptomyces*
Rickettsias	*Chlamydia, Rickettsia*
Mycoplasmas	*Mycoplasma*
Phylum Cyanobacteria	*Anabaena, Anacystis, Oscillatoria, Spirulina*

Finally, almost all prokaryotes have peptidoglycan in their cell walls, a substance whose composition is unique to the kingdom Monera. It should be emphasized that absence of characteristic eukaryotic organelles should not be construed as a total absence of internal membranes and other structures from the prokaryotic cell.

Membranous mesosomes are frequently associated with formation of new cell walls during cell division, and a cell's DNA is often seen in electron micrographs to be attached to a mesosome. Many aerobic bacteria have elaborate internal membrane systems to which respiratory enzymes are bound, and photosynthetic bacteria may have extensive and highly organized internal membranes laden with photosynthetic pigment systems.

Though many prokaryotes are not motile, some can move by means of flagella: whiplike filaments that extend singly or in tufts from one or both ends of the cell, or all around it. In contrast to the flagella of eukaryotes, which usually consist of a circle of nine pairs of microtubules surrounding two central microtubules, bacterial flagella consist of a single fibril made of the protein flagellin.

The bacterial flagellum rotates about its base rather than beating like a eukaryotic flagellum or cilium. Thus, flagellum architecture and behavior provide another major difference between prokaryotic and eukaryotic cells.

METABOLIC DIVERSITY IN THE KINGDOM MONERA

Although many types of prokaryotes can obtain energy either by fermentation or by cellular respiration and are therefore called *facultative anaerobes* (capable of being either anaerobic or aerobic), others can live only by fermentation and are, in fact, poisoned by oxygen. These oxygen-sensitive fermenters are *obligate anaerobes*. (Some facultative anaerobes can conduct only fermentation but are not damaged by oxygen when it is present.) At the other extreme, some monera are *obligate aerobes*, being unable to survive for extended periods in the absence of oxygen.

Respiratory electron transport in the absence of oxygen as an electron acceptor is carried out by some of the monera. These forms use oxidized inorganic ions such as nitrate, nitrite, or sulfate as electron acceptors. Included among these organisms are the denitrifiers.

Nutritionally, four broad categories may be recognized within the kingdom Monera. Organisms of the first category, the *photoautotrophs*, include the phylum Cyanobacteria and the *phototrophic bacteria* (purple sulfur bacteria, green sulfur bacteria, and some others). Photoautotrophs use light as their source of energy and carbon dioxide as their source of carbon.

The cyanobacteria perform photosynthesis as do the photosynthetic eukaryotes, with chlorophyll a as the key pigment, and produce oxygen as a by-product of noncyclic photophosphorylation. In contrast, the purple and green sulfur bacteria use *bacteriochlorophyll* as their key photosynthetic pigment, and they do not release oxygen. Instead, they produce

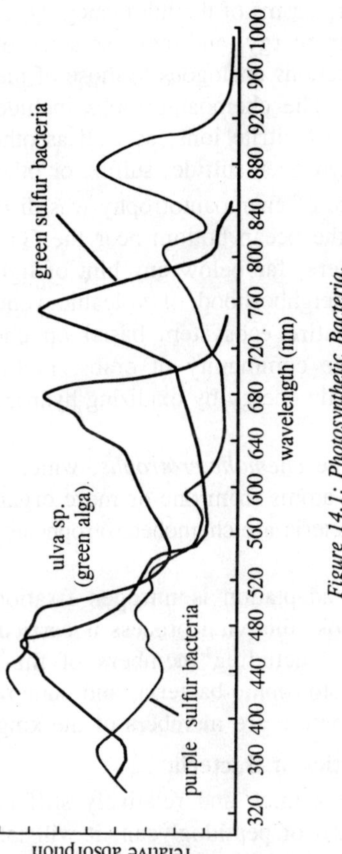

Figure 14.1: Photosynthetic Bacteria.

particles of pure sulfur because they use hydrogen sulfide (H_2S) instead of H_2O as an electron donor for photophosphorylation. Bacteriochlorophyll absorbs light of longer wavelength than that used by all other photosynthesizing organisms.

Thus, for example, the green and purple bacteria can grow in water beneath fairly dense layers of algae, because the wavelengths of light that they need are not appreciably absorbed by the algae. The second nutritional category is made up of the *photoheterotrophs*. These bacteria use light as their source of energy but must obtain their carbon atoms from organic compounds made by other organisms.

The photoheterotrophs are the purple *nonsul fur* bacteria (also included in the phototrophic bacteria). They use such compounds as carbohydrates, fatty acids, and alcohols as their organic "food."

Chemoautotrophs, organisms of the third category, oxidize inorganic substances to obtain their energy; and they use some of that energy to fix carbon dioxide in reactions analogous to those of the photosynthetic carbon reduction cycle. The chemoautotrophs include the nitrifiers, which oxidize ammonia or nitrite ions, as well as other bacteria that oxidize hydrogen gas, hydrogen sulfide, sulfur, or other materials.

One spectacular case of chemoautotrophy was discovered in 1977 by scientists exploring the ocean bottom near the Galapagos Islands. At a depth of 2500 meters, far below any hint of light from the sun and in the immediate neighborhood of volcanic vents in the ocean floor, they found an entire ecosystem based on chemoautotrophic bacteria, feeding a large community of crabs, mollusks, and giant worms. The bacteria obtain energy by oxidizing hydrogen sulfide (H_2S) released from the vents.

Finally, there are the *chemoheterotrophs*, which typically obtain both energy and carbon atoms from one or more organic compounds. The great majority of bacteria are chemoheterotrophs-as are all animals, fungi, and many protists.

Another metabolic adaptation is nitrogen fixation. As noted in other chapter of this book, this vital process is carried out by a wide variety of prokaryotes, including members of the cyanobacteria, *actinomycetes*, some phototrophic bacteria, and numerous others. The only nitrogen fixers in nature are members of the kingdom Monera.

Structural Characteristics of Bacteria

Most bacteria have a thick and relatively stiff cell wall. If the wall contains a great deal of peptidoglycan, it will take on a blue to purple color when treated with the Gram stain; bacteria with such walls are called *gram-positive*. *Gram-negative* bacteria contain less peptidoglycan and appear pink to red following Gram-staining.

This difference is somewhat useful in classifying bacteria; but it should be noted that a variety of cell wall structures are found among the monera. Three shapes are particularly common among the bacteria, as shown in Figure elsewhere in this chapter and various figures in this chapter.

These are spheres (*coccus*; plural: cocci), rods (*bacillus*; plural: bacilli), and curved or spiral forms. Cocci can occur singly or in two- or three-dimensional arrays as chains, plates, or blocks of cells. Bacilli and spiral forms occur singly or in chains; but the chains do not really signify multicellularity, since each cell is fully viable and independent. Most bacteria reproduce by the fission of one cell into two. Chains arise merely by the adhesion of cells after fission. A wide variety of other structural features are exhibited by certain groups of bacteria.

Some form stalks by which they are attached to their substrate. The stalk may be an extension of the cell wall or an extracellularly secreted product. Sheathed bacteria constitute filaments that approach but do not attain true multicellularity.

The cells occur in chains enclosed within a delicate tubular sheath; and when cell division occurs, it occurs simultaneously in all cells of the filament. Sheathed bacteria reproduce by releasing flagellated cells from the open end.

KINGDOM MONERA, PHYLUM BACTERIA

Gliding Bacteria

Cells of the *gliding bacteria* are rods that "glide" from place to place. (The genus *Thiothrix* in Figure elsewhere in this chapter and the genus *Beggiatoa* in Figure elsewhere in this chapter of this chapter are two examples of gliding bacterial groups.) The physical basis of the gliding movement is not yet known.

The cells are capable of a form of amoeboid movement, and a secreted slime may also be involved in their locomotion-they leave slimy trails behind them as they move over soil or dead organic matter. Gliding bacteria form remarkable reproductive structures similar to those of cellular slime molds. A group of cells aggregates, and from the cell mass there arise characteristic reproductive structures called fruiting bodies.

The fruiting bodies may be simple globes over a millimeter in diameter, or they may be somewhat more complex, branched structures. Then either single cells transform themselves into thick-walled spores, or whole clusters of cells form a cyst resistant to drying. Both spores and cysts can germinate under favorable conditions to yield the typical, gliding vegetative cells.

Spirochetes

The spirochetes have rather thin and flexible walls. They possess unique structures called axial *fibrils* or *axial filaments*, composed of flagella along the cell body between the cell wall and an outer envelope. The cell body is a long cylinder coiled spirally. The flagella constituting the axial filaments begin at either end of the cell and overlap in the middle.

The axial filaments are thought to be responsible for motility of these organisms and there are typical basal bodies where they insert into the cell wall, but the precise mechanism by which they work is unknown.

Many spirochetes are parasites in humans, including *Treponema pallidum,* the organism that causes the venereal disease syphilis. Others live free in mud or water, characteristically under anaerobic conditions.

Curved and Spiral Bacteria

The curved and spiral bacteria are diverse in properties, sharing little more than a curved form and a gram-negative reaction. Some, notably members of the genus *Spirillum*, live free in fresh or salt water, whereas others are parasitic. Some species cause diseases in animals; several subspecies of *Campylobacter fetus* are increasingly recognized as the cause of intestinal inflammation and other damage to humans.

A particularly interesting genus in this group is *Bdellovibrio.* Some species of *Bdellovibrio* penetrate and reproduce within various other bacteria-one bacterium parasitizing another!

Gram-Negative Rods

The *gram-negative rods*, as a group, demonstrate the advantage and weakness of the classification scheme employed here. The advantage is that such groups are readily recognized in the laboratory by their shape and staining properties. The disadvantage is that the group is so large and diverse that it can scarcely be a "natural" group with close evolutionary ties among its members.

Some gram-negative rods are aerobic, others are facultative anaerobes, and still others obligate anaerobes. Nitrogen fixing genera such as *Rhizobium* (Figure 8 in Chapter 18) are included, as are *Nitrobacter, Thiobacterium,* and other anaerobes that use nitrogen or sulfur compounds instead of oxygen for respiration.

Escherichia coli, probably the most-studied organism of all, is a gram-negative rod. So, too, are many of the most famous human pathogens, such as *Yersinia pestis* (plague), *Shigella dysenteriae* (dysentery), *Vibrio cholerae* (cholera), and *Salmonella typhimurium* (a common agent of food poisoning in humans).

Gram-Positive Rods

There are two principal subgroups of *gram-positive rods*. One produces *endospores*—highly resistant structures containing a copy of the bacterium's [illegible], some ribosomes and other cytoplasmic constituents, a thick peptidoglycan coat, and an outer spore coat. Members of this group include the many species of *Bacillus,* including *B. anthracis,* the agent of anthrax in sheep and humans, and *B. thuringiensis, a* species used agriculturally against insect pests of the order Lepidoptera (moths, butterflies, and their relatives).

The genus *Clostridium* includes *Clostridium denitrificans,* a free-living bacterium that plays an important role in the planet's nitrogen cycle; two producers of potent toxins, *C. botulinum* (various forms of botulism) and *C. tetani* (tetanus); and *C. perfringens* (food poisoning, gas gangrene).

The toxins produced by *C. botulinum* are among the most poisonous ever discovered; one milliliter can kill about two million mice, and the lethal dose for humans is about *onemillionth* of a gram. Other gram-positive rods do not form endospores. These include bacteria of the genera *Lactobacillus* (a lactic acid producer), *Listeria,* and others.

Actinomycetes

Just as gliding bacteria bear a superficial resemblance to cellular slime molds, the *actinomycetes* resemble filamentous fungi. Actinomycetes develop vegetatively into elaborately branched systems of filaments that lack any cross walls whatsoever (Figure 14). Such a mat of filaments is called a *mycelium.* Presumably, each branching system contains many copies of the genetic material, just as branched filamentous fungi contain large numbers of nuclei.

Some actinomycetes reproduce by forming chains of spores at the tips of the filaments, a process resembling asexual spore formation in many fungi. Nevertheless, the actinomycetes are true prokaryotes. In the species that do not form spores, the branched, filamentous growth ceases and the structure breaks up into typical cocci or rods.

The actinomycetes include several medically important members, such as *Actinomyces israelii,* a cause of infections in the oral cavity and elsewhere; *Mycobacterium tuberculosis,* the species that causes tuberculosis; and *Streptomyces,* the genus that produces streptomycin and several other antibiotics. We derive most of our antibiotics from members of the actinomycetes.

Rickettsias and Mycoplasmas

Yet another group of bacteria includes *rickettsiae* and related organisms. Once grouped with viruses because of their size and growth characteristics, these extremely small intracellular parasites, approximately 1 [Lm in length and 3 μm in diameter, have cell walls and chemical characteristics similar to some gram-negative bacteria. With one exception, rickettsias have never been grown outside of living cells.

Rickettsias are agents of several serious diseases in humans, notably Rocky Mountain spotted fever (more common in the Southeastern United States than in the Rocky Mountains) and typhus. They are frequently carried by arthropods, particularly fleas and ticks, but do not seem to cause any disease symptoms in their arthropod hosts.

Chlamydiae are often lumped with the rickettsiae because of their small size (0.2 to *1.5* μm in diameter) and their growth habit (obligately intracellular parasites). These tiny spheres are unique prokaryotic cells due to a complex reproductive cycle in which two different types of cells are seen. In humans, various strains of chlamydiae cause eye infections (especially trachoma), venereal disease, and forms of pneumonia.

Even smaller than rickettsiae and chlamydiae are the mycoplasmas-the smallest cellular creatures ever discovered, some having diameters between 0.1 and 0.2 Rm. The mycoplasmas are "small" in another crucial sense: they have less than half as much genetic information (DNA) as do the other prokaryotes.

It has been speculated that the amount of DNA in a mycoplasma may be about the minimum amount required to code for the absolutely essential properties of a cell. Most mycoplasmas are parasites found within the cells of animals and plants. As intracellular parasites, they are not subjected to the osmotic challenges faced by free-living bacteria; and they have no peptidoglycan-containing cell wall.

As a result, they take on irregular shapes; and they cannot be killed with penicillin, which manifests its antibacterial effect by interfering with wall synthesis.

Methanogens

Ten species of microscopic prokaryotes, previously assigned to various bacterial groups, share the property of producing methane (CH_4) by the reduction of carbon dioxide. All of these *methanogens* are obligate anaerobes, and they use methane production as the key step in their energy metabolism.

In 1977, Carl Woese of the University of Illinois established that all of the methanogens are, in fact, closely related to one another-and only distantly related to the other species of bacteria and cyanobacteria. This assignment was based on a detailed study of the base sequences of RNA samples isolated from the ten methanogens and from a variety of other prokaryotes. Woese suggested that methanogens are the modern representatives of a group as ancient as those different ones that gave rise to the other prokaryotes.

He has suggested, in fact, that the methanogens should be treated as a separate kingdom in their own rightthe kingdom *Archaebacteria*. Pending further clarification of the status of the methanogens, we shall consider them to be a group within the phylum Bacteria. Methanogens release approximately two billion tons of methane into Earth's atmosphere each year, accounting for all of the methane in our air, including that associated with mammalian flatulence.

Approximately one-third of the methane production comes from methanogens in the guts of grazing herbivores such as cows; a few energy-conscious souls have suggested that the methane from belching cattle might be trapped for use as fuel.

Gram-Negative and Gram-Positive *Cocci*

Cocci, you will recall, are spherical bacterial cells; and, like the rodlike bacilli, both gram-negative and gram-positive cells are found, providing a structural basis for grouping species. Some of the gram-negative cocci use oxides of nitrogen or sulfur as terminal electron acceptors for respiration.

In terms of human infections, *Neisseria gonorrhoeae,* the cause of the common venereal disease gonorrhea, gets the most publicity; *N. meningitidis* causes a frequently fatal infection of the linings of the nervous system; other genera, such as *Acinetobacter* and *Moraxella,* also cause infections.

The gram-positive cocci are numerous; species of the genus *Staphylococcus* are about 1 μm in diameter and are called staphylococci. They are abundant on the human body surface, and are responsible for boils and numerous other skin problems. *Staphylococcus aureus* is the best-known human pathogen; it is found in 20 to 40 percent of normal adults (50 to 70 percent in hospitals) and causes a variety of respiratory, intestinal, and wound infections, in addition to skin diseases.

Staphylococci produce toxins that are a major cause of food poisoning and toxic shock syndrome. *Streptococcus* is another important genus of grampositive cocci. Cells of this group are known as streptococci. These cells divide along a single axis and stay together after fission, forming chains of cocci.

In Figure elsewhere in this chapter, *Streptococcus mutans* (an acid-producing oral species that can erode tooth enamel) is shown; *S. pneumoniae* (formerly called *Diplococcus pneumoniae)* was the first species of organism in which it was proven that DNA was the hereditary material. There is not a major organ system in the human body that is not subject to one form of streptococcal infection or another.

BACTERIA AND DISEASE

One of the most productive eras in the history of medicine was the late nineteenth century, a time during which bacteriologists, chemists, and physicians established the fact that many diseases are caused by microbial agents.

The German physician Robert Koch laid down a set of rules by which the relationship between a disease and a microorganism could be tested. According to Koch, the disease in question could be laid to a particular microorganism if (1) the microorganism could always be found in diseased individuals, (2) the microorganism taken from the host could be grown in pure culture, (3) a sample of the culture produced the disease when injected into a new, healthy host, and (4) the newly infected host yielded a new, pure culture of microorganisms identical to that obtained in step (2).

These rules-called *Koch's postulates*—are still important among modern procedures for the investigation of new diseases. In other chapter of this book we considered the immune system and other modes of protection against diseases of microbial origin. We also examined, briefly, the problems faced by a pathogenic bacterium in establishing itself in a host.

The consequences of an infection for the host depend upon a number of factors. One is the *invasiveness* of the pathogen: its ability to multiply within the body of the host. Another is its toxigenicity: ability to produce chemical substances injurious to the tissues of the host. Often bacterial toxins can kill the cells of a host that has not previously been exposed to them.

Corynebacterium diphtheriae, the agent of diphtheria, has low invasiveness and multiplies only in the throat; but its toxigenicity is great, so that virtually the entire body is affected. In contrast, *Bacillus anthracis,* which causes anthrax (a disease primarily of cattle and sheep), has low toxigenicity but an invasiveness so great that the entire bloodstream ultimately teems with the bacteria.

It should be kept in mind that in spite of our frequent mention of human pathogens in the foregoing sections, only a small minority of the known bacterial species are agents of disease. Far more species play positive roles in our lives and in the biosphere-participating in the digestive processes of animals, in the processing of nitrogen and sulfur in soils, as decomposers in all ecosystems, and as key participants in many of our own industrial and agricultural processes.

KINGDOM MONERA, PHYLUM CYANOBACTERIA

Of all known groups of Monera, the cyanobacteria (blue-green bacteria or blue-green algae) are without question the most independent nutritionally. They perform photosynthesis by using chlorophyll *a* and liberating oxygen gas; they can carry out fermentation under anaerobic conditions; and many can fix nitrogen on a large scale.

They require only water, nitrogen gas, oxygen, a few mineral elements, and carbon dioxide. Despite their ability to do the kind of photosynthesis otherwise characteristic only of eukaryotic photosynthesizers, they are true prokaryotes.

They contain none of the familiar membranebounded organelles of eukaryotic cells; they do not have a discrete nucleus; their chromosomes lack proteins; and their cell walls contain peptidoglycan. Even so, the cyanobacteria contain elaborate and highly organized internal membrane systems, the photosynthetic lamellae or thylakoids. They are also the only prokaryotic photosynthesizers that contain chlorophyll *a,* except for one bacterial genus, *Prochloron.*

The cyanobacteria, in contrast to many of the artificially defined groups of monera, form a closely related, homogeneous, logical grouping. They are placed in a separate phylum from the other bacteria because of their mode of photosynthesis.

However, lest we forget the complexity of prokaryote taxonomy, it should be mentioned that a few leading microbiologists classify the cyanobacteria as a subgroup of the gliding bacteria because motile forms use the gliding type of locomotion.

Cyanobacteria can be free-living, colonial, or filamentous. Some filamentous forms show differentiation into at least three different cell types: vegetative cells, spores, and *heterocysts*. Heterocysts are important structures for two reasons. First, when filaments reproduce by fragmentation, the weak point may be the heterocyst.

More important, however, heterocysts evidently lack the oxygenevolving portion of photosynthesis and, therefore, are more anaerobic. As a consequence, the extremely oxygen-sensitive nitrogenase required for nitrogen fixation survives; and it is in the heterocysts that nitrogen fixation occurs. All of the known cyanobacteria with heterocysts fix nitrogen, and the forms that lack heterocysts do not.

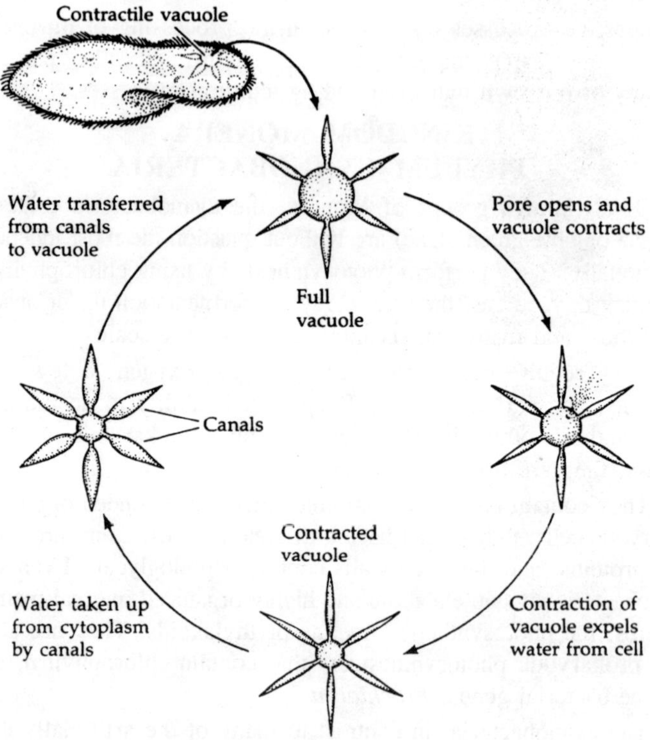

Figure 14.2: Contractile Vacuoles.

Although a form of sexual reproduction is encountered in the phylum Bacteria, it is absent in the *cyanobacteria*. Reproduction among the blue-greens is by fission, either to produce a new vegetative cell or to produce a resistant spore. Recently, viruses have been discovered that can infect cyanobacteria and then transfer genetic material from one organism to another by transduction, but true sexuality has never been observed.

THE KINGDOM PROTISTA

The protists are another heterogeneous group of organisms. Although they are quite distinct from monera, protists are difficult to discriminate cleanly from members of the other kingdoms of eukaryotic organisms. All protists are *eukaryotic,* and they are *unicellular* or *colonial.* (Some biologists also include certain multicellular organisms in the kingdom Protista, but we have avoided this practice.)

Protists, too, are startling in their diversity. Nutritionally, some are autotrophs, whereas others are absorptive heterotrophs, and still

Table 14.3: Major Phyla of the kingdom Protista.

Phylum	*Common Name Or Description*	*Examples*	*Form of Locomotion*
Mastigophora	Flagellates	*Euglena*, *Volvox*, *Trypanosoma*	Use flagella for locomotion
Sarcodina	Amoebas and their relatives	*Amoeba*, *Entamoeba*, Radiolarians, Foraminiferans	Use pseudopods for locomotion and for capturing food
Sporozoa	Amoeboid parasites	*Plasmodium*	Have no means of locomotion
Ciliophora	Ciliates	*Paramecium*, *Blepharisma*, *Vorticella*	Use cilia for locomotion

others are ingestive heterotrophs. Some switch with ease between the autotrophic and heterotrophic modes of nutrition. One phylum consists entirely of nonmotile organisms, but the others include cells that move by amoeboid motion, by ciliary action, or by means of flagella.

Members of all but one of the protist phyla have contractile vacuoles that help them cope with their hypotonic environments. The organisms have a more negative water potential than the environment and, hence, constantly take in water by osmosis.

Cells in one of the phyla (Sporozoa) possess rigid cell walls that resist osmotic water uptake. In the other phyla, excess water is collected in the contractile vacuole, located near the surface of the cell. When the contractile vacuole is full, a tiny pore opens, connecting the vacuole with the outside world; then the vacuole quickly contracts, pushing its contents out of the cell.

A beautifully simple experiment confirms that bailing out water is the principal function of the contractile vacuole. One observes some cells under the microscope and notes the rate at which the vacuoles are contracting-they look like little eyes winking. Then one takes other samples of cells and places them in solutions of differing water potential.

The less negative the water potential, the more hypertonic are the cells, so that water should be rushing into them faster and faster. And, in fact, the contractile vacuoles pump more rapidly. Conversely, if the solute concentration of the medium is increased until it is isotonic with the cells, the contractile vacuoles cease pumping.

In other chapter of this book, we introduced the concept of endosymbiosis (organisms living together, one inside the other). As one of the most bizarre examples, we selected the protist *Myxotricha paradoxa,* which has a variety of bacteria living inside it and on its surface. Endosymbiosis is very common among the protists; and, in some cases, the endosymbionts are themselves protists.

All radiolarians, for example, harbor photosynthetic protists or unicellular plants as endosymbionts. As a result, the radiolarians appear greenish or yellowish, depending on the type of endosymbiont they harbor. This arrangement is beneficial to the radiolarian, for it can make use of the food produced by its photosynthesizing guest; and the guest presumably profits from metabolites made by the host or simply by being given physical protection.

It is believed that the other eukaryotic kingdoms-the fungi, plants, and animals-arose from the kingdom Protista in different ways. There are real difficulties in deciding just where to draw the line between, say, the protist and plant kingdoms. Certain organisms are described by some biologists as protists and by others as plants.

A good case can be made for either assignment, and it is our belief that there is no single, "right" way to make all the choices. In this and the next two chapters, we have adopted a particular plan for making such assignments. We do not claim that it is necessarily the best way to do it; rather, it is a way.

KINGDOM PROTISTA, PHYLUM MASTIGOPHORA

In an important sense, the phylum *Mastigophora*, the flagellates, can be regarded as the most fundamental of all the eukaryotic phyla. If every trace of life on Earth were removed except the members of

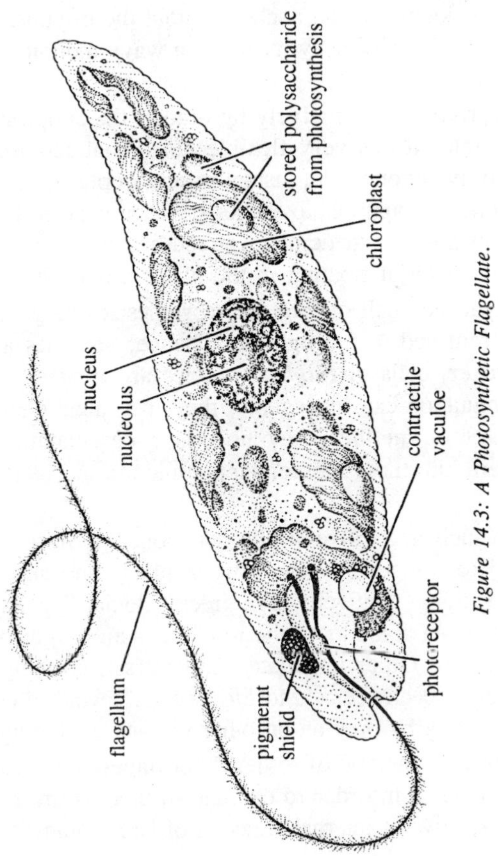

Figure 14.3: A Photosynthetic Flagellate.

this one group, a large percentage of the species would probably survive-or, to be more precise, they would survive so long as a supply of fixed nitrogen was available, because there are no nitrogen fixers in the phylum.

Not only would they sustain life entirely by themselves, but they would provide a favorable starting point for a renewal of evolutionary diversification of both the plants and the animals. No other single phylum outside the prokaryotes has the right combination of suitable biochemical talents and diversity of adaptive types among its members to approach such a potential.

Figure elsewhere in this chapter depicts a cell of the genus *Euglena*. Like most other members of its phylum, this common freshwater form possesses a complex cell plan, including a well-formed nucleus. It propels itself through the water with one of its two flagella, which sometimes doubles as an anchor to hold the organism in place. The flagellum provides power by means of a wavy motion that spreads from base to tip.

Euglena reproduces vegetatively by mitosis-the simplest and most direct way possible. It has very flexible nutritional requirements. In sunlight it is fully autotrophic, using its chloroplasts to synthesize organic compounds through photosynthesis. When kept in the dark, the organism loses its photosynthetic pigment and begins to feed exclusively on dead organic material floating in the water around it.

Such a "bleached" cell of *Euglena* resynthesizes its photosynthetic pigment when returned to the light and, hence, becomes autotrophic again. If, however, cells of *Euglena* species are treated with certain antibiotics or mutation-causing agents, they lose their photosynthetic pigment completely; neither they nor their descendants are ever autotrophs again-but these descendants function perfectly well as heterotrophs.

Because of their great diversity in nutrition, the Mastigophora are sometimes said to bridge the gap between plants and animals at the unicellular level. Some relatively large green colonial flagellates appear quite similar to green algae or to the motile aquatic stages of some of the terrestrial plants. Other flagellates, in contrast, strongly resemble tiny animals. Some species related to *Euglena* are devoid of chloroplasts and make their living by preying on other protists, including *Euglena*.

An impressive variety of other "zooflagellates" (animallike flagellates), so labeled in order to distinguish them from the plantlike "phytoflagellates," live as internal parasites of larger animals, including humans. Within the guts of certain wood-eating roaches and termites live an array of huge zooflagellates possessing some of the most bizarre and complicated body forms found anywhere among the protists.

Some idea of the diversity of this phylum is conveyed by Figure elsewhere in this chapter. The genera *Gonium* and *Volvox* are both photosynthetic and might well have been treated along with the green algae in other chapter of this book, whereas *Trypanosoma* and the cellulose-digesting flagellate from the cockroach *Cryptocercus* are sometimes considered animals.

The Mastigophora also span the gap between single-celled and many-celled organisms. Surprisingly large and well-organized colonies of cells are formed in such freshwater groups as the genus *Volvox*. The cells are not differentiated into tissues and organs as in the plants and animals, but the colonies show vividly how the preliminary step to this great evolutionary development might have been taken.

In addition, the intermediate stages between the onecelled state of *Euglena* and the extreme colonial state of *Volvox* are preserved in such loosely colonial forms as *Gonium* and *Pandorina*. Some of the Mastigophora are pathogens for humans. One of the most dreaded diseases of Africa is sleeping sickness, or nagana.

The vector (intermediate host) for nagana is an insect, the tsetse fly. Massive efforts have been made to eliminate the tsetse fly by the use of DDT and other insecticides, but these have met with only partial success. The tsetse fly has catholic tastes and will bite livestock and wild animals as well as humans, infecting them with parasitic flagellates of the genus *Trypanosoma*.

The trypanosomes multiply in the human bloodstream and produce toxic substances. When these parasites invade the nervous system, the symptoms of sleeping sickness appear-and are followed by death. Other disease-causing flagellates include *Giardia lambia,* a contaminant of water supplies that causes intestinal disorders, and *Trichomonas vaginalis,* which causes a common but usually mild venereal disease.

KINGDOM PROTISTA, PHYLUM SARCODINA

The members of the phylum *Sarcodina* (or Rhizopoda-"root-foot") are the amoebas and their relatives and have often been portrayed in popular writing as simple blobs-the simplest form of "animal" life imaginable. A superficial examination of a typical amoeba, illustrated in Figure elsewhere in this chapter, shows how such an impression might have been obtained.

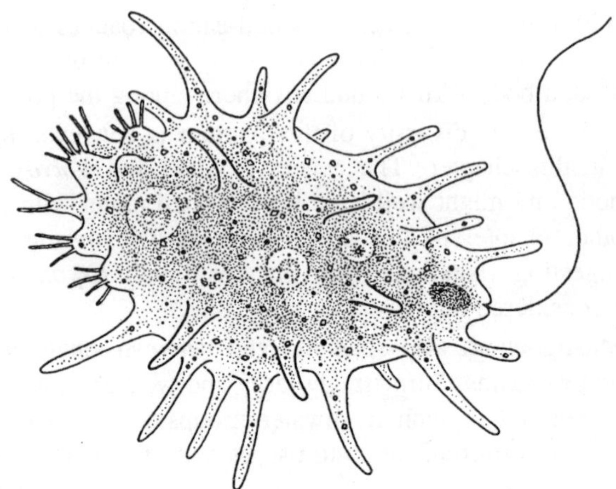

Figure 14.4: Amoebas.

Amoebas consist of a single cell with no definite shape. They feed on small organisms and particles of organic matter by phagocytosis, engulfing them with pseudopods: extensions of the constantly changing body mass. Particles of food are sealed off in food vacuoles within the cytoplasm of the amoeba.

The material is then slowly digested and assimilated into the main body of the organism. Pseudopods are also the organs of locomotion. Despite its apparently "primitive" characteristics, the amoeba is probably not a primeval organism.

Compelling evidence points to the conclusion that its simplicity is a secondarily derived condition in evolution. The phylum Sarcodina apparently originated from ancestors within the phylum Mastigophora. Some intermediate forms still exist. The example shown, *Mastigamoeba aspera*, is such an exactly intermediate link that it could equally well be placed in either phylum, the Mastigophora or the Sarcodina.

Amoebas of the free-living genus *Naegleria,* some of which can enter humans and cause a fatal disease of the nervous system, have a two-stage life cycle, one stage having amoeboid cells and the other flagellated cells.

Amoebas are, in fact, rather advanced forms of protists, most of which are specialized for life on the bottoms of lakes, ponds, and other bodies of water. Their creeping form of locomotion and manner of engulfing food particles require them to remain close to a relatively rich supply of sedentary organisms and organic particles. In humans, the amoeba *Entamoeba histolytica* is a major cause of dysentery.

The remaining Sarcodina form an astonishing array of even more specialized forms. All are animallike, existing as predators, parasites, or scavengers. None is photosynthetic. There are *shelled amoebas* that live in casings of sand grains glued together or in spiny or scaly shells secreted by the organism itself.

Foraminiferans are marine creatures that secrete shells of calcium carbonate. Their pseudopods are long, threadlike, and branched, and interconnect with one another to create a sticky net, which foraminiferans use to catch smaller plankton (free-floating microscopic organisms). The shells contain numerous microscopic pores through which long, fine pseudopods reach out to capture food.

When a foraminiferan reproduces, it does so by an equal mitotic division; and the daughter cells abandon the old shell and make new ones of their own. The discarded skeletons of infinite legions of ancient foraminiferans make up extensive limestone deposits in various parts of the world, forming a covering hundreds to thousands of meters deep over millions of square kilometers of ocean bottom.

Foraminiferan skeletons also make up the sand of some beaches. A gram of such sand may contain as many as *50,000* foraminiferan shells. The shells of individual foraminiferan species have distinctive shapes, and they are easily preserved as fossils in marine sediments. Each geological period had its own distinctive foraminiferan species.

For this reason, plus the fact that they are so abundant, foraminiferan remains are especially valuable as indicators in the classification and dating of sedimentary rocks and serve as indicators in oil prospecting. *Heliozoans* are freshwater sarcodines surrounded by a bristling array of long pseudopods. Like the foraminiferans, they drift in the water and use their pseudopods to trap smaller organisms.

A third group with the same feeding technique is the *radiolarians*. Found exclusively in the sea, they are perhaps the most beautiful of all microorganisms. Almost all radiolarian species secrete siliceous (glassy) skeletons from which needlelike pseudopods project.

The skeletons of the different species are as varied as snowflakes, and many of them have elaborate geometrical designs. So intricate are their shells that photographs do not do them justice-the drawing in Figure elsewhere in this chpater was made from detailed microscopic observation. A few of the radiolarians are among the largest of the protists, with skeletons measuring several millimeters across.

Uncountable numbers of radiolarian skeletons, some as much as 700 million years old, form the sediment under some seas in the tropics.

KINGDOM PROTISTA, PHYLUM SPOROZOA

The *sporozoans* are exclusively parasitic organisms that derive their name from the fact that some of them produce sporelike infective stages. Sporozoans lack contractile vacuoles. They generally have an amoeboid body form, but this in no way indicates a relationship to the Sarcodina.

The development of the trait is a common evolutionary event in parasitic protists. This mark of "degeneracy" has appeared, for example, even in parasitic dinoflagellates, which some biologists assign to the plant kingdom (although others would include the dinoflagellates in the protists).

Sporozoans, like many obligate parasitic counterparts among the animals, display elaborate life cycles featuring asexual and sexual reproduction by a series of very dissimilar life stages. Often these stages are associated with two kinds of host organisms. The best known sporozoa are the *malaria* parasites of the genus *Plasmodium,* a highly specialized group that spends part of its life cycle within vertebrate red blood cells.

Although malaria has been almost eliminated from the United States, it continues to be a major problem in some tropical countries; indeed, malaria is one of the largest diseases in terms of number of people infected. Plas*modium* is transmitted to humans by female mosquitoes of the genus *Anopheles.*

Plasmodium enters the human circulatory system when a hungry, infected *Anopheles* penetrates the human skin in search of blood. The parasite cells find their way to the liver and the lymphatic system, change their form (into "merozoites"), multiply, and reenter the bloodstream, attacking red blood cells. In approximately 2 days, the attackers multiply repeatedly, producing up to 36 new *Plasmodium* cells.

The victimized red cell then bursts, releasing a new swarm of parasites to attack other red blood cells. If another *Anopheles* bites the victim, some of the parasitic *Plasmodium* cells are taken into the mosquito along with the blood, thus infecting the mosquito.

Within its body, the parasites attack cells of the mosquito's gut, reproduce, and move into the salivary glands, thence to be passed to another vertebrate host. Because *Plasmodium* cannot be passed directly from one animal to another, malaria is best combated by the removal of stagnant water in which mosquitoes breed. The use of insecticides

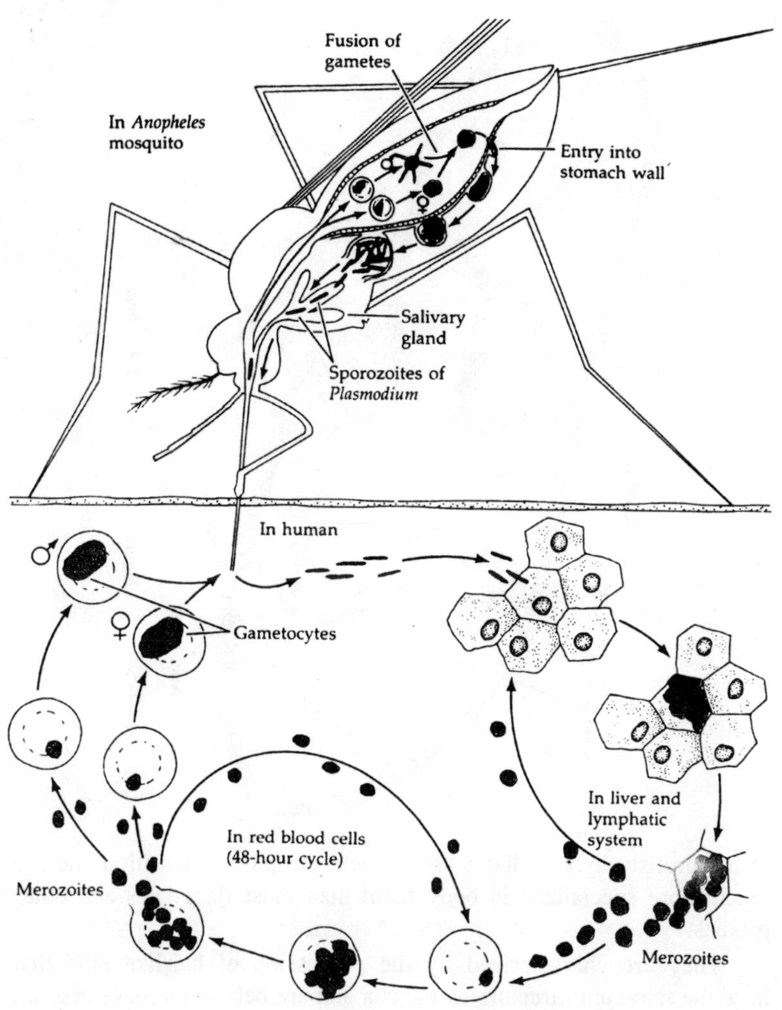

Figure 14.5: Life cycle of Plasmodium.

to reduce the *Anopheles* population is effective where the possible ecological, economic, and health dangers of the insecticide can be rationalized.

KINGDOM PROTISTA, PHYLUM CILIOPHORA

The phylum *Ciliophora*, consisting of the ciliates, ranks with the flagellates (Mastigophora) as the most diverse and ecologically important

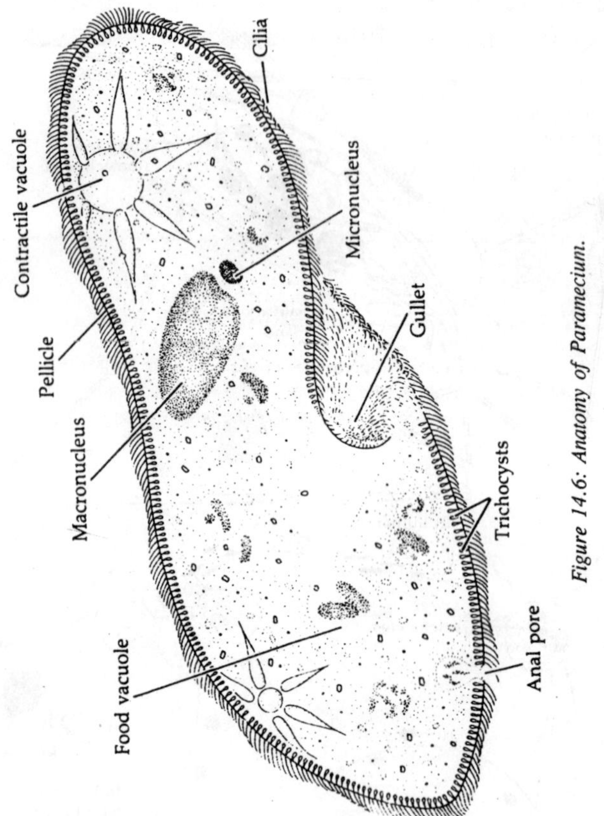

Figure 14.6: Anatomy of Paramecium.

of the protist phyla. Ciliates are all heterotrophic in nutrition and are much more specialized in body form than most flagellates and other protists.

They are characterized by the possession of hairlike cilia that have the same ultrastructure as flagella and are believed to have evolved from them. A second characteristic of the Ciliophora is the posses sion of two types of nuclei: a large *macronucleus* and, within the same cell, from 1 to as many as 80 *micronuclei*.

The little micronuclei are the essential carriers of the genetic information. The macronucleus is sometimes called the vegetative nucleus because it is not essential in reproduction but does play a vital role in the expression of genetic information in the phenotype.

The astonishing complexity of structure and behavior of ciliates is exemplified by Paramecium, a famous and frequently studied genus.

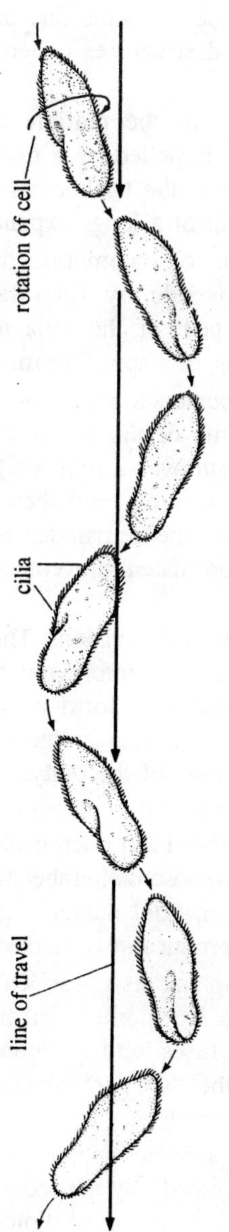

Figure 14.7: Locomotion of Paramecium.

The slipper-shaped body is covered by an elaborate pellicle, a structure composed principally of an outer membrane and an inner layer of closely packed, kidney-shaped structures called alveoli that embrace the cilia.

Also present as a layer of the pellicle are unique defensive organelles called trichocysts. Expelled by a microscopic explosion in a few thousandths of a second, the trichocysts emerge as sharpened darts driven forward at the tip of a long, expanding shaft.

The cilia provide a form of locomotion that is generally more precise than that made possible by flagella or pseudopods. A paramecium can direct the beat of the cilia to propel itself either forward or backward, moving in a spiraling manner.

When a paramecium encounters a barrier or an unpleasant stimulus, it can back off swiftly. (Some of the larger ciliates hold the speed record for the kingdom Protista-over 2 mm/sec.) A few of the cilia of Paramecium are sensory in function, and they are somehow able to transmit stimuli back through the remainder of the cytoplasm in a way that permits rapid, coordinated movements on the part of the entire organism.

Paramecia reproduce by cell division. The *micro-nuclei* divide mitotically, but the macronucleus simply pinches apart to give two daughter macronuclei. An elaborate form of sexual behavior called *conjugation* occurs when two paramecia line up tightly against each other and fuse in the oral region of the body.

During the next several hours there is an extensive reorganization and exchange of nuclear material. Each micronucleus divides meiotically, a process that reduces the chromosome number from diploid to haploid. All but one of the resulting haploid nuclei break down; and the last one divides mitotically and produces two haploid "gametes."

The macronuclei break up and disappear. Of the two haploid nuclei in each cell, one remains in its "home" cell and the other migrates to the partner cell, where it fuses with its counterpart. The exchange is fully reciprocal-each of the two paramecia gives and receives an equal amount of genetic material.

The two organisms now separate and go their separate ways, each having been genetically "refreshed" by the recombination that occurred during conjugation. The new, recombined diploid nucleus of each cell divides mitotically, producing what is destined to be the new macronucleus and a second nucleus that gives rise to the appropriate number of micronuclei by further mitotic divisions.

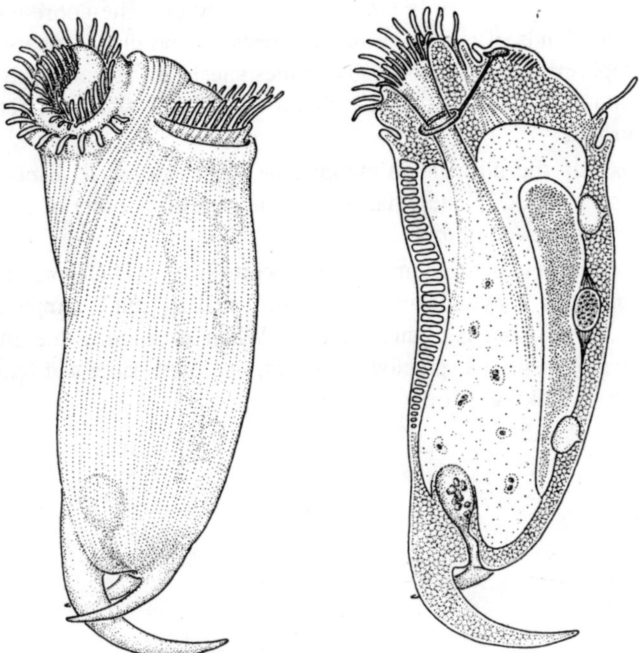

Figure 14.8: Exceptional Ciliates.

As pointed out in Chapter 20, conjugation in *Paramecium* is *a sexual* process because genetic recombination occurs; but *reproduction* is not an immediate consequence-two cells began the process, and the same two cells are still there at the end.

As a rule, each clone of paramecia must periodically go through the process of conjugation. It has been shown by laborious experimentation that, if some species are not permitted to conjugate, the asexual clones can live through no more than approximately 350 cell divisions before they die out.

CYTOPLASMIC ORGANIZATION IN THE CILIATES

Most ciliates possess all of the traits just described for *Paramecium*. Some, however, are notable for the exceptional degree of development of individual organelle systems. Certain ciliates, for example, have the equivalent of legs. Fused cilia called *cirri* move in an independent, but coordinated, fashion and enable the organism to walk over surfaces. This degree of coordination is made possible by nervelike *neurofibrils* leading to individual cirri.

When the neurofibrils are experimentally cut, the coordination is lost. Many kinds of ciliates possess *myonemes*: musclelike fibers within the cytoplasm. Contraction of myonemes causes an astonishingly quick retraction of the stalk of forms such as *Vorticella* when the organism is disturbed.

Possibly the ultimate in cytoplasmic organization is displayed by highly specialized ciliates that live in the digestive tracts of cows and many other hooved animals.

They possess not only myonemes, neurofibrils, and elaborately fused cilia, but also a cytoplasmic "skeleton" and a "gut" complete with "mouth," "esophagus," and "anus." When examining the intricate structures of these and some other ciliates, one must pause and remember that one is looking at only one cell!